PAKISTAN
ON THE
BRINK

ALLEN LANE

PAKISTAN
ON THE
BRINK

The Future of Pakistan,
Afghanistan and the West

AHMED RASHID

ALLEN LANE

ALLEN LANE

Published by the Penguin Group
Penguin Books Ltd, 80 Strand, London WC2R 0RL, England
Penguin Group (USA) Inc., 375 Hudson Street, New York, New York 10014, USA
Penguin Group (Canada), 90 Eglinton Avenue East, Suite 700, Toronto, Ontario, Canada M4P 2Y3
(a division of Pearson Penguin Canada Inc.)
Penguin Ireland, 25 St Stephen's Green, Dublin 2, Ireland (a division of Penguin Books Ltd)
Penguin Group (Australia), 250 Camberwell Road, Camberwell,
Victoria 3124, Australia (a division of Pearson Australia Group Pty Ltd)
Penguin Books India Pvt Ltd, 11 Community Centre, Panchsheel Park, New Delhi – 110 017, India
Penguin Group (NZ), 67 Apollo Drive, Rosedale, Auckland 0632, New Zealand
(a division of Pearson New Zealand Ltd)
Penguin Books (South Africa) (Pty) Ltd, 24 Sturdee Avenue, Rosebank,
Johannesburg 2196, South Africa

Penguin Books Ltd, Registered Offices: 80 Strand, London WC2R 0RL, England

www.penguin.com

First published in the United States of America by Viking Penguin,
a member of Penguin Group (USA) Inc. 2012
First published in Great Britain by Allen Lane 2012
001

Printed in India by Gopsons Papers Ltd., Noida

A CIP catalogue record for this book is available from the British Library

Trade Paperback ISBN: 978–1–846–14587–2

ALWAYS LEARNING  **PEARSON**

*This book is dedicated to the love and support of my sisters
Sultana and Rukhsana,
my teacher and mentor Ralph Blumenau,
and of course always for Angeles, Rafa, and Saara.*

The nation that will insist upon drawing a broad line of demarcation between the fighting man and the thinking man is liable to find its fighting done by fools and its thinking by cowards.

Sir William F. Butler, *Charles George Gordon* (1889)

CONTENTS

ABBREVIATIONS

AfPak   Afghanistan-Pakistan

ANA   Afghan National Army

ASEAN   Association of Southeast Asian Nations

ASF   Afghan Security Forces

BND   Bundesnachrichtendienst, the German intelligence service

CENTCOM   U.S. Central Command

CIA   Central Intelligence Agency

CTC   CIA's Counterterrorism Center

EU   European Union

FATA   Federal Administered Tribal Areas

FC   Frontier Corps

GHQ   General Headquarters of the Pakistan Army

IEC   Independent Election Commission

IED   improvised explosive device

IMF   International Monetary Fund

ISAF   International Security Assistance Force

ISI   Inter-Services Intelligence

KP   Khyber-Pakhtunkhwa

LT   Lashkar-e-Taiba

MI6   Britain's external intelligence service

NATO   North Atlantic Treaty Organization

NDU   National Defense University

NSC   U.S. National Security Council

PML-N   Pakistan Muslim League—Nawaz

RAW   Research and Analysis Wing of Indian intelligence

SCO   Shanghai Cooperation Organization

SOF   U.S. Special Operations Forces

TTP   Tehrik-e-Taliban Pakistan

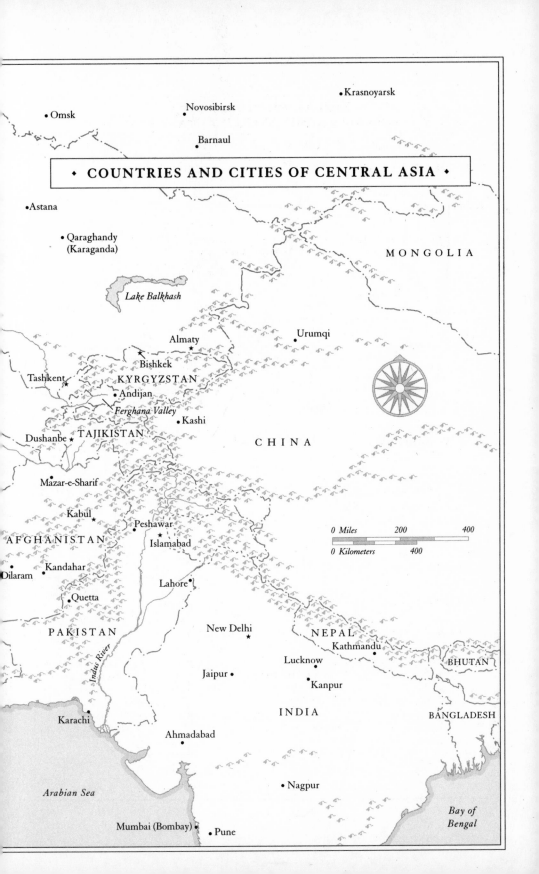

✦ COUNTRIES AND CITIES OF CENTRAL ASIA ✦

• Krasnoyarsk

Novosibirsk •

• Omsk

Barnaul •

•Astana

MONGOLIA

• Qaraghandy
(Karaganda)

Lake Balkhash

Urumqi •

Almaty •

Bishkek ★

Tashkent ★   KYRGYZSTAN

• Andijan

Ferghana Valley

Dushanbe ★   TAJIKISTAN

• Kashi

CHINA

• Mazar-e-Sharif

Kabul ★

Peshawar •

AFGHANISTAN   ★ Islamabad

• Kandahar

• Dilaram

• Quetta

Lahore •

PAKISTAN

New Delhi ★

NEPAL

Kathmandu •

Lucknow •

BHUTAN

Jaipur •

• Kanpur

Karachi •

INDIA

BANGLADESH

Ahmadabad •

0 Miles   200   400

0 Kilometers   400

Indus River

Arabian Sea

• Nagpur

*Bay of
Bengal*

Mumbai (Bombay) •   • Pune

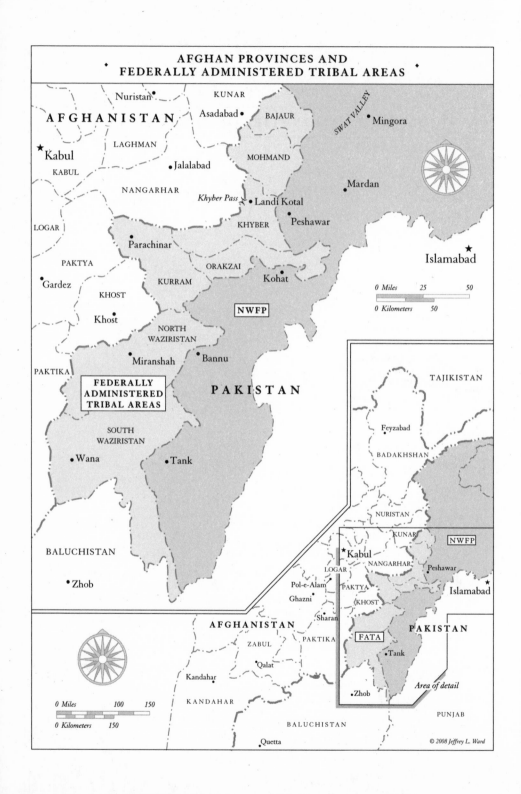

AFGHAN PROVINCES AND
FEDERALLY ADMINISTERED TRIBAL AREAS

AFGHANISTAN

Nuristan

KUNAR

Asadabad

BAJAUR

SWAT VALLEY

Mingora

LAGHMAN

MOHMAND

Kabul

KABUL

Jalalabad

Mardan

NANGARHAR

Khyber Pass

Landi Kotal

KHYBER

Peshawar

LOGAR

Islamabad

Parachinar

ORAKZAI

PAKTYA

Kohat

Gardez

KURRAM

0 Miles   25   50

0 Kilometers   50

KHOST

NWFP

Khost

NORTH
WAZIRISTAN

PAKTIKA

Miranshah

Bannu

PAKISTAN

TAJIKISTAN

FEDERALLY
ADMINISTERED
TRIBAL AREAS

Feyzabad

SOUTH
WAZIRISTAN

BADAKHSHAN

Wana

Tank

BALUCHISTAN

NURISTAN

KUNAR

NWFP

Zhob

Kabul

NANGARHAR

Peshawar

LOGAR

Pol-e-Alam

PAKTYA

Islamabad

Ghazni

KHOST

AFGHANISTAN

Sharan

PAKISTAN

ZABUL

PAKTIKA

FATA

Tank

Qalat

Kandahar

0 Miles   100   150

KANDAHAR

Zhob

Area of detail

0 Kilometers   150

PUNJAB

BALUCHISTAN

Quetta

© 2008 Jeffrey L. Ward

PREFACE

IN JANUARY 2009, when Barack Obama was inaugurated as the first black president of the United States, hopes of Americans and Europeans were high that he would make a greater U.S. commitment to Afghanistan in terms of money, troops, economic development, and state building—and above all, to finding a political solution to end the war. Obama's promise to do all of that, and his expressed desire for a regional solution that would bring Afghanistan's neighbors together in order to help the peace process, were even more welcome.

Obama did commit more of everything to Afghanistan, and many fields (such as education, health, media, the building of a new Afghan Army, and the degrading of Al Qaeda) have seen substantial improvements. However, the country has also seen a steady deterioration at almost every level—military, political, economic, and human. Violence has increased substantially, and the Taliban insurgency is now a nationwide movement. Tragically, as the endgame approaches, the administration still lacks a political strategy: the U.S. military and intelligence are in the driver's seat. The United States and NATO now plan to leave by 2014. The administration makes statements about Western forces transitioning and about handing over authority to the Afghan government and army, but it offers no clarity about how that can be accomplished in the midst of a civil war.

The escalation of the war has helped prolong and deepen an already long-running crisis in Pakistan. Its political and military leadership has shown neither the courage nor the will nor the intelligence to carry out major reforms in the country's foreign and economic policies. The Pakistani state still fosters many extremist jihadi fighters belonging to various groups, even as the Pakistani Taliban directly threatens that very state. The military has allowed the Afghan Taliban factions and their leaders safe sanctuary and support ever since 2001—something the Americans knew well but failed to raise effectively. Social services are near collapse, law enforcement is abysmal, economic hardship is widespread, natural disasters occur with little or no government assistance, and the majority of the population has no security.

Undeniably, the military and political situation in both Afghanistan and Pakistan has deteriorated considerably during Obama's tenure in office. Moreover, for two years, the critical U.S.-Pakistan relationship has been in a steady process of breakdown or deterioration. Obama and his senior officials share a major part of the blame because their failure to act as a team has resulted in contradictory policies, intense political infighting, and uncertainty about U.S. aims and objectives in the region. Regional players have been allowed to manipulate these very contradictions. The legacies of the cold war and the war on terror are still with us. Against the backdrop of an American and European recession, we are still trying to wipe clean those historical legacies so that we can get on with improving our world.

China and India are making huge economic advances, the Muslim world has seen the upswing known as the Arab Spring, struggles for democracy are occurring in countries that have hitherto known nothing but dictatorship, and women worldwide have made enormous strides. Sadly, such progress made has not been duplicated in South and Central Asia. This vital part of the world, the birthplace of Al Qaeda, remains beset by extremist groups and nuclear weapons. Yet Afghanistan and Pakistan have a greater impact on the world's stability than any other place on earth. We ignore efforts to forge peace and stability there at our peril.

This is my third book on the wars in Afghanistan, and on political developments in Pakistan and Central Asia, framed by the U.S. administrations that have tried to tackle these issues. For three decades, I have traveled, reported, written, and spoken about the wars and political events I have witnessed. During those thirty years, I have spent an inordinate amount of time trying to help politicians and diplomats find a solution to Afghanistan.

I have spent much of my adult life writing this trilogy. The first book, *Taliban*, covers the Afghanistan of the 1980s and 1990s and the rise of the Taliban and Al Qaeda, seen through the eyes of one of the few reporters on the ground there. It is very much a reporter's notebook. My second book, *Descent into Chaos*, is an attempt at a comprehensive history of the first eight years after September 11, 2001, during which the United States went to war in Afghanistan, and Pakistan became a reluctant partner. It covers the presidency of George Bush and looks at events from the different perspectives of Pakistan, Afghanistan, and Central Asia.

This third book, *Pakistan on the Brink*, is neither a reporter's notebook, a historical epic, nor a comprehensive history. It describes selected events during the first term of the Obama presidency; the focus is on the current crisis and on the solutions that are needed to ensure a future peace. It resembles a book of essays, each dealing with a different aspect of the same problem, discussing the processes that have led to the present impasse. As such, it can be opened anywhere, and any chapter can be read separately from the rest.

All parties to the conflict in Afghanistan and to the deterioration in Pakistan have made terrible mistakes. Almost all the major players have shown arrogance, hubris, rigidity, and stubbornness; all have, to some degree, lived in the past and been unable to change their thinking. As an observer of these events, however, I have also found this period to be a time of exhilaration and hope. No one who has covered the never-ending Afghanistan wars, as I have, can expect to be an optimist, but I am constantly looking for that open window and hoping it will stay open long enough for peace to emerge.

I hope younger readers will one day read my trilogy as a single document that covers a terrible period of mankind's history, from which crucial lessons were learned that made it impossible to repeat such death and destruction. Even though the same miseries have been inflicted on the same people, only in different eras under different masters, I believe fervently that we do learn from our mistakes, and that is where hope lies.

I would like to express my immense gratitude to my publisher and editor, Wendy Wolf of Viking Penguin, for forcing this book out of a very reluctant author who wondered if anyone really would want to read another book of mine. To my agent, Flip Brophy, who has backed me up all these years, and knows just when to push me forward and when I should say nothing, I can only offer my deeply felt thanks. Flip is a New York gem.

I would also like to thank Bruce Giffords, Carla Bolte, Noirin Lucas, and Janet Biehl at Viking.

I would like to thank all manner of friends, diplomats, generals, academics, bureaucrats, politicians, and heads of state who have given me time and attention in the United States, Britain, Pakistan, Afghanistan, Tajikistan, India, Belgium, Germany, Poland, France, Sweden, Norway, Spain, and the Netherlands, as well as at the United Nations. Above all I would like to thank my family for once again standing beside me and helping me write this book.

Ahmed Rashid

Lahore, November 2011

ONE

Osama and Obama, Legacy and Inheritance

AROUND MIDNIGHT on Sunday, May 1, 2011, two MH-60 Black Hawk helicopters took off from the U.S. air base in Jalalabad in eastern Afghanistan to carry out Operation Neptune Spear. They were packed with twenty-three soldiers of Navy SEAL Team 6, the most highly trained American special forces unit, also known as the Naval Special Warfare Development Group. The helicopters were wrapped in the latest stealth and noise-suppressant technology, but they still flew low, hugging the ground and the bends in the mountains, skimming the tree lines and avoiding towns and highways, as they crossed some 120 miles into Pakistan's territory. The radar cover on Pakistan's western border was minimal, the United States knew, because no air attack threatened from Afghanistan. Later four heavily armed MH-47 Chinook helicopters also took off from Jalalabad, carrying a second unit of SEAL Team 6, in case the first had to fight their way out.

The sleepy residents of Abbottabad, a small hill station in northwestern Pakistan thirty-five miles from Islamabad, heard the helicopters only when they were literally over their heads. Abbottabad, a bucolic fresh-air town whose rolling green hills made it resemble a

British country seat, is one of the nation's most important and safest military centers. Here the Pakistan Military Academy Kakul trains all officers joining the army and serves as headquarters for three military regiments. Kakul is the West Point of the Pakistan Army, and most of the town's residents are retired army officers.

As the two lead Black Hawk helicopters neared the target—a large, well-protected compound on the edge of town—one of them suffered a loss of power and was forced into a hard landing at the compound's edge. Nobody was hurt, and the downed helicopter was quickly destroyed. The original plan to rappel down into the compound using ropes from the helicopters was abandoned, and the second helicopter now landed in a field just outside it. Twenty-three SEALs, a Pakistani-American interpreter who spoke both Urdu and Pashto, and a tracking dog made the assault. They blew holes in the compound's massive eighteen-foot-high and three-foot-thick walls and entered the main house. They moved in the dark through the three-floor mansion, blowing up metal doors that had been placed in front of the staircase and shooting dead two men and one woman who had hosted and cared for their target.

Then the SEALs entered the third-floor bedroom of Osama bin Laden and shot him dead with two bullets, one to his head and another to his chest. He had promised never to surrender after 9/11 and he did not try to do so now.[1]

The soldiers carried out a DNA test on the corpse of the most wanted man in the world, then carried it to the waiting helicopter. His son Khalid, age twenty-two, had been killed on the staircase as the SEALs came up. Bin Laden's three wives and fifteen children were handcuffed but left in the compound. Before leaving, the SEALs scooped up enormous amounts of electronic equipment that was lying around—more than one hundred flash drives, ten computer hard disks, five computers, and mobile phones—with enough data to fill a library; the CIA would need months to read and analyze it. Bin Laden must have felt extremely safe in this house, where he had lived since 2006, not only because there were no cohorts of bodyguards and only a few weapons present, but because so much data was lying in the open. The only precaution he had taken was to sew a five-hundred-euro note and two telephone numbers into his cape.[2] The lack of security indicated that one or more unknown Pakistanis must have been protecting him.

His corpse was taken first to the U.S. base at Bagram, Afghanistan, and then to the aircraft carrier USS *Carl Vinson* in the northern Arabian Sea. Here his body was washed according to Islamic custom, placed in a white sheet, and weighted. His funeral prayers were read, and in the early hours of Monday morning, he was slipped into the sea from the lower deck. President Barack Obama announced his death in a dramatic late-night speech from the White House, declaring that "justice has been done." The news touched off an outpouring of joy in Washington and New York, especially at the site of the former Twin Towers. The mood in Afghanistan was equally upbeat, mixed with the trepidation that Bin Laden's death might encourage the Americans to pull out their troops earlier than planned. The mood in Pakistan was more mixed and much more dangerous—at first disbelieving, then somber, and finally angry. The reason for the anger was not that Bin Laden had lived so safely in Abbottabad for so many years, but that U.S. forces had invaded Pakistan's sovereignty.

Osama bin Laden was more than just an icon. His ideology of global jihad, and Al Qaeda's acts of terrorism, changed the way we all live, our security concerns, how we travel, and how we conduct politics and business; it deeply scarred relations between the Muslim world and the West. The Costs of War project at Brown University estimates that since 2001, the wars in Afghanistan, Iraq, and Pakistan have killed 225,000 people, including soldiers, and created more than 7.8 million refugees. The total cost is estimated at $4 trillion. Although the global economic collapse of 2008 affected the world far more than the war on terror, the costs of the wars—and of the security put in place to thwart terrorism—probably contributed enormously to the economic downturn.[3] Despite the celebration at his death and declamations that Al Qaeda was a spent force, the ideology of global jihad that Bin Laden espoused will not disappear quickly, for it has taken root in far too many Muslim fringe groups.

In the decade since the September 11 attacks, Al Qaeda has voraciously expanded its global network. It has set up branches in every European country, penetrated Muslim communities in the United States, and spread widely across Africa and the Middle East. In the aftermath of the Arab Spring, when people's movements overthrew dictatorships in Tunisia, Egypt, and Libya, the biggest challenge will be to ensure that Al Qaeda does not penetrate these societies or in any way determine their political future. Al Qaeda has transformed itself over the years: once a highly centralized organization, in which recruiting, training, policies, and planning all came from its top leaders, it is now a far looser and more amorphous terror network. It has promoted itself as a franchise, lending its name to extremist groups around the world, over whom it has no control and whose policies it does not run. It has spread through the Internet and YouTube and through word of mouth and example. It will not quickly allow itself to be destroyed. Bin Laden's death was a watershed moment, the end of an era, but it does not spell the end of Al Qaeda. Al Qaeda has adapted extremely well to previous setbacks and changed circumstances, and it will adapt again to cope with Bin Laden's death.

The American search for Bin Laden started in the early 1990s, after the discovery of his involvement in the killing of U.S. soldiers in Somalia in 1993 and Saudi Arabia in 1996 and the first attack on the World Trade Center in 1993. After Bin Laden declared in February 1998 that every Muslim has a duty "to kill Americans wherever they are found," that search became more determined.[4] September 11, 2001, turned him into the most wanted man in the world—and a folk hero in many parts of the Muslim world.

The United States spent a fruitless decade chasing a man on the run, but then in 2010 the breakthrough came when CIA agents finally tracked down one of his trusted couriers, a Pakistani born in Kuwait with the nom de guerre Abu Ahmed al-Kuwaiti. Ahmed had been with Bin Laden since the battle of Tora Bora in 2001, which had been Bin Laden's last fight with his American pursuers before leaving for Pakistan. Since 2002, Al Qaeda prisoners had been mentioning Ahmed's name to U.S. interrogators. Only in 2004 was his nom de guerre confirmed, when Hassan Ghul, a top Al Qaeda operative who had been captured in Iraq, described how close Ahmed was to Bin Laden.

He was positively identified in August 2010.[5] The CIA would eventually tail him to a large house in Abbottabad, which had no telephone or Internet lines and was surrounded by high walls and from which nobody ever seemed to come and go. Ahmed and his brother, who were known locally as Arshad and Tariq Khan, had custom-built this house for Bin Laden in 2005. Their real names were later discovered to be Abrar and Ibrahim Said Ahmed, and their family had lived in the village of Martung, just north of Abbottabad, before settling in Kuwait.[6]

After discovering the house, the CIA undertook massive ground and satellite surveillance of the compound, even renting a house nearby. From there agents observed, inside the compound, a tall, unidentified man taking daily walks. They called him "the pacer."[7]

The Americans had several options. They could bomb the house, flattening it and killing the civilians living nearby. They could use drone missiles to target more precisely. Or they could mount a commando attack. On March 14, 2011, Obama held the first of five national security meetings to discuss the options. The decision to attack was kept secret from most of the administration and from all U.S. allies, including Britain and Pakistan. Obama made the decision to go ahead on April 29, the Friday before the assault. That weekend he would visit tornado-hit Alabama and also crack jokes at a White House dinner for journalists and celebrities.

The political fallout from Bin Laden's death was most dire in Pakistan. For years, every Pakistani leader had denied that Bin Laden was in their country. As early as 2005, President Pervez Musharraf had frequently said—without providing any evidence—that Bin Laden was dead and that looking for him was no longer a high priority for Pakistan. That same year, he had arrogantly berated British prime minister Tony Blair, telling him that Pakistan had "completely shattered Al Qaeda's vertical and horizontal links" and that "it is absolutely baseless to say that Al Qaeda has its headquarters in Pakistan."[8] The army's all-powerful Inter-Services Intelligence Directorate (ISI) would immediately harass any journalist who wrote that Bin Laden was alive and active in Pakistan.

Now, in the eyes of the world, Pakistan's leaders had turned out to be liars or worse. U.S. congresspeople and several world leaders expressed strong suspicions that elements in the army, in the ISI, or in extremist Islamic groups trained by one or the other had provided Bin Laden with a security network. Pakistan denied these accusations, and to date nothing has emerged to link the government with Bin Laden. But the matter is unlikely to rest with their protestations of innocence and victimhood.

Pakistan has been through terrible moments before, but it has never been placed in such an embarrassing position. The surrender of the Pakistan Army to India and the loss of East Pakistan in 1971 left the country with a huge sense of shame and anger. It has muddled though other wars and defeats at the hands of India, through devastating floods and earthquakes, and through enormous political turmoil. The military has ruled Pakistan for thirty-three of its sixty-four years, and the army has dissolved elected governments four times.[9] As Pakistani historian Farzana Shaikh observes, "Pakistan is, of course, no stranger to chaos. But what makes this moment in Pakistan's history exceptional is the threat it is seen to pose, simultaneously, to the security of its own citizens, to the welfare of its regional neighbors, and to the stability of the wider international community. These new concerns bear little or no comparison to the more 'contained' moments of chaos that have scarred Pakistan."[10]

At one a.m. on May 2, Gen. Ashfaq Parvez Kayani, the head of the Pakistan Army, was at home in his study when he received a call from the director general of military operations, Maj. Gen. Ishfaq Nadeem, telling him about a helicopter crash. Pakistani helicopters did not fly at night, so this was clearly a foreign intruder. Kayani called Air Chief Marshal Rao Qamar Suleman, who scrambled two American-made F-16 jet fighters, but the U.S. raiders had already reentered Afghanistan. Local army and police units in Abbottabad did not arrive at the scene until well after the Americans had left. Around two a.m., President Obama called his Pakistani counterpart, Asif Ali Zardari, to give him the news that Bin Laden had been killed in Pakistan. Zardari was stunned but managed to gather his thoughts enough to congratulate Obama. A little later Admiral Mike Mullen, chairman of the Joint Chiefs of Staff, telephoned his friend Kayani.

In several meetings, the country's top leadership—President Zardari, General Kayani, Prime Minister Yousaf Raza Gilani, and Lt. Gen. Ahmed Shuja Pasha, the head of the ISI—could not agree on how to react. In shock, disbelief, and anger, they discussed the serious consequences for Pakistan. Initially Gilani, like Zardari, hailed Bin Laden's killing "as a great victory," and the Pakistani Foreign Office had welcomed the news. This mild reaction was prompted by Obama's first words, in which he praised Pakistan for cooperating with the United States. Even though there had been no cooperation with the United States, Pakistan's civilian leaders had no desire to take on the Americans. Then for the next four days, there was a news blackout and silence from the authorities, which bewildered the public.[11]

Then much harsher criticism began to be voiced in the United States. Leon Panetta, the CIA chief, said that Pakistan had not been prewarned of the raid because "it was decided that any effort to work with the Pakistanis could jeopardize the mission—they might alert the targets." John O. Brennan, Obama's counterterrorism adviser, said that Bin Laden must have had a support network, but "whether or not that was individuals inside of the Pakistani government is unknown." These words, the toughest possible, demonstrated to the world the U.S. administration's level of mistrust for Pakistan.[12]

Finally the army retaliated. On Thursday, May 5, after meeting with his nine top generals, called the Corps Commanders, Kayani issued a blistering statement. Calling the raid "a misadventure," he said that "any similar action violating the sovereignty of Pakistan will warrant a review on the level of military/intelligence cooperation with the United States." He would immediately reduce "to the minimum essential" the number of U.S. military trainers, contractors, and CIA personnel in the country.[13] He ignored the issue of Bin Laden's presence in Pakistan and instead made paramount the issue of the breach of Pakistan's sovereignty; he and the other generals wanted to protect Pakistan's honor. The civilian leaders picked up the army's cue. On a visit to Paris, Gilani uttered the memorable words that "there is an intelligence failure of the whole world, not just Pakistan alone." On May 9, the government called a joint session of parliament, ostensibly to berate the ISI, but it ended up endorsing the army's position. "Singing from the GHQ (General Headquarters) hymn sheet, it also demanded a review of Pakistan-US cooperation," wrote one astute observer.[14]

It wasn't just the U.S.-Pakistan relationship that was in a crisis—it was Pakistan itself. The raid had certainly breached its sovereignty, but Bin Laden had breached it for years by living undetected or tolerated in Pakistan. The government's unwillingness to come clean on Bin Laden's presence in Pakistan led to further public confusion. Many Pakistanis refused to believe that he had died in the raid and argued that the Americans had faked the whole episode—like the landing on the moon. On May 3, Al Qaeda admitted in an Internet posting titled "You lived as a good man, you died as a martyr" that Bin Laden was dead—"the blood of the holy warrior sheikh, Osama bin Laden, God bless him, is too precious to us and to all Muslims to go in vain." They had no problem believing that he had lived in Pakistan, because most of the leaders of other terrorist networks were also living there, but Pakistanis still refused to believe he was dead.[15]

The public was also demoralized that the armed forces, which consume 30 percent of the national budget, had proved to be so incompetent, and criticism emerged in the media. The military tried to deflect it by warning off journalists and by allowing the public's deep-seated anti-Americanism to flourish. Strident anti-American feelings intensified in the military. Suddenly Kayani's own soldiers appeared more unwilling than ever to fight the Pakistani Taliban in what they were convinced was an American war.

A rash of statements from world leaders and the international media held the Pakistan Army either totally culpable in hiding Bin Laden or totally incompetent in not discovering his whereabouts, leading to further public outrage and despair. For years, President Hamid Karzai of Afghanistan had told the United States and NATO that Pakistan was hosting Al Qaeda and the Taliban; now he lashed out at them for not believing him: "Year after year, day after day, we have said the fighting against terrorism is not in the villages of Afghanistan . . . [but] is in safe havens. It proves that Afghanistan was right."[16] Senator Carl Levin, chairman of the Armed Services Committee, summed up the mood of the U.S. Congress by saying that "the Pakistani army and intelligence have a lot of questions to answer." There were calls to reduce, even cancel, Washington's $2 billion–$3 billion annual military aid to Pakistan.[17] European leaders, equally skeptical, demanded that Pakistan come up with answers, but the country's leadership was not prepared to provide them.

Later in May, a devastating series of suicide attacks and bomb blasts by the Pakistani Taliban and Al Qaeda killed more than 160 people and wounded 350. The most serious attack was on a naval base in Karachi on May 22, when six suicide fighters held off an entire garrison and destroyed $70 million worth of U.S.-supplied naval reconnaissance aircraft. A few days later the prominent journalist Syed

Saleem Shahzad, who had reported on links between the navy and Al Qaeda and had allegedly been picked up by the ISI for it, was found dead. The ISI vehemently denied detaining him, but Washington was later to accuse the government of orchestrating his killing. According to the New York–based Committee to Protect Journalists, Pakistan became the most dangerous place in the world for journalists to work—not just because of the Taliban but also because of the security agencies. Shahzad's death had followed the harassment of many journalists by the so-called media wing of the ISI, run by senior naval officers. They were in the habit of threatening journalists and their families on the phone or in face-to-face meetings or in messages sent to them through third parties. Eight journalists were killed in 2010, and another eight in the first seven months of 2011.

On August 6, the Taliban exacted a kind of revenge when they shot down a Chinook transport helicopter, killing forty people aboard, including thirty-two U.S. military personnel. It was the largest death toll of Americans in a single day in the war and included seventeen SEALs—some of whom belonged to the SEAL team that had taken down Bin Laden.[18] Two Taliban shot at the helicopter with rocket-propelled grenades, and one rocket exploded inside the helicopter. It was deemed a lucky shot. A few weeks later a U.S. drone missile fired into North Waziristan in Pakistan and killed Al Qaeda's newly appointed number two, the Libyan-born Atiya abd al-Rahman. He was considered a key aide first to Bin Laden and now to his successor, Ayman al-Zawahri, and his death was a major blow.

The war in Afghanistan would continue, but Pakistan is now considered the most fragile place in the world, both because of what might happen there politically and because of what it can foster elsewhere. It is the most unstable country and the most vulnerable to terrorist violence, political change, or economic collapse. Its multiple long-term and short-term problems seem insurmountable by the present military and civilian leadership. It is not yet a failed state, but as its febrile state worsens, it is sliding down the path of becoming one. It still has a powerful army and a corrupt and run-down but functioning bureaucracy, judiciary, and police force; its economy would be viable if its problems were properly addressed, and its population is hard-working. Pakistanis perform outstandingly well in academia, the arts, television, fashion design, pop music, and of course cricket. But they lack adequate social services such as health care, full literacy, a modern educational system, population control programs, and real economic growth.

The civilian political elite has failed to give the country leadership. Holding virtually all the political and economic power, the elite lacks all sense of responsibility toward the public, refuses to pay taxes, and is immeasurably corrupt. Whenever elections are held, invariably after a long bout of military rule, the political elite has failed to govern effectively. The development of an alternative democracy is stuck. At the same time, a powerful military dictates the country's foreign policy, especially toward India, Afghanistan, and the United States, eats up over 30 percent of the national budget, and runs several unaccountable intelligence services. For several decades, the army has used Islamic extremists to pursue its foreign policy agendas in India and Afghanistan, but that practice has now backfired and created an internal extremist movement called the Pakistani Taliban, which I will discuss in greater detail in the next chapter. Moreover, the military also controls the fourth-largest nuclear weapons arsenal in the world, with more than one hundred nuclear weapons.

These long-term problems, if not tackled immediately, may well plunge Pakistan into the failed-state category very soon. The UN estimates that Pakistan's 185 million population will grow to 275 million by 2050. Despite its primarily agricultural economy, Pakistan can barely support its existing population, and it is difficult to see how water, food, land, and services will be available for 90 million more people. One-third of Pakistanis today lack drinking water, another 77 million have unreliable food sources, and half the school-age children do not go to school. The literacy rate is 57 percent, the lowest in South Asia and not much better than the 52 percent that prevailed at the creation of Pakistan in 1947. Half the population are not even looking for jobs, since they know they won't be able to find them. The country needs at least a 9 percent annual growth rate to employ its under-twenties, who make up 60 percent of the population. The 37 percent of Pakistanis who are under the age of fifteen give Pakistan one of the world's largest youth bulges.[19] In an economy whose 2.6 percent growth rate fails to provide them with jobs or food security, a never-ending stream of young men face a future of little promise and are ready to sign on to jihad.

Pakistan's short-term problems are worsening on a daily basis, creating far-reaching regional and global problems. Since 2005, a Taliban insurgency has aimed to topple the government, defeat the army, and install an Islamic extremist state. The Pakistani Taliban currently control large tracts of the northwest, and other extremist groups from around the country have joined them in destabilizing major cities such as Karachi and controlling large tracts of the southern Punjab. Ethnically, the Afghan and the Pakistani Taliban movements are mostly tribal Pashtuns: Afghanistan has 12 million Pashtuns, but

Pakistan has another 30 million. They are a constant source of man-power for fighting the Americans in Afghanistan and the army in Pakistan.

A full-scale revolt is under way in the country's largest province, Baluchistan: the rebels are fighting the army and demanding separa-tion from Pakistan. Both sides in the Baluchistan conflict are com-mitting some of the worst atrocities Pakistan has ever witnessed. In Karachi, with its 18 million people, in Sind province, and in the North-ern Areas, unattended ethnic inequality has led to insurgency and acute ethnic conflict. Intolerance is growing, and minority religious groups, such as Christians and Hindus, who have lived peacefully with the majority Sunni Muslims for decades, are now fleeing the country. Muslims from other minority sects—Shias, Ahmedis, Ismai-lis, and others—are being visibly targeted, and those who can afford to are also settling abroad. After years of low revenue collection, fail-ure to develop new industries and trading partners, joblessness, and chronic inflation, the economy is collapsing. Acute shortages of gas, electricity, and water have led to the closure of industry. Pakistanis have carefully watched the 2011 Arab Spring, but many fear that such a movement in Pakistan to destabilize or remove the existing regime would lead not to greater democracy but to a bloody revolution led by Islamic extremists.

As far as the United States is concerned, Pakistan should be the keystone country in the region, but after 2001, two American admin-istrations virtually ignored its worsening domestic crisis, as long as Pakistan kept delivering some degree of cooperation in the U.S.-led war in Afghanistan, which to the Bush administration meant one thing: that Pakistan capture members of Al Qaeda. The challenge for President Obama was to reshape U.S. policy so as to salvage the Pakistani state and so that the Pakistani military's strategic interests were not permanently at odds with U.S. interests in the region. As the end of U.S. involvement in Afghanistan approaches, the United States could no longer afford to ignore Pakistan.

The Western timetable for withdrawal from Afghanistan was drawn up at one of the largest NATO summit meetings ever held, in Lisbon on November 19, 2010. Heads of state of forty-nine countries agreed to a withdrawal of most of the 150,000 U.S. and NATO forces by 2014 and a transfer of responsibility to Afghan security forces. When Barack Obama became president in January 2009, there were 32,000 U.S. troops in Afghanistan. The Bush administration, in its final months, had approved another 11,000 troops. Obama ordered an escalation of 21,700 more troops in March 2009, then added another 33,000 with his surge decision that December. For a short period, there were just under 100,000 U.S. troops in the country. In 2011, Obama announced that 10,000 U.S. troops would leave that year, while another 23,000 would leave by the summer of 2012, leaving behind 65,000 for the final departure by 2014. NATO's 50,000 troops would follow the American withdrawal timetable. By 2014, Americans will have been fighting a thirteen-year war—longer than the First and Second World Wars combined.

The Afghans, who have been at war since 1978, are exhausted. Most Afghans want U.S. troops to leave but are divided between wanting a peace settlement and wanting to share power with the Taliban. While the Pashtuns favor a total U.S. withdrawal and a deal with the Taliban, the non-Pashtuns in northern Afghanistan and many of the 5 million population of Kabul prefer to see the war continue until the Taliban are defeated. The new urban elite does not want to see the United States abandon Afghanistan as the Soviets did after their withdrawal in 1989. Many Afghans fear that once the West leaves, their country will plunge back into civil war. And will their powerful neighbors continue their interference in landlocked Afghanistan or agree to a stability pact and noninterference? The elephant in the room is Al Qaeda and its extremist Afghan and Pakistani allies, based in Pakistan. Nobody can predict how they will react to a U.S. withdrawal.

Stabilizing Afghanistan and Pakistan and ensuring that Al Qaeda plays no role in either country has become even more vital in the aftermath of the revolutions sweeping through the Arab world in 2011. The Arab Spring has given the heart of the Muslim world a real opportunity for faster economic progress, democracy, literacy, and stability. But it has also given Al Qaeda enormous opportunities to reenter the Middle East and disrupt or co-opt the ongoing revolutionary process. The only organized political parties were the Islamists in countries such as Egypt, Tunisia, and Libya, where autocratic rulers were overthrown through mass movements. The fear was that Al Qaeda could return on the backs of these Islamist parties. A state failure in Pakistan or Afghanistan, unleashing a flood of extremists from these two countries, would quickly destabilize the Middle East and destroy the changes there. Instability in the Afghanistan-Pakistan region would also directly affect India and its ongoing war with domestic Islamic extremism. The states of Central Asia— Tajikistan, Uzbekistan, Turkmenistan, and Kyrgyzstan— are particularly vulnerable because extremists from these countries, who have spent the past decade hiding out in Pakistan, are now making their way through northern Afghanistan back to their homelands. The fragile and authoritarian states of Central Asia may well become the next battleground for Al Qaeda and militant Islam.

The U.S.-NATO plan depends on making peace with the Taliban, leaving a self-sustaining Afghan government and army to take over the responsibilities of security and governance and development. Regional stability is essential if Afghanistan is to survive. This optimistic plan does not really reflect the deep pessimism felt on the ground in both Afghanistan and Pakistan, but it may succeed.

The truth is that the West can no longer afford to fight in Afghanistan. A global recession began in 2008, and even before it ended, another one was around the corner in 2011. At this writing (November 2011), three European countries—Ireland, Portugal, and Greece—are on life support, courtesy of international lending institutions such as the European Central Bank. European countries are cutting down on defense spending by as much as 30 percent. Soldiers who risked their lives on the front lines in Afghanistan or Iraq are being demobilized, unemployed the moment they get home. On paper, NATO has 2 million troops under arms, but it can provide and equip only 40,000 to continue fighting in Afghanistan—too few to make a difference. When NATO bombed Libya in the summer of 2011, it ran out of ammunition. Opposition to the Afghan war in European countries is overwhelming, with public polls running as high as 70 percent against it. In the United States, public opposition to the war tops 60 percent, as jobs are now the single most important issue.

Since 2009, the United States has spent over $100 billion a year on the troop surge in Afghanistan, while in 2011 the U.S. defense budget has reached a staggering $671 billion. Between 2001 and 2010, the United States spent a total of $444 billion in Afghanistan, including $25 billion each for economic development and for Afghan security forces.[20] The recession at home, not major successes on the battlefield, will determine the endgame in Afghanistan. Worse, the Taliban insurgency is more intense than ever, the Afghan government is weaker than ever, and Pakistan is more vulnerable and lacks a positive relationship with Washington.

Barack Obama's first thoughts today are on his 2012 reelection bid. In a recession-hit United States, and with the Republicans in control of Congress, Obama needs to show that he can bring American troops home and declare some kind of victory. By the time of NATO's Lisbon summit in November 2010, none of Obama's key civilian advisers in the White House or the State Department believed that the war could be won militarily. Some among the CIA and the uniformed military in the Pentagon disagreed, but even they did not believe that outright victory was possible. Yet they were unable to contemplate a withdrawal that smacked of defeat or even talks with the Taliban.

A few weeks after Lisbon, on December 16, the White House released its cautious strategic policy review on Afghanistan. "The momentum achieved by the Taliban in recent years," it noted, "has been arrested in much of the country and reversed in some key areas, [but] these gains remain fragile and reversible. Consolidating those gains will require that we make more progress with Pakistan to eliminate sanctuaries for violent extremist networks."[21]

In other words, the United States was admitting that the Taliban could in time overturn all that the 2009–10 troop surges had achieved and that it had made no progress in persuading Pakistan to end its sanctuaries for the Afghan Taliban, even as the Pakistani Taliban expanded their attacks in Pakistan itself and were joined by Islamic extremist groups that had previously been trained by the ISI and had fought in Indian Kashmir. The most pressing issue for the Americans was the network run by Jalaluddin Haqqani in eastern Afghanistan, which was allied to both the ISI (who guaranteed their sanctuary in North Waziristan by refusing to go after them) and Al Qaeda (which provided the latest technology, training, and inspiration). The Haqqani network had access to hundreds of suicide bombers from the most militant madrassas in FATA and had the singular ability to mount devastating suicide attacks in major Afghan cities.

After a decade, NATO has achieved none of its strategic aims—rebuilding the Afghan state, defeating the Taliban, stabilizing the region—so what assurances can it now plausibly give that it will do so by 2014? Despite grandiose plans for a transition, nobody in Washington or other capitals can agree upon or visualize what the "end state" in Afghanistan will look like. What would talks with the Taliban or the regional countries resolve for the Afghans? Would such talks bring peace?

If there is to be a transition in Afghanistan, what will NATO be transitioning to? A stable, popular Afghan government, or one that is mired in corruption and incompetence? A well-trained, fighting Afghan Army, or one that is high on drugs and illiterate? A stable police force, or one whose desertion rate is the highest in the world? A functioning bureaucracy, judicial system, and ministries, or ones that can barely deliver services to the public, such as exist today? Even with the best outcome, the Afghan state will still be a basket case, dependent on receiving over $8 billion in aid each year just to maintain its army and bureaucracy. And large tracts of the country are under the control of the Taliban.

A Western ambassador in Kabul posed the problem clearly to me in November 2010: "Are we creating a sustainable government? Are we getting the politics right? Will there be an Afghan Army and civil service to take over when we leave, or will we just switch off the lights when we go?"

The West has rapidly built up the Afghan Army and police, but the bare bones of a functioning country are still missing. Primarily the United States and NATO have failed to create an indigenous Afghan economy that is not dependent on foreign aid or on employment on U.S. bases and that gives people real jobs and incomes. When the American troops leave, tens of thousands of Afghan drivers, cooks, guards, and clerks will be out of a job, because they will have no place in the local economy. After 9/11, President Bush declined to invest in rebuilding Afghan infrastructure, such as roads, dams, and water and power supplies. As a consequence, real economic growth, including the creation of long-term jobs, has been extremely limited.

In 2011, only 6 percent of Afghans received electricity. Kabul—the largest city, with 4 million people—received partial full-time electricity only in January 2009, via a 20-megawatt power line from Uzbekistan. Richard Holbrooke, Obama's special representative for Afghanistan-Pakistan who unfortunately died on the job in December 2010, initiated a new program to improve the economy and invest in agriculture, but it needed time and better security. Citizens in need of help or justice cannot get it from the government, and the capacity of its ministries to spend development funds and create programs is minimal.

If the bare bones of an Afghan state are still missing, so is Afghan leadership. President Hamid Karzai has lost the trust of many Afghans and the international community, as he has failed to improve governance, tackle corruption, or carry out free and fair elections. He seems pathologically unable to maintain a reasonable working relationship with American and NATO officials. If there is to be an effective transition toward self-government, then clearheaded, visionary Afghan leadership is needed. Yet Karzai appears to be wrapped in contradictions and enigmas, while he plays the role of victim and martyr, feeling constantly mistreated and undermined by the Americans.

As the endgame approaches, intense competition has developed among Afghanistan's six neighbors: Iran, Pakistan, China, Turkmenistan, Uzbekistan, and Tajikistan. These countries have a long and bloody record of monumental interference in Afghanistan. Now they seem to be preparing to move in once again, recruiting their proxies among the Afghan warlords and spreading money and influence in the country. Afghanistan cannot be stable unless its neighbors—and its larger, more powerful near neighbors, India, Russia, and Saudi Arabia—agree on noninterference. Obama pledged to achieve that through regional diplomacy when he was inaugurated, but little has since been accomplished.

The neighbor most vital for any peaceful resolution in Afghanistan is Pakistan, which has its own ambitions and interests in the country, which it feels must be fulfilled. Otherwise Pakistan's military can become deal breakers, unless they are satisfied. After 9/11, the military regime of President Pervez Musharraf provided sanctuary to all the defeated Taliban leaders (for reasons that I explained in *Descent into Chaos*).[22] In 2003, the ISI helped the Taliban restart their insurgency in Afghanistan and provided them with the supplies, training camps, and infrastructure, even as Musharraf kept the Bush administration on his side by capturing or killing leading members of Al Qaeda.

Neither Bush nor, it seems, Obama has had a strategic vision sufficiently broad to persuade Pakistan to shut down the sanctuaries and refocus its strategy. Under General Kayani, the army has become even more obsessed with India and the threat of Indian influence in Afghanistan, and even more insistent on running the country's foreign policy—even as its bloody war against the Pakistani Taliban is whittling away its influence. With a corrupt, incompetent civilian government that lacks all sense of public service or responsibility, the Pakistani public has nowhere to turn.

Tensions between the United States and the Pakistan military escalated through 2010 and 2011. For the army, the killing of Bin Laden was the humiliating last straw, and a deep chill set in, just when the two countries needed more than ever to work together. In 2011, the region appeared more divided than it had been a decade earlier.

Every issue discussed in this book shows how the exit from Afghanistan and the transition will be extremely difficult. How will Afghanistan survive? Can Pakistan be assured a safe future, with all its problems and its nuclear weapons? If the West is to depart Afghanistan by 2014 and leave behind relatively stable regimes in Kabul and Islamabad, it will need a multidimensional political, diplomatic, economic, and military strategy. In the next three years, will the United States and Europe be capable of pursuing such a strategy, or will they leave a bigger mess than in 2001? Finding a solution to these problems is the purpose of this book.

TWO

Pakistan in Crisis

WHEN BARACK Obama took office in January 2009, the crisis for Pakistan's people, the region, and the international community was far larger than even the perceptive president could have realized. Two weeks before he became president, he understood that Pakistan—whose problems, policies, and needs the Bush administration had largely ignored—might pose a greater danger to regional stability than even Afghanistan. Yet without Pakistan's help and compliance, no successful U.S. withdrawal from Afghanistan or reduction in Taliban violence could happen. The term *AfPak* is used for the region colloquially, but in every aspect and plan, Pakistan had to come first. What was the United States to do about Pakistan the problem, Pakistan the ally, Pakistan the asset—and eventually Pakistan the partial solution? There were no immediate answers.

Now in the autumn of 2011, relations between the two countries have slipped catastrophically to the lowest point ever—worse than anyone can remember, in an always-tumultuous roller-coaster relationship. The United States and Pakistan are just short of going to war. Obama has tried to address the Pakistan issue with far more comprehensive policies than Bush ever did, but he has failed to sustain them or to unite his administration around them or to provide sufficient political or monetary support to change the Pakistan Army's all-consuming psychological obsession with India.

Pakistan has a litany of problems, some of which involve the military. It refuses either to acknowledge or to end its covert support for the Afghan Taliban. It drags its feet on seeking a settlement with India. The antistate Pakistani Taliban is growing. The military refuses to handle politically the separatist insurgency that has erupted in Baluchistan province. Extremism in the army's ranks and concerns about the safety of Pakistan's nuclear weapons cause international apprehension. The military leadership fears that its officers and soldiers are becoming more intensely anti-American and so more susceptible to extremist propaganda.

On the other hand, the civilian government and the political parties refuse to address a wave of extremist intolerance against minority groups, both non-Muslim and Muslim. They take no responsibility for providing services to the public, while indulging in large-scale corruption. They allow an unprecedented economic meltdown to become worse by declining to carry out reforms or listen to international advice. An energy crisis turns the lights off for up to eighteen hours a day and undermines production. They fail to disarm militants or address the situation in Karachi, where ethnic and criminal blood-letting leaves scores of people dead every month. Pakistan faces diplomatic isolation, as its relations with all major countries except for China are souring dramatically. Devastating floods in 2010 and 2011 and an epidemic of dengue (malarial) fever in Punjab in 2011 were unavoidable, but governmental concern and aid delivery were totally inadequate. Pakistanis are beginning to fear the worst: international isolation, anarchy, civil war, a coup by Islamic militants.

As I discussed in *Descent into Chaos*, U.S.-Pakistan relations in the aftermath of 9/11 were tortuous. A deadly branch of the Taliban emerged in Pakistan, which, despite many warnings by experts, the army never anticipated. But to understand why Pakistan's political and military elites have taken the direction they have, we need to take a longer view of the country's weaknesses and strengths.

Four factors have prevented Pakistan from stabilizing and becoming a cohesive state. First, its political elite has failed to establish a coherent national identity capable of uniting the nation. The very subject remains deeply contentious: Is Pakistan an Islamic state, or is it a state for Muslims that has space for other religions and ethnic minorities? Is it not a democratic state as envisioned by its founder Muhammad Ali Jinnah? Are its people Muslims first, Sindhis or Punjabis second, and Pakistanis third? Or are they Pakistanis first and foremost?

The military defines Pakistani national identity defensively, in terms of the country's vulnerability, as a national security state, with a permanent mistrust of India. The politicians in power have never seriously tried to challenge this isolating self-definition by offering alternative policies, such as promoting good neighborliness, ending support for Islamic extremism, fostering economic development, and providing education. The Pakistani Taliban, for their part, would define Pakistan in religious terms: they call for the establishment of a state based on Sharia or Islamic law and for a caliphate, a supranational entity that would dissolve Pakistan's borders and aid and abet Islamic extremism and Al Qaeda. The extremists lack sufficient support to seize state power, but they have a proven ability to disrupt the state and foment anarchy.[1]

By 2011 the Pakistani Taliban were a much more dangerous entity than even the Afghan Taliban. The Pashtun tribesmen who made up the original core of the Pakistani Taliban had been joined by militants from Punjab, Karachi, and other places that had been involved in the war in Kashmir. They provided a sophisticated, educated, and urban edge to the terrorist war they now waged against Pakistan's security forces and civilians. Second, all these groups had camps in FATA, where they willingly trained foreigners, especially European Muslims from countries such as Britain, Germany, and Sweden; these students then returned home to become terrorists. Third, they were far more ideologically extreme than their Afghan brothers and could depend on a far larger pool of recruits as fighters and suicide bombers. By 2011 the main Afghan Taliban had expressed their desire to talk with the Kabul government and the Americans, but the Pakistani Taliban were still adamant about Pakistan's destruction.

The second factor dividing the country is Pakistan's national security paradigm: Is it to remain India-centric, as determined by the military? Or is it to adopt an alternative vision, as advocated by civil society and the progressive political elite? The long-running civilian-military rift that underlies these two views has contributed to the army's rule of Pakistan for nearly half the country's existence. Whenever the army feels that its control over national security is being challenged—usually in the midst of a political-constitutional-economic crisis, when an incompetent and corrupt civilian government is at the helm—it invariably overthrows the government and imposes military rule. This has happened four times in Pakistan's history, and military rule has often lasted a decade or more.

In the military's view, Pakistan is constantly threatened by outside enemies, in particular India but at times also Afghanistan, Iran, or the United States. In order to stand up to this perceived threatening environment, it maintains an army of 600,000 men, the seventh largest in the world. Its total security forces number more than 1 million men, armed with nearly one hundred nuclear weapons. The military consumes between 25 and 30 percent of the budget. It is able to secure those state resources because the political elite is supine and corrupt, parliament does not insist on accountability, and the army retains control of foreign policy, national security, and the nuclear arsenal. No enlightened military leaders have arisen to try to change this status quo, despite the spread of democracy and the demise of authoritarian forms of government around the world.

Third, Pakistan has become an abnormal state that uses Islamic militants—jihadi groups, nonstate actors—in addition to diplomacy and trade to pursue its defense and foreign policies. These nonstate actors have deeply antagonized its neighbors, all of whom have, at one time or another, felt their pressure. After September 11, 2001, the army's policies did not change, even though the whole world was now deeply aware of the threat posed by Islamic extremist forces and was less than tolerant toward them.

Yet Pakistan's location gives it enormous geostrategic potential. It borders Central, South, and West Asia, is a gateway to the sea for China, and is situated at the mouth of the Arabian Gulf; no other country in the world has such potential to become a hub for trade and business or the transcontinental transport of energy. Even India would find it far more useful to use Pakistan as an investment hub, and a leaping-off point to access Central and West Asia, than to be in conflict with it. The country lacks major natural resources like oil, but if it were at peace with its neighbors and with itself, Pakistan would become the great trading crossroads of the world, ensuring stability in the region. Islamic militant proxies would have no need to terrify the neighbors. Yet the army and the political elite have never tried to create such a Pakistan—they have always perceived the country as vulnerable and indefensible, and regarded every other government as a potential threat. Because of these fears, they support strategic depth and a pliable Afghan government that could aid Pakistan in times of war with India. This absurd theory, which I contradicted in my 2000 book *Taliban*, nonetheless persists and prevents the military from developing a rational policy toward Afghanistan.

The fourth factor perpetuating Pakistan's fragility is the inability of its ethnic groups to find a working political balance with one another, and the failure of Pakistan's political system, its parties, and its army to help them do so. Punjab, the second-largest province geographically, contains 60 percent of the country's population. Seventy percent of the army and a large part of the bureaucracy are drawn from Punjab. Punjab is also the most ethnically homogeneous province, with the vast majority of its population being Punjabi. The Baluch, Sindhis, and Pashtuns have at one time or other all felt underprivileged and resentful of the Punjabis. Punjabis constitute 60 percent of the population so all the other nationalities put together cannot equal Punjab's weight in determining economic or national policy. Moreover, the other three provinces—Baluchistan, Sind, and Khyber-Pakhtunkhwa (KP)—are often at odds with one another over issues such as distribution of water and electricity. For the smaller provinces, Punjab also constitutes the center of the state because it is from Punjab that the bulk of the army and the bureaucracy is recruited. As a result of Punjab's dominance, resentment from the smaller provinces has ebbed and flowed over the years. They have mounted everything from political resistance and civil unrest to terrorism and separatist guerrilla wars; the current insurgency in Baluchistan province is the fifth of its kind. Hence the absence of a shared national identity that transcends ethnicity, tribe, religion, and language is a lingering problem for Pakistan. If Pakistan were a trading hub and a regional crossroads, using all its territory, all its ethnic groups would have a stake in it.

The military and the political elite are both to blame for perpetuating the four factors and for failing to forge Pakistani unity. The major political parties are run as family dynasties rather than democratic institutions, and they have rarely offered modernizing policies that would reform the economy or society; they have rarely tried to live up to their responsibilities to the people. Civilian rule in the 1990s by Benazir Bhutto and Nawaz Sharif, who were twice popularly elected to power and twice deposed by a combination of the army and the presidency, made Pakistan a byword for corruption and mismanagement. Meanwhile the long bouts of military rule, in which politicians were jailed or exiled, have made it unthinkable for educated young people to enter politics. The politicians' failure has sustained the army's strong anticivilian prejudice and more recently fueled public antagonism toward politicians and the democratic system. Such conditions have only helped Islamic extremists present themselves as incorruptible, clean alternative rulers.

These internal conflicts within the country's elite have prevented the rulers from noticing major shifts and challenges in the global environment. They have allowed history to pass them by, with the result that Pakistan has missed out on all recent global developments. The end of the cold war in 1991–92 spelled the end of superpower aid for all third-world countries: in order to survive, middle- and low-income countries were forced to practice good neighborliness, build regional trade alliances, develop new industries, and find new markets for their goods. Hence the rapid expansion of the European Union (EU), the Association of Southeast Asian Nations (ASEAN), the Shanghai Co-operation Organization (SCO), and other such economic blocs.

But Pakistan spent the 1990s at loggerheads with all its neighbors. Early in the decade, the conflict with India escalated dramatically as the army supported jihadi groups to fight in Indian Kashmir, while Islamabad's support for the Taliban regime kept relations with Iran and the Central Asian republics tense and competitive over Afghanistan. Many Pakistanis talked of building roads, railways, and oil pipelines that would link Central Asia, via Afghanistan, with the port of Karachi; many talked of the potential of the new Chinese-built port of Gwadar on the Baluchistan coast. But nothing could come of such dreams as long as a civil war raged in Afghanistan, an insurgency continued in Baluchistan, and an isolated Pakistan continued to support the Taliban. The peace and economic dividend at the end of the cold war that benefited many countries rolled by Pakistan unnoticed.

Meanwhile globalization built interlinked prosperity and new industries in many third-world countries. India surged ahead: it adapted quickly to globalization, carrying out major economic reforms and encouraging its private sector. India's boom could have accelerated a similar expansion in Pakistan if the two neighbors had had better trade ties. But instead, globalization passed Pakistan by. Many educated Pakistanis had no idea of the dramatic economic changes being wrought on the world stage, as Pakistan continued to export its traditional raw materials like cotton and rice, fought its proxy wars in Kashmir and Afghanistan, and stagnated. In the past twenty years, it has not developed a single new industry or cultivated a major new crop, even though it is an agricultural country. Globalization made it vital for Pakistan to spend money on education, to upgrade the skills of its workforce, and to invest in new industries. Instead Musharraf fueled a consumption-based economy that rested on personal and state debt.

September 11, 2001, was another wake-up call for Pakistan to end its dependence on jihadi groups as a surrogate for conducting foreign policy. After Al Qaeda's attack on the U.S. mainland, the world was clearly going to consider Islamic extremism the new enemy, and the United States would clearly use that threat to justify military intervention in other states. President Bush's message to Islamabad—"You are either with us or against us"—was aimed at gaining Pakistan's support for the invasion of Afghanistan, but it was also a clear warning for the future. Hitherto the United States had closed its eyes to Pakistani support for jihadist groups because of the presumed threat from India, but now that such groups had actually attacked the United States, Washington was no longer prepared to allow state sponsorship of them.

But Pakistan's reaction was myopic. Musharraf thought he could still manipulate and massage the Bush message. While agreeing to support the United States against Al Qaeda, the ISI allowed jihadi groups to intensify their attacks in India and Kashmir—which, after the attack on the Indian parliament in 2001, nearly led to war with India. In 2003, the ISI helped revive the Taliban insurgency in Afghanistan. By 2005 (as I pointed out in *Descent into Chaos*), a major confrontation between the United States and Pakistan was clearly inevitable, and it did occur in 2010 and 2011.

The last decade has also brought fundamental changes in national belief systems around the world—but not yet in Pakistan. A country's military strength, its nuclear weapons, its geostrategic ambitions, and its influence over its neighbors are worthless if—as is the case with Pakistan—its economy is weak, its people are illiterate, and its youth are jobless. The rapid economic growth of India and China was the harbinger of their strength and regional influence. Pakistan, by contrast, has undertaken no major economic or social reforms since the early 1990s. The ruling elite refuses to tax itself or to invest its wealth in modernizing industry and agriculture; the state-run industries are bleeding the country; and the army refuses to cut its expenses, even as it has expanded its own tax-free businesses and property empires. Only 1.8 million people pay income tax, and farmers pay no income tax, even though they are the best off due to the rapid rise in food prices. Corruption is rampant, and social services, especially education, remain abysmal, because every year the government's spending on health and education is cut as military expenses increase. Literacy is at a miserable 57 percent, the lowest in South Asia. Neither the politicians nor the army has ever called for a massive literacy campaign.

For the past twenty years, the country has lived off IMF loan programs, which have never been fully completed or complied with because the various governments have refused to carry out the reforms demanded by the IMF. Other countries provide large amounts of aid, but Pakistan has very little to show for it. Between 2001 and 2010, the United States gave a total of $20.5 billion. Germany, Britain, Japan, and other donors, along with the World Bank and the Asian Development Bank, provided about half again that sum. Out of the U.S. funding, $14.4 billion went to the Pakistan Army for operations along the Afghan border, while only $6.1 billion was used as economic aid, and most of that ($4.8 billion) was for budgetary support.[2] The United States was also generous on the humanitarian front when a dreadful earthquake hit northern Pakistan in 2005 and when floods destroyed much of the country's infrastructure in 2010.

When Richard Holbrooke first visited Pakistan in 2009, Pakistanis admitted bluntly that they had nothing to show for all the U.S. aid— not a hospital, a dam, or a university. Holbrooke set about rectifying the situation by arranging aid for the decrepit electrical power system: he and Senator John Kerry shepherded through Congress the Kerry-Lugar-Berman bill, which offered Pakistan's civilian sector $7.5 billion over five years or $1.5 billion a year. It was the first time the United States would provide so much aid for the social and economic sector. The bill passed in 2009, and Obama signed it into law. Initially the army put up strong objections to the bill because it was conditioned on Pakistan doing more in the war on terror and strengthening democracy. Within two years, however, U.S. military aid was suspended due to the breakdown of U.S.-Pakistan relations after the killing of Bin Laden. Thereafter the possibility arose that China would step in to bail out Pakistan. But despite China's massive support for the government and the military—it provides nuclear reactors and weapon systems as well as strategic infrastructure projects—it has rarely given cash to Pakistan for budgetary support or for counterterrorism campaigns, both of which the United States was providing.

The government and the military further exacerbate Pakistan's crisis-ridden state by constantly feeding the public false narratives:

that the United States, India, and Israel are conspiring to undermine Pakistan and ultimately to dismember the country; that the reason for the increase in Islamic extremism in Pakistan is the U.S. occupation of Afghanistan; that the United States and India are arming and funding the Pakistani Taliban to weaken Pakistan; that Osama bin Laden was never killed in Abbottabad; that the United States is intent on capturing Pakistan's nuclear weapons; and that if the United States were to leave Afghanistan, terrorism and suicide bombings would cease and everything would return to normal. Indian external intelligence, RAW (Research and Analysis Wing), abetted by the CIA, is said to be funding separatists in Baluchistan and Sind to carry out acts of terrorism, while India lays down deep roots in Afghanistan.

These lies and myths confuse the public and youth, prevail over objective or rational analysis, and make it easier to spread conspiracy theories. The political, intellectual, and media elites have never challenged them in a sustained way—many journalists are on the government or ISI payroll or receive other perks and privileges. Among the majority of academics, too, intellectual standards and honesty have been sorely lacking, except for a few superb scholars who refuse to compromise. Government servants, especially those in the foreign and interior ministries, tend to be subservient to the army, and groupthink disallows any real debate over policy.

But because of these narratives, the rulers, for example, can relatively easily divert discussion of the death of Bin Laden from the main issue—what he was doing for so many years living next to the Pakistan military academy in Abbottabad—to the issue of the United States violating Pakistan's sovereignty. Talk about Pakistan's vulnerability and India's demonhood can dominate the TV talk shows and newspapers, having an enormous impact on public perceptions. The military and government deny unrelentingly that Pakistan is doing anything untoward against its neighbors or is helping extremists. For ten years, Islamabad has denied that Al Qaeda, the Afghan Taliban, or the Haqqani network was ever based on its soil, even though most of their leaders have been captured or killed in Pakistan. In recent years, the military has admitted to the Americans that these groups are present in Pakistan, because the army is also intent on getting negotiations going between these groups and the United States. But the army will never admit it in public.

In a social atmosphere where anything is believable, the extremists benefit most. The false narratives give excellent cover to anti-Indian jihadist groups, such as Lashkar-e-Taiba (LT), that have been trained by the ISI and that have working relationships with Al Qaeda and the Taliban. The Pakistani state does not merely protect these jihadist groups and allow them to recruit and train cadres and mobilize funds; it portrays them not as terrorists but as benign social workers. After the LT mounted attacks in Mumbai in 2008, Pakistan held LT leaders under discreet house arrest for a few weeks, then freed them. This nonpunishment infuriated the United States, India, and the international community.

Higher education has suffered enormously. The best teaching staff has left the country, so universities are unable to educate their students adequately. This is especially true in the army. The Pakistan Army's prime institution, the National Defense University (NDU) in Islamabad, has seen a sad loss of intellectual rigor. In the past, the NDU, where all midcareer officers take courses, prided itself on allowing officers to hear dissident views and encouraged rigorous discussion. I lectured at the NDU for fifteen years, until Musharraf banned me, along with half a dozen other writers and intellectuals who held different views on the army's policies. Musharraf insisted, for example, that the 1999 Kargil war with India was a victory. Most Pakistanis and the world think the war was a humiliating defeat, but neither Musharraf nor the NDU will hear of it. Under Musharraf and Kayani, too, lecturers have been encouraged not to question the army's dominant role in the polity. The NDU has even begun to give courses to civilians, politicians, and elected members of parliament: it teaches them the army's interpretation of national security and politics—rather than learning from them the importance of democracy and civilian control over the armed forces. Anne Patterson, the U.S. ambassador who lectured there, was shocked to "receive astonishingly naive and biased questions about America." She said officers have no chance to hear alternative views, even though many of them have children studying in the United States.[3]

The constantly tense military-civil relations dominate Pakistan's politics. Three of the country's four military dictators were forced out of power by a mass movement and simultaneously a constitutional crisis, an economic depression, and an increase in ethnic separatism. Every time a military regime is bought down, Pakistanis have to go back and reinvent the wheel of democracy. After a decade of military rule, civilian governments are invariably incompetent and corrupt and only await their denouement at the hands of the next military coup. No elected government has yet been able to fulfill its whole term mandate before being voted out of office through another election. Every military dictator, too, has been forced out, usually by his inability to get himself elected for a second term as a civilian rather than as a military president. In 2007, President Pervez Musharraf wanted to take off his uniform, end his long stint as army chief, and get elected as president for a second term, this time as a legitimate civilian. Few were prepared to accept that, even in the army. The political crisis that he generated before his resignation gave the extremists time and space to expand their area of operations. Ironically it was the army and his chosen successor as army chief, Gen. Ashfaq Parvez Kayani, who ultimately forced Musharraf out, by refusing to back him any longer.

———

The chaos and violence that preceded Musharraf's ouster portended the country's present political meltdown. In 2007, after a year of secret diplomacy and intense U.S. and British political pressure, Musharraf reluctantly agreed to allow Benazir Bhutto to return home from exile to contest a general election. Corruption charges against her would be dropped, and she could emerge as prime minister; in return she would support Musharraf for a second term as president. But in March 2007, Musharraf tried to force the Supreme Court chief justice Iftikhar Muhammad Chaudhry to resign. Failing, Musharraf suspended him and placed him under house arrest. The public and lawyers were indignant, and Chaudhry's cause—a free and independent judiciary—led to street protests across the country. Then on October 6, 2007, defying public sentiment, Musharraf got himself elected president by a puppet parliament for the second term. (In Pakistan, the president or the head of state is elected by a majority of votes in parliament while the chief executive or prime minister is elected through general elections.)

On October 18, Benazir Bhutto returned to Karachi to a rapturous welcome. The day she arrived, a huge bomb exploded next to the truck she was traveling in, killing 140 people and leaving hundreds wounded. Bhutto demanded an international investigation into the attack. The carnage, and Musharraf's refusal to accept her demand, led to mounting public anger at Musharraf and acute strains between the two. The military had clearly neglected her security, despite promises made to the Americans. Senior members of her Pakistan Peoples Party (PPP) were convinced that elements from the intelligence agencies were responsible for the blast. Civil-military relations deteriorated even further.

Bhutto's return to Pakistan had raised enormous hopes that she would restore democracy, curb extremism, and rebuild the economy. She had matured immensely since she was twice prime minister and had allowed her husband, Asif Ali Zardari (then known as "Mr. 10 Percent"), to fix business deals. This time Zardari had been told to stay home in Dubai and mind the kids. Bhutto was shocked by the growth of extremism, and as she toured the country, she took an ever-hardening line against the militants. "Extremism," she said, "looms as a threat but it will be contained . . . if the moderate middle can be mobilized to stand up to fanaticism. I return to lead that battle."[4] The militants were determined to stop her, while the army mistrusted her coming to power on the backs of the Americans and scorned her peace overtures to India and Afghanistan.

Pakistan was then in the midst of the first wave of suicide attacks: the Pakistani Taliban had recently coalesced around Al Qaeda, young Pashtun tribal and radical leaders from the tribal areas, and mainstream Punjabi extremist groups that had fought in Kashmir. Radicalized through the madrassa (Islamic school) network by years of fighting in Afghanistan, and angry at the army for cooling down the Kashmir jihad, they aimed to overthrow the Pakistani state. The Pakistani Taliban targeted the army, government officials, and civilians while also helping the Afghan Taliban fight the Americans in Afghanistan.

The Federally Administered Tribal Areas (FATA), where the militants coalesced, consist of seven tribal agencies that border Afghanistan and the province of Khyber-Pakhtunkhwa (KP, formerly the North West Frontier Province). The British had constituted these areas as a no-man's-land between British India and Afghanistan, drawing the Durand Line right through the tribal areas, splitting them between Afghanistan and British India. Neither Afghanistan nor the Pashtun tribes have ever recognized this border, calling it arbitrary and claiming that the territory now in Pakistan belongs to Afghanistan. (For a far more extensive description of FATA and events there in the ongoing conflict, see my *Descent into Chaos*.)

Briefly, the tribes in FATA have been particularly receptive to radicalization because of their history of poverty, underdevelopment, and religious conviction, and their constant state of rebellion to protect their rights. With a population of just 3.5 million people, FATA has an immensely rugged terrain and little in the way of a modern economy, education, or prospects for its youth. Forty-six percent of the population works outside FATA. The literacy rate for women is one of the lowest in the world at 3 percent, while for men it is only 15 percent, compared to Pakistan's national average of 57 percent. The influx after 2001 of Al Qaeda and the Afghan Taliban into this region has acted like an economic and religious engine, driving the process of radicalization.

Tribal resistance to the army began in 2004. The militants turned back each attack, enough to produce army defeats and humiliating cease-fires. That further emboldened them. Army attempts to raise local militias to fight them were a failure. The militants abandoned their traditional tribal chiefs and elders, who usually supported the government, and killed more than one thousand of them. Tens of thousands of tribesmen fled FATA. By 2010 the militants controlled almost all of FATA.

In 2007, the various militant tribal militias formed the Tehrik-e-Taliban Pakistan (TTP); that same year militants openly confronted security forces at the siege of the Red Mosque, in the heart of Islamabad. The army was forced to storm the mosque complex, killing more than one hundred people. Those militants who survived escaped to FATA and became suicide bombers. In 2007, there were fifty-six suicide bombings that killed 865 Pakistani security forces and civilians, compared with just six suicide attacks the previous year.[5] The losses in 2007 exceeded the total losses for all years between 2001 and 2006. An internal civil war had begun. By 2011, more than 35,000 people would be killed, including 3,500 security personnel.

Meanwhile the political confrontation intensified. On November 3, to preempt a possible Supreme Court verdict against his reelection as president, Musharraf declared a state of emergency and arrested thousands of people, including Bhutto. Condemnation of Musharraf's "second coup" was worldwide. His actions even dismayed the army, which feared that his growing unpopularity would also affect them. Under pressure, Musharraf gave up his uniform and handed over the role of army chief of staff to Gen. Ashfaq Parvez Kayani, who had headed the ISI since 2004. Musharraf was now hugely unpopular, viewed as arrogant and overweening—his dictatorship now confined to a single person, his cabinet redundant, and parliament a rubber stamp.[6] People wanted a return to full democracy and Musharraf out of power. They looked to Bhutto to lead them. But on December 27, 2007, their hopes were traumatically dashed when she was assassinated just two weeks before the date of the general election.

Her popularity and the widespread belief (never proved) that Musharraf's intelligence agents were responsible for her death led to violent countrywide protests for three days. The government produced a tape recording of an alleged telephone conversation involving Baitullah Mehsud, one of the leaders of the Pakistani Taliban, ostensibly taking responsibility for the murder. The real perpetrators are still not known. Musharraf made some callous remarks about her death that incensed the public. "You need three qualities today if you want to fight the extremists and the terrorists," he told *Newsweek*. "Number one, you must have the military with you. Well, she was very unpopular with the military. Very unpopular. Number two, you shouldn't be seen by the entire religious lobby to be alien—a nonreligious person. The third element: don't be seen as an extension of the United States. Now I am branded as an extension, but not to the extent she was."[7]

The PPP chose Bhutto's nineteen-year-old son, Bilawal Bhutto Zardari, as the new party chairman. As he was still studying at Oxford University, her immediate political successor became her controversial husband, Asif Ali Zardari. When the delayed election took place on February 18, 2008, Musharraf's party did badly with twenty-three sitting ministers losing their seats. The PPP won 87 seats, against the 66 seats won by the main opposition party, the Pakistan Muslim League–Nawaz (PML-N), led by Nawaz Sharif. Zardari formed a coalition government with smaller parties that had done well in the provinces and initially with the support of Nawaz Sharif.

The voter turnout was just 45 percent, the lowest ever recorded and nearly 20 points less than the 63 percent turnout for the first free and fair elections in 1970. FATA recorded the lowest turnout in its history—only 12 percent. All this indicated public disenchantment with democracy. The PPP suffers from personalized dynastic leadership, corruption, a feudal political base, incompetence, and a lack of technocrats. However, it is the only national party in Pakistan that still has support in all four provinces. All the other parties, including the PML-N, have become regional parties representing an ethnic group or a province.

Zardari's electoral alliance included the Awami National Party (the main Pashtun anti-Taliban party in KP province), the Muttahida Quami Movement in Sind (the party of the Urdu-speaking population), and nationalist groups in Baluchistan. The election produced the first genuine national government that had support from all the major ethnic groups. It raised hopes for stability and progress.

The extremists challenged the election by creating mayhem in the streets. In the first ten weeks of 2008, seventeen suicide bombings killed nearly three hundred people and left the country reeling. The Pakistani Taliban controlled the main roads out of Peshawar and besieged the city; only months later did the army regain control. Kidnappings for ransom rose dramatically in KP and FATA, where on June 25 Baitullah Mehsud executed twenty-eight members of a tribal peace group who had met with the Pakistani Taliban. The new government had no clear plan on how to deal with the escalating violence and left all decision making to the army.

The war in FATA left 1.5 million people displaced, while the year-long unrest created a severe economic and energy crisis, with chronic shortages of gas, electricity, and fuel. Musharraf, a recipient of more than $10 billion in aid from the United States, had failed to build a single electricity-generating station. Zardari set up the Friends of Pakistan forum to beg traditional donor countries for more money, but they refused to oblige until the government first carried out major economic reforms. To stave off a default, the government signed an agreement with the IMF for a loan of $11.3 billion, promising to implement economic reforms. After a decade of military rule, General Kayani wanted to distance the army from Musharraf and improve its image. He also wanted to be his own man and that meant getting rid of Musharraf, which the PPP was more than willing to agree to. Under pressure, Musharraf finally resigned on August 18, 2008. Zardari, who had so far stayed in the background, now decided to play a public role and was soon elected as the new president.

————

This was the long-running political crisis that the Obama administration inherited. Pakistan, the supply chain of the U.S.-led war in Afghanistan, was undergoing a deep political, economic, and social upheaval. Meanwhile Obama was priming his administration to push Pakistan harder in dealing with the Afghan Taliban it was hosting. On the campaign trail, he had talked about the importance of Pakistan, but he knew his options were limited. "Make no mistake: we can't succeed in Afghanistan or secure our homeland unless we change our Pakistan policy. . . . The greatest threat to that security lies in the tribal regions of Pakistan, where terrorists train and insurgents strike into Afghanistan," he said in July 2008. "We cannot tolerate a terrorist sanctuary, and as President, I won't."[8]

FATA was now the main base for Al Qaeda and Western jihadis, who were coming there in ever-increasing numbers to receive training. The Americans were deeply worried that the Pakistan Army was mounting all too few operations in FATA; that it was instead striking peace deals with militants who refrained from attacking Pakistani forces but eagerly attacked U.S. forces in Afghanistan; and that it refused to disturb the Haqqani network in North Waziristan. Admiral

Mike Mullen, chairman of the Joint Chiefs of Staff, made it his personal mission to build a relationship with Kayani and persuade him to take the high road—he invested much time and energy in it.

In late September 2008, Kayani reappointed two generals whom he considered his most effective and loyal officers. Lt. Gen. Ahmed Shuja Pasha became head of the ISI, replacing Lt. Gen. Nadeem Taj, a Musharraf loyalist; and Maj. Gen. Tariq Khan became head of the Frontier Corps (FC). Pasha was a graduate of the German staff college and spoke German fluently. He and Kayani had been joined at the hip when dealing with the U.S. military and the CIA, trying to mollify them while refusing to yield to their demands to "do more." Kayani was to extend Pasha's tenure twice, and even after Osama bin Laden was killed in Pakistan and politicians demanded Pasha's head, he refused to let him resign. Tariq Khan was to do an excellent job in turning around the paramilitary and largely Pashtun FC, which was underpaid and overworked, raising its morale and providing it with better equipment through U.S. support.

The militants showed their disregard for the new government in September by exploding a massive truck bomb that blew up the Marriott Hotel in Islamabad, killing 53 people and injuring 266. The blast was heard thirty miles away, and fire gutted the whole building. In October, another suicide attack in FATA, aimed at anti-Taliban tribal elders, killed 85 and wounded 200 tribesmen. The country was on fire. Then the far worse attack in Mumbai, India, carried out by Pakistan's Lashkar-e-Taiba, set the world alight as India alleged the involvement of the ISI.

Kayani did not immediately respond by taking action in FATA, so Washington delayed sending promised arms and releasing funds to the military. In his first meeting with the civilian government in June,

Mullen made it clear that the United States perceived the threat from FATA. "I believe fundamentally if the United States is going to get hit, it's going to come out of the planning that the leadership [of Al Qaeda] in the FATA is generating, their planning and direction," he said.[9] As had been secretly agreed by the U.S. administration when Obama ordered the first surge of U.S. troops to Afghanistan, the CIA stepped up drone missile attacks, firing off twenty-two missiles in the last four months of 2008, compared to twelve in the first eight months. But these attacks did not alter the balance of power in FATA, where the Taliban and Al Qaeda still ruled.

Pakistan was now inescapably becoming an unstable state, a continuing supporter of the Afghan Taliban even as the army went up against its homegrown Pakistani Taliban. The army had clearly underestimated Obama's resolve to deal more harshly with Pakistan than Bush had ever done. Yet as Obama sent more troops and aid to Afghanistan, Americans had started to ask why he was doing so when the real problem was in Pakistan.

President Zardari and the civilian government, although dependent on American support, did not want to risk antagonizing the army. On the contrary, he yielded to the army on every count, even as his government demonstrated more and more ineptitude. The army was determined to prevent any U.S. military presence on its soil; it would remain hostile to India and protect Pakistan's sovereignty, even though foreign extremists like Al Qaeda had long ago broken such boundaries.

THREE

Pakistan: Who Betrayed Whom?

AT THE heart of Pakistan's rapid decline, its worsening relations with the West and neighboring countries, and its image as the center of global terrorism is the army's continued reliance on proxy jihadi forces. Some of them are ready to carry out the state's bidding, but others will just as easily turn against the military. In the 1990s, their main target was Indian Kashmir, but when the Taliban emerged, Pakistani militants went to Kandahar to fight for them. The United States was embarrassed but shrugged its shoulders—the Clinton administration had no policy toward Pakistan or Afghanistan in the 1990s. India could look after itself, and if Pakistan considered India its long-term foe, there was nothing much the Clinton White House wanted to do about it. But after September 11 everything changed—except Pakistan's policies.

Pakistan's strategic location, which should have been a vital economic asset to the country, was now a liability, as it became the central hub for the U.S. war in Afghanistan and as jihadis from surrounding countries flocked there. Pakistan's new global identity was not as a model of innovation or modernity but as a refuge for multiple extremist groups. A decade after 9/11, its failure to address the extremist threat culminated in the breakdown of its relations with the United States and NATO. I outlined in detail the role of the Afghan and Pakistani Taliban in Pakistan in *Descent into Chaos*. But much of the blame must be laid on the Bush administration, whose sole focus was catching Al Qaeda, even though more American troops were dying at the hands of the Taliban than Al Qaeda. President Musharraf had agreed with Bush to provide intelligence on Al Qaeda, which the ISI did, but as far as the Taliban were concerned, there was no such agreement or commitment. It took four years after the Taliban insurgency restarted for the White House to begin to take the Taliban as a serious threat. Ryan Crocker, the last Bush administration ambassador to Pakistan, told me in 2007, just before he left Islamabad, that he had never received an order from Washington to raise the issue of Taliban sanctuaries with the Pakistanis.

Pakistan had first used proxy forces just after it gained independence in 1947, when it sent thousands of Pakistani Pashtun tribesmen to battle Indian forces in Kashmir, triggering the first India-Pakistan war. Sixty years later the grandchildren of those Pashtuns would be urged to go kill Americans in Afghanistan. In 1962, following India's defeat by China, the military regime of Gen. Ayub Khan secretly sent several thousand soldiers disguised as guerrillas to stir up rebellion among the population in Indian Kashmir. Code-named Operation Gibraltar, the infiltration was a failure, but it led to the second all-out war between the two countries, which Pakistan lost.

In 1971, the army created similar proxy forces in East Pakistan (now Bangladesh) in order to help it subdue the separatist Bengali insurgency, which was being backed by India. These proxy forces, some Bengali but mostly Urdu-speaking Biharis as well as cadres of the Jamaat-e-Islami, carried out several massacres.[1] Pakistan's defeat by India and the loss of East Pakistan—half the country—created strong feelings of humiliation within the military, which encouraged it to continue using proxies as an effective tool to weaken India and achieve revenge. The military was to further bankroll the Sikh insurgency in Indian Punjab and, over the years, several tribal uprisings in northeastern India. A vicious tit for tat ensued, as India in turn funded and supported Baluch, Sindhi, and Pashtun separatists in the 1970s and later. Baluchistan has undergone five insurgencies. In the 1980s, India backed the pro-Soviet Communist regime in Kabul, which launched its own terrorist campaign in northwestern Pakistan to counter the presence of the Afghan mujahedeen.

Also in the 1980s, the ISI made a bold move to exert distributive control over billions of dollars in arms supplies and cash supplied by the CIA for the mujahedeen. Military dictator president Zia ul-Haq stipulated to President Reagan that if Pakistan were given total control of the CIA program and funds, it would only risk the wrath of the Soviet Union. The Americans complied, and the ISI expanded enormously, becoming not just the arbiter of foreign policy through its covert programs but also the most powerful and intrusive political player in the country. Up to 30,000 foreign jihadis came to fight alongside the mujahedeen, and many of them were to stay on in Pakistan. The military took enormous credit for the defeat and breakup of the Soviet Union. After 9/11, Pakistan believed it could carry on in a similar way with the Americans—help out the CIA with Al Qaeda, but assert its sovereignty and carry on with its own agenda in Kashmir and Afghanistan.

In 1989, the ISI used the residue of U.S. funds for Afghanistan to support a mass movement in Kashmir against India that would last a decade. Many of Pakistan's generals were to remain influenced by the expansionist foreign policy and the use of jihadis cultivated by Zia ul-Haq, who took the country literally from one jihad to the next without a break. Several Pakistani militant groups such as Harkat-ul-Jihad-al-Islami (founded in 1984) and Lashkar-e-Taiba (founded in 1982) were born in the crucible of the anti-Soviet Afghan war, before moving on to greater exploits in Kashmir in the 1990s. At home, there was a rapid growth in madrassas, weaponization, drugs, and crime, making these groups self-sufficient, as ISI funding for extremist groups was reduced. As long as the Indian giant remained cowed and pro-Pakistan forces were successful in Afghanistan, no Pakistani government came up with plans to deradicalize the militants and to undertake economic and educational reforms.

Pakistan began to lose control of these groups in 1997, when the Taliban leader Mullah Muhammad Omar handed over all training camps for foreigners in Afghanistan to Osama bin Laden. In these camps, Kashmiri and Pakistani extremists mixed with young militants from all over the Muslim world and from Europe, just as an earlier generation had done in the 1980s in Afghanistan. Al Qaeda's indoctrination had an enormous impact on them: some embraced the idea of global jihad, joined Al Qaeda, and went on to provide it with skills and facilities. Both before and after 9/11, all Pakistani insurgent groups used Afghanistan as an arena for virtual battle experience, increasing their militancy, raising their numbers, and sharpening their skills. These Pakistani groups would later turn against the regime in Islamabad and flourish as the Pakistani Taliban.

After the defeat of the Taliban after 9/11 in Afghanistan, Musharraf and the military began the long process, overseen by the Americans, of capturing and killing Arab Al Qaeda members who had fled to Pakistan. The United States gave cash rewards to Pakistani security officers who had been involved in actions to kill and capture members of Al Qaeda. A tiny minority of Pakistani officers from the ISI and from Pakistan's special forces had jihadist sympathies and disagreed with this policy; they left the army and joined militant groups. They, too, became important to Al Qaeda, for they organized some of the deadliest attacks against the Pakistan Army, starting with two attempts to assassinate Musharraf in December 2003 that almost succeeded.

Musharraf's determination to wipe out Al Qaeda and its growing Pakistani support base was undercut by his double-edged policy of helping the Afghan Taliban relaunch their insurgency in Afghanistan. Paramount in the military's thinking was the fear of India encircling Pakistan first from its eastern borders and now along its western borders. He based this contradictory initiative on several strategic assumptions made by the ISI: that the Afghan Pashtuns, whom Pakistan favored, had lost their dominance to the non-Pashtun warlords of the Northern Alliance, whom the United States favored; that the United States would quickly leave Afghanistan after its invasion of Iraq; that the United States would give India increasing influence in Afghanistan and would eventually dump Pakistan, as it had after the Soviet withdrawal in 1989; and that the pro-Indian Kabul regime would help India undermine Pakistan's western borders. With these assumptions in mind, Musharraf's next step was to ensure that the Afghan Taliban remained a proxy force for Pakistan and to persuade their defeated and dispirited units to unite and relaunch an insurgency in Afghanistan. Even though many Taliban preferred making their peace with Karzai, the ISI persuaded them not to do so once the insurgency began.

The ISI helped the Taliban raise funds in the Arabian Gulf states and facilitated their acquisition of guns and ammunition. It set up training camps manned by its own officers in Baluchistan province, where many Taliban leaders had settled. It set up a secret organization to run the Taliban, even as it was cooperating with the CIA in apprehending Al Qaeda. Retired army and ISI officers, operating outside the traditional military structures, manned the secret organization. For several years, the United States failed to detect this support base or understand how it operated.[2] The main Taliban under Mullah Omar set up offices in Quetta and Peshawar; its leaders in Quetta directed the insurgency in southern Afghanistan. Another Afghan Taliban ally, Gulbuddin Hekmatyar's Hezb-i-Islami party, operated out of northern Pakistan.

From their bases in Pakistan, the Taliban launched attacks into Afghanistan while recruiting Pakistani Pashtuns to provide them with base security and additional manpower, even as they radicalized them for their cause. Thus were born the Pakistani Taliban in FATA. They were local Pakistani Pashtun tribesmen who became radicalized after spending years in the company of either Al Qaeda or the Afghan Taliban and receiving generous payments for services rendered. At first, Musharraf ignored the threat, and the army went into denial mode about the existence of any terrorist bases in FATA. Finally in March 2004, under U.S. pressure, Musharraf launched the first attack against the Pakistani Taliban in South Waziristan. But the poorly trained and armed Frontier Corps units walked into an ambush and lost some two hundred men. The next month the army signed a peace agreement with the Pakistani Taliban leader Nek Muhammad. This pattern of attacking and then surrendering ground through a so-called peace treaty established a losing pattern for the army for the rest of the decade. Throughout this period, the veteran Afghan anti-Soviet fighter Jalaluddin Haqqani played a critical role for the army, creating temporary cease-fires or bringing Pakistani Taliban to talks with the military.

The tribal agencies of FATA were dominated by the network led by Haqqani and his sons. Haqqani was based in the town of Miranshah, the capital of the North Waziristan tribal agency, but the Afghan Taliban and Pakistani militants who came to operate from other parts of FATA all paid homage to Haqqani. He had become extremely close to both the ISI and Al Qaeda in the 1980s and was honored even by the Americans for his fierce fighting against the Soviets. He subsequently joined the Taliban movement in 1994 and became a minister in the Taliban government in Kabul in 1996. After 9/11 the CIA and ISI tried to persuade him to withdraw his support from the Taliban and Al Qaeda but he refused to do so. His present influence in Afghanistan is largely in three of the eastern Pashtun provinces: Khost, Paktika, and Paktya.

With the army's intense focus on the future of Afghanistan and the threat it now faced from homegrown Taliban, Musharraf began secret negotiations with the Indians. In 2004 both countries agreed to a cease-fire along the disputed Line of Control, the border that divided Indian Kashmir from Pakistani Kashmir. Significantly, that cease-fire has held ever since, even though both countries still maintain large numbers of troops on the border. As a result, young Punjabi militants from parties that had once fought in Kashmir became frustrated, split away from their mother parties, and came to FATA to fight for the Afghan Taliban. The tribal agencies were soon littered with camps of Punjabi militants who had received Haqqani's permission to set up shop. In FATA, they underwent further radicalization and were provoked by U.S. drone strikes and by the Red Mosque siege to take up arms against Pakistan. The conviction spread among them that the Pakistan Army was the lackey of the Americans and an enemy of Islam, so now God ordained them to overthrow Pakistan's state through an Islamic revolution.

The ISI lost control over these groups, which killed and bombed their way through Pakistan's cities, targeting specifically the offices of the ISI and other intelligence agencies. Only Lashkar-e-Taiba (LT)— by now the largest, best-disciplined, and most highly trained extremist party, with some support in the army itself—remained loyal to the state and sought to fight only India. But even LT leaders came under pressure from their cadres to fight the Americans, and so by 2009 its leaders allowed a limited number of young fighters to play a role in Afghanistan.

Over the next few years, FATA was to turn into a battleground, but the army remained extremely selective about whom it went after. It hunts down only those who oppose the Pakistani state; it allows Afghan Taliban such as Jalaluddin Haqqani, who remains loyal to Pakistan, to thrive in North Waziristan. Likewise, it leaves alone Pakistani Taliban commanders—such as Hafiz Gul Bahadur and Maulvi Nazir Nazir from South Waziristan—who only fight U.S. forces in Afghanistan. Such dubious deals cannot be sustained, as under such a regime everyone thrives, including those militants determined to destroy Pakistan.

Recently, the United States has pressured Pakistan to go after the Afghan Taliban and the Haqqani network, but given Pakistan's critical role in the U.S. war effort in Afghanistan, it was reluctant to push too hard. Initially some 80 percent of the American military goods and fuel bound for U.S. and NATO troops in Afghanistan arrived at the port of Karachi and underwent a long truck drive through Pakistan to reach either Kandahar (via Quetta and Chaman in Baluchistan) or Kabul (via Peshawar and the Khyber Pass). In 2009, despite numerous attacks on truck convoys by Pakistani Taliban and bandits, the United States still moved most of its cargo through Pakistan.

But the strains on the relationship were forcing the Americans to look elsewhere, because periodically when relations between U.S. and Pakistani forces on the Afghan border became tense, Pakistan would shut down the NATO traffic. By the summer of 2011, 50 percent of supplies had been redirected through the Northern Distribution Network—a patchwork of rail and road routes through Russia, Siberia, Central Asia, and the Caucasus. One-third of supplies now pass through Azerbaijan, while the rest is carried from the European Baltic ports through Russia and Central Asia. U.S. military planners have swiftly reduced the supplies going through Pakistan just as the two countries' relations have started to fall apart.[3]

The relationships and alliances grew ever more complicated and confusing. The ISI continued to provide the CIA with intelligence on Al Qaeda and on Western jihadis, large numbers of whom were still arriving in FATA for training. Most contentious of all, the ISI cooperated with the CIA in allowing missiles fired by Predator drones to target high-level Al Qaeda and later Pakistani Taliban in FATA. The CIA ran the Pakistani air base at Shamsi in Baluchistan province, so some of the drones that killed militants in FATA actually took off from Pakistani soil. The drones have become the target of widespread public anger at the government, the army, and the Americans. Drone strikes began in June 2004, and during the Bush administration (which ended in January 2009), a total of only forty-four were fired.

Obama sees them as a strategic rather than a tactical weapon and has authorized four times as many, or one strike every four days.

Pakistani critics maintain that while the drones kill militants, they also kill hundreds of civilians. The Americans have tried to downplay this and claim only a few dozen civilians as the strikes become more accurate. As of July 2011, 250 drone strikes have killed between 1,500 and 2,300 people; of those who died, only an estimated 33 were known terrorist leaders.[4] When the CIA has insufficient intelligence, it conducts what it calls "signature strikes," aimed at killing clusters of people whose identities are not known but who are considered likely enemy. The United States makes no attempt to justify these strikes as self-defense or to consider that innocent people are being killed.[5]

The drone program is controlled by the CIA's Counterterrorism Center (CTC), which had three hundred employees in 2001 but has grown to more than two thousand by 2011. Because of its high level of operational secrecy, those running the drone program are almost unaccountable except to the CIA itself. The CIA has expanded beyond intelligence gathering and analysis to become a military force capable of making decisions as to who should live and die, without the accountability that the U.S. Army would have to face in similar circumstances. In 2011, the CIA is running thirty Predator and Reaper drones, a network of Pakistani agents inside FATA to provide targeting information, and a clandestine Afghan militia that enters Pakistan to provide intelligence on the Taliban.[6] Earlier U.S. agreements with Pakistan about where and how many drones would be fired no longer hold, and in 2011 Pakistan has demanded, futilely, that all drone strikes cease.

Both sides are trapped in their own double-dealing. The Americans cannot discuss drones, because they are a classified CIA operation, while Pakistan pretends it never sanctioned the drones or provided intelligence to the United States, for fear of riling up the militants and the public. As a result, the Americans can conveniently ignore Pakistan's demands, while Pakistan can do nothing to counter the public's strong anti-American sentiment and the militants' conviction that the army is providing intelligence to the Americans. The U.S.-Pakistan agreements over the use of drones should have been made partially public to show that this is a joint program and that the drones are strictly targeting militant leaders. Instead, the lies on both sides have piled up until the entire justification of the program has collapsed. The program has no legitimacy for Pakistanis and the same goes for international human rights groups. Even in Washington the CIA's authority over the drones has left the State Department out on a limb, because while State may have been pursuing talks with the Taliban, the CIA was bombing them.

In 2010, as violence by the Taliban intensified in both countries, more Pakistanis were asking why the military had pursued a policy of subterfuge with its own people for so many years. The principal reason was to keep India off balance and to keep India's influence in Afghanistan constantly under threat. In the mid-1990s, when the Pakistan-backed guerrilla war in Indian Kashmir was at its height, a Pakistani general explained to me the war's strategic value. It kept 700,000 Indian troops and paramilitary forces in Kashmir at very low cost to Pakistan; at the same time, it ensured that the Indian Army could not threaten Pakistan, created enormous expenditures for India, and kept it bogged down in military and political terms. Rightly or wrongly, this was also the key to Pakistan's strategy in Afghanistan— to keep the pot simmering but never allow it to come to a boil.

In 2008, India signed a nuclear weapons deal with the United States, became wealthy and powerful, received U.S. support for a seat at the UN Security Council, and became the new destination for Western investors. But Pakistan has escalated its fears of the Indian threat. The military has become more reckless in its use of jihadi groups. The Mumbai attack in 2008 by Lashkar-e-Taiba was brazen, as was Pakistan's subsequent refusal to ban LT or disarm the jihadi groups in Punjab. Likewise, the attacks on the Indian embassy and other facilities in Kabul, which began in 2008, were easily traceable back to the Haqqani network and to intelligence operatives in Pakistan.

The Mumbai attack brought India and Pakistan close to war. On November 26, 2008, just six weeks before Obama's inauguration, ten Pakistani terrorists belonging to LT attacked nine locations, including three hotels and a Jewish center in Mumbai, India's largest commercial hub. The attacks and the sixty-hour siege killed 160 people, including 12 foreigners and 6 Americans, and wounded 300. One of the gunmen, Ajmal Kasab, a Pakistani from a village near Multan, was captured alive and admitted to being trained by LT and a retired ISI officer in Karachi.

India ratcheted up its armed forces' readiness, and U.S. secretary of state Condoleezza Rice and Admiral Mike Mullen rushed to Delhi and Islamabad to try to prevent a war. India demanded that Pakistan hand over suspects who emerged from the interrogation of Kasab. The Pakistanis refused and for months even denied that Pakistanis from LT were involved. For the Americans, Pakistan had suddenly become a deeply untrustworthy and unpredictable ally, while LT had become the new Al Qaeda, with global jihadist intentions. It is doubtful that the Pakistan military high command was involved in Mumbai, although some elements in the ISI may have been. The terrorists' aim was to create a war situation with India, to relieve the army's attacks on the Pakistani Taliban in FATA. Indian prime minister Manmohan Singh had to exert considerable pressure to restrain the hawkish elements that wanted to punish Pakistan. However, India broke off all talks with Pakistan.

When Obama appointed Richard Holbrooke AfPak special envoy, he initially tasked him with trying to bring India and Pakistan to a peaceful understanding, or at least to the table to talk. India raised objections, saying it would not be tied to Pakistan in any AfPak formula. Indian officials arrived in Washington and berated Secretary of State Hillary Clinton and Holbrooke. Unwilling to risk a break with India, the State Department immediately demurred, saying that Holbrooke would not be mediating between the two countries but would only keep India informed of progress in AfPak. Obama succumbed and took India off the Holbrooke beat. Thus Holbrooke's attempts to find a regional settlement for Afghanistan were hobbled from the start. For Pakistan's military and public, it was a massive letdown—an Obama promise had been made and then broken. It spelled the beginning of the end of Pakistani trust in Obama. To the military, it showed Obama to be weak, vacillating, and untrustworthy, and it confirmed for many Pakistanis that the United States would always buckle in the face of Indian pressure and change its policy goalposts for the sake of India.

The Pakistani media became increasingly anti-American, depicting Pakistan's sacrifices in the war on terror and the lack of U.S. appreciation for them. Pakistanis began to compare India with Israel, which could do no wrong in American eyes, and Pakistan with the Palestinians, to whom the Americans always gave short shrift. The

Obama administration's missteps and Pakistan's overexpectant hopes contributed to the breakdown of relations in 2011. The American answer to the proxy war between India and Pakistan in Afghanistan was tepid and devoid of strategic thinking. In a crisis, such as the one generated by the Mumbai attacks, U.S. diplomacy did play a major role in getting both sides to climb down from a war. But the United States refused to get involved in moving the two countries toward peace and a settlement of their rivalry.

Pakistan had long argued that its need for "strategic depth" to counter India necessitated its interference in Afghanistan. In other words, Pakistan needed a friendly government in Kabul that, in case of war with India, would give its army support and space. By 2001, however, many Pakistani retired officers and academics had exploded that thesis as meaningless. The fact that both countries now brandished nuclear weapons made "strategic depth" irrelevant. Nobody would have time to look for it, just before or after a nuclear war. Nonetheless, even after 9/11, the U.S. military looked with great sympathy on Pakistan's thesis. Pakistan has continued to try to retain some level of parity with India in both its conventional armaments and its nuclear weapons.

However, the irony is that Pakistan has carried out its aims of parity with India by using U.S. aid and carrying out Washington's bidding in the region. According to Pakistan historian Farzana Shaikh, "It is then Pakistan's rivalry with India that has facilitated U.S. intervention in Pakistan—intervention largely encouraged by Pakistan's dominant military. In this transactional relationship of mutual dependence rather than mutual respect, the price for services rendered is all that has really mattered. And Pakistan . . . has concluded that it has been dealt a raw deal by America."[7] Pakistan has never come to terms with the fact that it has been able to use the United States only to a very limited extent vis-à-vis India, and today India's burgeoning relationship with the United States makes even that impossible.

In July 2011, a string of high-level U.S. visitors to India, and U.S. and Indian companies investing in each other's territory, culminated when Secretary of State Clinton asked India to play a larger role in the region. "India's leadership has the potential to positively shape the future of the Asia-Pacific," Clinton said in Chennai on July 20. "We think that America and India share a fundamentally similar vision for the future of this region."[8] America's newfound love for India was loathsome to Pakistan, but Pakistan's military and political leaders never explained to the public that things had changed, that Pakistan could no longer have a relationship with the United States as a hedge against Indian power, and that Pakistan needed to repair its relations with India, which was steaming ahead of it in every field.

In fact, the Bush administration had done several favors for Pakistan, apart from allowing the Taliban to take refuge in Pakistan. In 2006, Pakistan was caught red-handed trying to smuggle the full components of a nuclear bomb-making plant to Libya; and the CIA and MI6 produced evidence that Pakistan had sold nuclear technology to Iran for cash, to North Korea in exchange for ballistic missile technology, and to other clients. Musharraf's military regime found itself in the world's proverbial doghouse. The military produced a convenient scapegoat in Pakistani scientist Dr. Abdul Qadir Khan, but he undoubtedly was not the only culprit, and the military itself was suspected of being involved. But Bush rode to the rescue and allowed Musharraf to blame Khan personally, accusing him of getting rich and selling nuclear secrets. Khan accepted all the blame for the proliferation on public TV and was sworn to secrecy for his own safety.

The government then locked him up in a well-guarded house arrest for many years so that the truth could not emerge.

Musharraf wanted a second-strike nuclear capability; the military wanted to place nukes on missiles because it lacked the high-technology planes necessary to deliver bombs; they wanted to produce more plutonium to build more bombs; and they wanted to add to their single Chinese-donated nuclear reactor at Khushab, in Punjab, by buying two more reactors. The military, which ran and protected the nuclear program, achieved all these aims over time because the Bush administration had no clear nuclear nonproliferation strategy, and even as it signed a nuclear agreement with India, it provided no incentive to either country to restrict the expansion of nuclear weapons programs. Bush was not as concerned about Pakistan's nuclear weapons as he was about maintaining close cooperation with the ISI in catching Al Qaeda.

But fears about security inside Pakistan's nuclear facilities were constant. At least seventy thousand people worked in Pakistan's nuclear industry, including security personnel. Any one of them could become susceptible to extremist propaganda. After 9/11, the United States gave Pakistan more than $100 million to secretly bolster the security and fail-safe mechanisms around its bombs. The army, which controlled the nuclear program, did not want it disclosed that it was taking money from the Americans to make its bombs safe. Some exchange of safety technology between the United States and Pakistan also appears to have taken place. By 2010, Pakistan had more than one hundred nuclear weapons, a second-strike capability, and miniature bombs that it could place on long-range mobile missiles. But the army was still not satisfied that this was a sufficient deterrent against India and wanted more.

Nobody knows how much Pakistan actually spends on the nuclear program, because it is a state secret and is presumably hidden in other budget lines like pensions and health. Meanwhile Pakistan is the only country that opposes the proposed international Fissile Material Cut-off Treaty, which would cap fissile material stockpiles—a key Obama foreign policy aim. Pakistan says India has access to fissile material through its civilian nuclear program, so Pakistan will have to keep producing and stockpiling fissile material until it is satisfied it has enough.

As the Taliban attacks became more audacious and widespread in Pakistan, concerns arose about the safety of Pakistan's nuclear components. Bombs were always separated from their triggers and other components and stored separately; but what would happen if extremists were able to get inside information about one of these sites and raided it? The experts deemed two Taliban attacks very sensitive. The first was the daring attack in October 2009 on the army's general headquarters. The complex houses the office of the Strategic Forces Command—the office that runs the nuclear program on a day-to-day basis. Ten extremist terrorists penetrated inside the base by wearing army uniforms, having an army jeep, and carrying forged army IDs. They held more than forty officers and guards hostage for twenty hours, before commandos blasted their way in. Ultimately fourteen officers and civilians were killed.

The second was the attack on the Mehran naval base in Karachi in May 2011. It took place only a few miles from the Masroor air base, where nukes are stored, and here it took eighteen hours before soldiers were able to end the siege, even though there were only four to six attackers. Both attacks were deemed inside jobs, in which soldiers on the base had provided the terrorists with classified maps and information.[9]

However slowly, Dr. Khan and his relatives began to speak about what had really happened to him. In 2008, his Dutch wife, Hendrina Khan, gave an interview to *Der Spiegel* directly criticizing Musharraf's remarks in his 2006 memoir, *In the Line of Fire*. Musharraf had written, "I can say with confidence that neither the Pakistan army nor any of the past governments of Pakistan was ever involved or had any knowledge of A.Q.'s proliferation activities." Hendrina claimed he was lying, as the army had packed all the consignments that went abroad and organized the planes that carried them.[10] Even more devastating was an interview that Khan gave himself, in which he claimed: "Logistics and security at our plant were in the hands of the army, and they checked each and every item that came in or left. How then could I have sent things to any country without the army's knowledge? . . . I took sole blame for this whole episode because the political leadership urgently asked me to do so. . . . I feel stabbed in the back by the very people who benefited most from my work—i.e., the army."[11]

Finally in 2011, through an intermediary who is suspected to be his daughter, Khan made documents available to the *Washington Post* that show that he transferred more than $3 million in payments by North Korean officials to senior officers in the Pakistan Army. A letter from the North Korean military spelled out the details of the bribes.[12] The Pakistani military believed that the United States was deliberately leaking this information to the media to discredit the army.

Even though the United States made a major concession, allowing the Pakistan Army to save face both at home and abroad by blaming

Khan for proliferation, the army continued to mistrust the Americans. The army's obsessive focus on India then prevented it from adopting a counterinsurgency strategy when it came to fighting its own antistate Pakistani Taliban. The U.S. military, and in particular Admiral Mullen, spent much of 2008 and 2009 trying to persuade General Kayani to allow the United States to retrain two divisions or even two brigades of Pakistan's regular forces to conduct counterinsurgency in FATA. Kayani refused, telling Mullen repeatedly that any war would be fought on the plains of Punjab with India rather than in the mountains of Waziristan. Furthermore, after Mumbai, India had adopted a new "Cold Start" strategy (to be able to deliver an attack against Pakistan within seventy-two hours), which precluded any major Pakistan Army deployment in FATA and negated the value of counterinsurgency training. In other words, the Pakistan Army had no use for counterinsurgency.[13] Kayani's views were shortsighted, especially as the Pakistani Taliban quickly developed an offensive capability. But President Asif Ali Zardari and Prime Minister Yousaf Raza Gilani refused to contradict Army Chief Kayani or initiate a debate about the issue in parliament or the media.

After months of cajoling, Kayani finally agreed to allow seventy American special forces officers to train Pakistanis in counterinsurgency, but for the time being the recipients of the training would be not regular army but Frontier Corps (FC). The FC was made up mainly of Pashtun tribesmen who were underarmed and undertrained, whose pay and morale were low, who had been plagued by desertions, and who had a deep reluctance to fight their fellow Pashtuns in the Taliban. The Americans obliged reluctantly and began to pay for better equipment for the FC.

The army's lack of training in counterinsurgency had proved devastating whenever it had been deployed in FATA. In August 2008, for example, the generals sent the army to the Bajaur tribal agency in FATA to rid it of Pakistani Taliban, promising a two-week campaign, but eight months later the army was still fighting. Counterinsurgency has a doctrine of "clear, hold, and build" that is aimed at protecting the people and their homes. In Bajaur, the army's tactics were the direct opposite: it moved out the population, flattened villages with artillery, and used bombing and bulldozers to create vast free-fire zones. Without a local population to provide them with intelligence, information, or protection, the troops became sitting ducks for the rebels. Some four hundred thousand people fled Bajaur and became refugees, creating an enormous humanitarian crisis, but the army refused to allow NGOs to come and help. Among those who fled were tribal elders and educated youth—all vehemently anti-Taliban—who, had they been protected, would have provided the necessary backup to military operations. Getting counterinsurgency right is about getting the strategic priorities right; for some years the military still perceived India and not the Taliban as the greater threat.[14]

But as early as 2000, a classified report, commissioned by the army, called "Pakistan's Security Imperatives in the Medium Term," concluded that Pakistan's security threat was primarily internal and related to Islamic extremism and that unless strategic thinking changed, a tiny, well-organized minority could drag the country in an undesirable direction. "The army continues to see terrorism merely as a latent threat and India as the more clear and present danger," said Lt. Gen. Mahmud Ali Durrani, the former national security adviser to Prime Minister Gilani. "We have not grappled with the issue of extremism seriously—neither the public, nor the government nor army."[15]

In FATA, Taliban militants appeared to learn more quickly than the army. The Pashtun Taliban began to copy lessons from the LT's campaigns in Kashmir. Suicide bombing had never existed in South Asia before 1990, but when the Tamil rebels introduced it in Sri Lanka, the LT in Kashmir and other groups quickly followed the example. The LT called them "fedayeen" attacks—rather than committing suicide with a bomb-laden vest, militants would attack an Indian outpost with the intention of fighting to the death. After Al Qaeda retreated into Pakistan after 2001, it enlisted its own suicide bombers—mainly Pakistanis and Central Asians—to attack U.S. troops in Afghanistan, even though Islam strictly forbids suicide.

The Haqqani network and Pakistan's Taliban commanders soon developed suicide bombing into a veritable industry, persuading or forcing gullible Pakistani and Afghan teenagers to become bombers and then selling them to commanders in the field. Manufacturing parts for suicide vests became a cottage industry in FATA, with different families and villages producing the belts, ball bearings, and detonators while the Taliban provided the explosives. Suicide attacks have now become a major tactic for both the Afghan and Pakistani Taliban. In 2010, a total of eighty-seven suicide attacks in Pakistan killed more than three thousand people.

Washington little understood the Pakistan Army high command's refusal to cooperate closely with the U.S. military, its rejection of counterinsurgency training, and its deep hatred for India. The United States promised joint actions and policies, then acted unilaterally. Acute disagreements among Holbrooke, the White House, and the Pentagon seriously hampered U.S. policy and allowed the Pakistanis to play off one against the other. Later the CIA, the State Department, and Pakistan disputed the use of drones. As predicted, the Obama administration began with a tough line toward Pakistan but developed no strategic plan to win over the military. On July 12, 2008, Admiral Mullen arrived in Islamabad to warn Kayani to eliminate the Haqqani network and Maulvi Nazir Nazir's Pakistani Taliban militia, which was attacking U.S. forces in Afghanistan. Mullen showed Kayani evidence that the ISI was working with both organizations. The military leadership nodded and did nothing. In December, after the Mumbai attack, Gen. Michael Hayden, the CIA director, arrived demanding that Pakistan close down the LT and dismantle its infrastructure. Pakistan refused.[16]

Pakistani generals seem oblivious to the fact that ending the Taliban insurgency in their country and helping stabilize Afghanistan should be a higher priority than countering an imagined Indian threat. They seem heedless of the fact that they need to end their policy of supporting certain Taliban while fighting others and instead start deradicalizing militant groups in Punjab, or that they need to end Haqqani's control over North Waziristan and push the Afghan Taliban into a dialogue with Kabul to end the war. They seem unaware that their present course is putting Pakistan's security in the hands of the Taliban; that the isolationist path is at odds with the army's own strategic interests as well as those of Afghanistan, the entire region, and the West; and that it will ultimately endanger Pakistan's internal security and future development. Tragically, there is no political challenger at home who can say these things to the generals and mold a debate around what the army's strategy should be.

On the contrary, both Zardari and Gilani appear to be terrified of General Kayani, and instead of using civilian power, such as the media and parliament, to raise these issues, both men want to avoid riling the army so they can have long and safe terms in office.

FOUR

Afghanistan: The First Surge and the Failure of Elections

AFGHANISTAN HAD been at war for thirty-one years. There had been only a brief interlude of peace between the winter of 2001–2 (when the Taliban had been defeated) and the spring of 2003 (when the Taliban restarted the insurgency). The enormous Afghan desire for security, peace, and economic development—which they expected of their American benefactors and occupiers—was not to be fulfilled.

During the brief respite of 2002, Afghans voted with their feet: some 3 million Afghan refugees in Iran and Pakistan rushed home, and thousands more arrived from richer climes in Europe and the United States, with money to invest and skills to serve their rickety new government. As I traveled across the country that year, I sensed enormous enthusiasm and expectation in the air. The Americans had promised so much—surely they would deliver. The interim president, Hamid Karzai, seemed honest, amiable, and sufficiently modern, with no record of acting like a warlord—a rarity in Afghanistan. The Americans had unleashed the warlords to destroy the Taliban, but now they would control them. The alienated Pashtuns would be won over. Contrary to all stereotypes that Afghans were paranoid about foreigners in their land, goodwill toward the Americans and others was everywhere. Children and adults followed the foot patrols of the five-thousand-strong International Security Assistance Force (ISAF)—mainly British troops—around Kabul in awe. Everyone was exhausted from the fighting.

Even my skeptical self—with three decades of waiting for an Afghan window of peace to open, only to see it shut a few months later and fighting erupt again—even I held my breath and believed that this time the window would stay open.

Then President Bush went on to invade Iraq—and a fraction of those U.S. troops, resources, money, and global commitments could have turned Afghanistan toward peace and prosperity. Suddenly all seemed lost once again.

Seven years on, in the weeks before his inauguration as president in the winter of 2009, Barack Obama clearly had Afghanistan and Pakistan on his mind. He had made withdrawing U.S. forces from Afghanistan a campaign issue. But before he even occupied the White House, he had to face more ongoing crises than any other U.S. president in history. The collapse of Lehman Brothers, the American stock market crash, and the bankruptcy of major banks and investment houses, followed by the worst recession since the Great Depression, were his major preoccupations. Well before his inauguration, Bush had enlisted him to look for solutions to these crises and to the growing crisis in Afghanistan.

A few days before the inauguration and with little notice, I was invited to have dinner with the president-elect along with a few other American foreign policy experts. I flew from Pakistan for my first meeting with an American president. He strode into the dining room with three senior aides, made some friendly remarks, and cracked jokes that instantly put everyone at ease. Unusually tall and thin, his body seemed to glide around the guests as he shook hands. His easy-going, informal manner appeared to be a major personal asset. He had just come from a long briefing by the Bush team on Afghanistan. I asked him whether Pakistan was discussed, and he replied that the crisis in Pakistan was discussed even more than Afghanistan. He said that until recently he had had no idea how bad the problems were in either country. Both countries would need an enormous amount of his attention, he now realized—far more than he had anticipated.

During the campaign, Obama's team had been very critical of Bush for deferring so many key decisions in the region to his successor: funding for the Afghan war effort and economic development, increasing U.S. troop levels, speeding up building the Afghan Army, and getting NATO to do more. For months, these decisions had been deferred. Bush would order policy reviews and then not implement their conclusions. Obama was entering a policy quagmire to which too little thought, attention, and action had been paid.

Much of the dinner discussion was taken up with what Obama could do internationally to revise the negative perceptions and ruinous unilateralism that had resulted from Bush's obsession with the war on terror. The Muslim world was acutely alienated but also was hopeful and curious about a U.S. president whose parentage and upbringing straddled so many identities. He was black with a white mother and an African Muslim father; had lived in Indonesia; had traveled to Pakistan, India, and Kenya; and had Muslim relatives—a unique and engaging background. (For years, many Americans believed he was a Muslim, which was not the case.)

I pointed out to him that many autocratic and dictatorial Muslim rulers were deeply apprehensive. They feared that Obama might be too radical, too demanding of them to reform their societies, and that their strategic alliances with the United States—partly because of oil—could be at risk. Pakistan's newly elected president, Asif Ali Zardari, and its powerful army chief, Gen. Ashfaq Parvez Kayani, had mixed feelings about Obama. The Pakistan Army had always had an easier time with Republican administrations than with Democratic ones. After 9/11, it had built a cozy relationship with Bush, who had lavished billions of dollars of aid on Pakistan and had not asked too many difficult questions about the whereabouts of the Taliban or how the aid was being spent. Eighty percent of the $11.8 billion funneled to Pakistan in aid between 2001 and 2008 had gone to the military, with an unprecedented lack of accounting by either Islamabad or Washington. The Pakistanis now feared it was coming to an end. Likewise, Afghanistan's Hamid Karzai had spent eight years dealing on a daily basis with top Bush officials and had had monthly fireside video conversations with Bush himself; he, too, was nervous about the new man in the White House, who had already declared that the video conversations were over.

Moreover, Americans who had criticized the Afghan and Pakistani leaders' policies would now hold senior positions in the new administration. In February 2008, Joseph Biden, the incoming vice president, had spoken harshly about Bush's policy failures in words that had deeply annoyed the Afghan and Pakistani leadership. "Six years after we've ousted the Taliban," Biden said, "Afghanistan is a forgotten war, and that country, in my view, is slipping into failure—or toward failure. The Taliban is back. Al Qaeda is regenerated along the border. Violence is up and drug production is booming, and the Afghan people have very little faith in the ability of their government to deliver a better future. . . . Pakistani cooperation in the fight against extremism . . . has been sporadic at best. The reason is that, until recently, the terrorists we're fighting and the extremists the Pakistani fear are not one and the same."[1] His words rang true to many people.

Obama was not ignorant about the challenges of Afghanistan, but none of his Chicago-based advisers knew anything about the region. His campaign had set up a large group of American experts on Afghanistan and South Asia—experienced academics or retired officials. They prepared papers and discussed policy, but Obama never personally met with them and never took their advice. He had visited Afghanistan once, in July 2008, a trip that also took him to Iraq. His aides had determined that the trip had to be made in total secrecy, which was absurd. The experts were never consulted as to what he should say or do there. (This trait was to become common in the early Obama presidency.)

On that trip, Obama made the mistake of first meeting with Governor Gul Agha Sherzai, a rival of Karzai's for influence in their common hometown of Kandahar. Sherzai was a corrupt and brutal warlord, a deeply unsavory character, and Karzai did not take kindly to their meeting in Jalalabad. When Obama met with Karzai, he reassured him that he would pay far more attention to Afghanistan than Bush had done, and that he would work on Pakistan to give up its Taliban sanctuaries. Karzai was far from convinced.

During his campaign, Obama had described the Afghan war as a necessity while Iraq was a war of choice and a mistaken one. The money that the United States had spent on the reconstruction of Afghanistan since 2001, Obama had said, was equivalent to three weeks' expenditure on military operations in Iraq. If he was elected, he would rectify that by increasing annual nonmilitary aid from $1 billion to $3 billion. Initially the U.S. military, already overstretched in Iraq, was nervous that Obama would put more demands on it. Admiral Mullen had famously said, "In Afghanistan we do what we can. In Iraq, we do what we must. . . . The [Afghan] war is by design and necessity an economy-of-force operation."[2]

Obama himself had a very low opinion of the merits of the Iraq war, while the Afghan war was clearly being lost. The Iraq war, he said, "distracts us from every threat that we face and so many opportunities we could seize. This war diminishes our security, our standing in the world, our military, our economy, and the resources that we need to confront the challenges of the 21st century."[3]

As he left office, George W. Bush was warned by his military commanders that the security situation in Afghanistan was going from bad to worse. More troops were needed, and the Afghan presidential elections, scheduled for April 2009, would have to be postponed. Bush passed the buck to Obama. But changing the election date demanded early action, so Bush asked Karzai to find a constitutional way to postpone it until August. (Even that was to prove to be too early, given the worsening security situation.)

Due to institutional inertia, Bush had rarely reevaluated U.S. strategic priorities in the region; his administration's ideological moorings saw the world in black and white—Iraq and Al Qaeda were the main threat, Afghanistan was an afterthought, Iran was an enemy, and Pakistan was an ally. Karzai kept raising with him the danger posed by the Taliban resurgence, but to no avail; meanwhile Pakistan saw Bush's inattention as a free pass to continue to support the Taliban while keeping pressure on Al Qaeda.

Until 2004, the United States had only 15,000 troops based in Afghanistan, which has a population of over 30 million. In 2007, as the Taliban insurgency was spreading, there were still only 25,000 U.S.

troops there. Frustrated U.S. officials in Afghanistan would tell me that Washington did no serious intelligence gathering on the Taliban threat until 2006. Neither the White House nor the Pentagon was interested in monitoring Quetta or the Baluchistan-Afghanistan border, from which the Taliban infiltrated. "[W]e didn't know enough . . . it took us almost six months to figure out what we were doing," Lt. Gen. David M. Rodriguez admitted in 2007. "We fought hard every day to understand how Afghanistan worked. But we had a very shallow knowledge."[4]

In the summer of 2008, the Taliban launched a bloody offensive that, in June, killed more Western troops—forty-three—than in any month since 2001. The Taliban's use of improvised explosive devices (IEDs) increased by 200 percent. They undertook audacious attacks inside Kabul, and in Kandahar a brilliantly planned jailbreak freed eleven hundred Taliban prisoners. As a result of the deteriorating situation in the provinces, some thirty-six Afghan and Western aid workers were killed in 2008 and another ninety-two were kidnapped. Forty percent of the country was now off-limits to the UN and aid workers, while many Afghans and the international community held Karzai's government in low esteem for failing to tackle corruption or improve governance.

But all this was temporarily forgotten on a cold day in Washington, January 20, 2009, when Obama took office. That day the Taliban mounted three attacks in eastern Afghanistan, including a double suicide bombing that killed 15 people. In the south, it was announced, 650 schools were closed down because of Taliban attacks, cutting off 200,000 children from education. There were just not enough troops to guard everyone. The United States had 161,000 troops in Iraq but only 32,000 in Afghanistan (along with 29,000 NATO troops). Even as Obama urged European governments to send more troops to Afghanistan, polls showed that three-quarters of European voters rejected that idea. International patience with the war was waning fast. In 2008, the death toll for U.S. soldiers in Iraq was down by one-third, but 151 died in Afghanistan, up from 111 in the previous year. The UN said that Afghan civilian deaths increased by 40 percent in 2008. Clearly the military situation was deteriorating.

The reviews of the situation in Afghanistan that Bush had ordered up were now awaiting Obama's attention. They had been produced by NATO, by the Joint Chiefs of Staff at the Pentagon, by the U.S. Central Command (CENTCOM), where Gen. David Petraeus was now in charge, and by the White House. (At CENTCOM, Petraeus had enlisted more than one hundred experts from all parts of the U.S. government and academia to carry out the review.)[5] To cut through the confusion, Obama asked Bruce Riedel, a former CIA official and a long-term expert on the region who had led Obama's South Asia team before the election, to merge all the reviews and come to conclusions for short-term needs in Afghanistan. Gen. David McKiernan, the commander in Afghanistan, had asked for 30,000 troops earlier in the year, a request to which Bush had not responded. Now McKiernan said he needed even more.[6] McKiernan's desperation was driven by the need to secure the ground for the Afghan presidential election in August. An intense debate ensued between the Pentagon and the White House as to how many troops to send.

On January 21, 2009, Obama appointed veteran diplomat and peacemaker Richard Holbrooke as his special envoy for both Afghanistan and Pakistan (which would now be called AfPak). Holbrooke put together a large interagency team and brought in academic experts so he could deal comprehensively with everything from military issues to economic aid, boosting education, and media spin. Realizing the importance the United States was giving Afghanistan, major Western countries followed suit, appointing their own special envoys.[7]

The debate on how many troops to send to Afghanistan (detailed in Bob Woodward's *Obama's Wars*) preoccupied the White House for months. Tragically, the near-exclusive focus on military engagement prevented greater discussion of important strategic issues: Afghanistan's economic, political, and social future; peace talks with the Taliban; and U.S. policy toward Pakistan.[8] Holbrooke's office issued paper after paper on these larger issues, but they were rarely discussed. The highly perceptive British ambassador to Kabul, Sherard Cowper-Coles, later wrote that "just plunging on with a strategy of pouring in more troops and more money, without doing something about governance and about the political offer to the Afghan people and something to engage the regional players, was a recipe for eventual failure."[9] Finally the White House and the Pentagon agreed that 17,000 soldiers and 4,000 trainers would be deployed as soon as possible. The first 8,000 soldiers—Marines—would go to Helmand province in the south, where the violence was worst: the south was the center for the insurgents, the main heroin production area, and the principal area of access to Pakistan and Taliban supply lines. Eight thousand British troops that had been deployed there since 2006 were too thinly stretched out and had failed to establish peace.

Helmand actually had only 1 percent of the total Afghan population. According to the new counterinsurgency strategy that Petraeus favored and that was being practiced in Iraq, U.S. forces should have been deployed in densely populated areas. But a year earlier the U.S. Marines had decided they wanted to move their men from Iraq to southern Afghanistan (a decision that was little discussed in the Bush

White House) and started building a massive base in the Helmand desert. Now Obama had no option but to commit Marines to Helmand, even though it made little military or political sense. In some ways, all the decisions presented to Obama were either precooked or predecided because of constraints or logistics. The Marine Corps and the Special Operations Forces (SOF) had parallel chains of command and did not come under the overall command of the U.S. military commander in Kabul, who led the joint U.S. and NATO forces in what was called the International Security Assistance Force (ISAF). This created considerable confusion, as Marines were allowed to decide where they would be based without first conferring with the overall military command. A year later, the Marine Corps was brought under ISAF command.

On March 27, 2009, Obama announced his plan to send an additional 21,000 troops to Afghanistan. His goal was "to disrupt, dismantle and defeat al Qaeda in Pakistan and Afghanistan, and to prevent their return to either country in the future." He doubled the number of civilian advisers and experts and increased funds for economic development and for building up the Afghan Army and police (but refused to define it all as nation building). He got tough on corruption within the Afghan government.[10] For Pakistan, he had harsh words: he demanded that it do more to root out extremism but imposed few sanctions—and dangled few carrots—to enforce the threat. The following week at the NATO summit in Strasbourg, and then at the European Union summit in Prague, Obama asked Europe to come up with more troops, but the response was tepid. Britain agreed to send 2,000 more and Poland another 400.

But Obama was stuck with securing the Afghan presidential election in August. Everyone—the United States, NATO, the UN, and many Afghans—understood that because of the country's high level of violence, the election was a disaster waiting to happen and that Karzai would ultimately rig it. Many believed that it should be postponed for a year or more or until violence was reduced, the insurgency was under control, and governance in Kabul was improved. The White House never properly debated the issue. The entire first year of the 2009 Obama surge in manpower and money would have to be spent on securing the country for the election, rather than on developing a long-term counterinsurgency and economic development strategy. Richard Holbrooke would shake his head and tell me that the election was a huge distraction from what really needed to be done on the ground. Through the summer, U.S. military offensives, aid money, and development projects were all directed at getting the public out to vote rather than building long-term security.

Karzai, who had become more controversial and unpredictable, insisted upon the election. In January 2008 at the World Economic Forum summit in Davos, Switzerland, I had a long dinner with him, alone, at the chalet where he was staying. I urged him to delay the election—which he could have done through parliamentary approval—and to consider stepping down and seeing to an orderly political and generational transition. No Afghan ruler had achieved such a feat for a century, as most had been killed by their rivals. He should anoint someone younger whom he trusted to run as the next president, I said, and then he could retire as the honored father of the nation.

He surprised me by saying he would think about it. We discussed several potential candidates, and the person he seemed to trust most was Hanif Atmar, then the education minister. (In 2010, the increasingly paranoid Karzai would sack Atmar on unsubstantiated charges.)

Then three months after Davos, Karzai told me in Kabul that he had to run "for the good of the country," that the election could not be delayed, and that he needed his second term to secure peace with the Taliban. I suspected that his advisers and his brothers, who were then mired in alleged corruption scandals, were putting pressure on him to run again. The political careers and incomes of a large number of people depended on Karzai's remaining in power.

Despite the compressed time given to organizing them, the 2004 presidential and 2005 parliamentary elections had been successful, with large voter turnouts, considerable public enthusiasm, and a wide choice of candidates. The Karzai team had done some heavy rigging and bribery in the south, but overall the political process had been advanced and helped legitimate the constitution and the leadership. In 2004, Karzai won his first full term as president against twenty-three other candidates, winning 55.4 percent of the vote with a voter turnout of some 60 percent. He was still relatively popular, and despite the lack of Western aid for rebuilding the country, Afghans still saw him as the leader most likely to secure that aid in the future. The most important factor: the Taliban insurgency was not strong enough to undermine the election.

Even in 2004, Afghans and Western officials had debated whether the election should be delayed. But in 2009—when the country faced a full-blown insurgency and had a barely functioning administration, economy, and army and could ill afford an election—such a debate never took place. The problem was that for the Americans, elections had become a litmus test determining everything else. A U.S. intervention in any third-world country now consisted of holding an early election so that the country could be dubbed a democracy, and then the United States could head for the exit. By contrast, the European philosophy, favored by the UN, was to first build governance and an economic infrastructure—nation building—so that elections could be both meaningful and sustainable.

Elections should come at the end of such a process, not at the beginning, and certainly not in the midst of an insurgency. The institutions that postelection democratic governance required were still nonexistent in Afghanistan. In 2009, the country had no party system, scant respect for parliament (which carried out little legislation), and no public mobilization or electoral awareness campaigns, while the elected officials of the provincial councils, which should have been greatly empowered, had been ignored. Instead the patronage alliances made by warlords and powerful candidates continued to dominate the political scene, as they had in 2004.[11] But in 2009, for very different reasons, the Americans and Karzai wanted elections and argued that any further delay would signal weakness to the Taliban.

In the run-up to the election, Karzai became deeply suspicious of Obama and believed he wanted to replace him as president. He was convinced that Holbrooke was inducing other leading Afghans to run against him. Acute mistrust and dislike of the Americans was widespread, which made it morally much easier for Karzai's supporters to rig the election. This time 17 million voters had forty candidates to choose from. The two best known were both disgruntled former cabinet ministers: the Tajik leader and former foreign minister Abdullah Abdullah and the Pashtun former finance minister Ashraf Ghani Ahmadzai. Karzai feared that he might not win the election outright and would be forced to go into a second round, which he wanted to avoid at all costs. His paranoia, fed by his aides and his brothers, led to astonishing conspiracy theories about evil U.S. and British intentions to rig the vote, making Karzai's supporters determined to ensure that the president won on the first ballot.

Meanwhile, throughout the summer of 2009, the Taliban were on the offensive, intent on disrupting the election. In the first six months of that year, their attacks had soared by 60 percent over 2008. In a single week in June, Taliban attacks had killed 250 civilians and soldiers in twenty-five provinces. (Afghanistan has thirty-four provinces.) It was the widest, deepest, and bloodiest Taliban offensive so far, and their control had expanded to nearly half of Afghanistan's 364 districts.

The critical battlegrounds were the two southern provinces of Kandahar and Helmand, which had large Pashtun populations. Karzai and his supporters were Pashtun, which was the largest ethnic group, and traditionally a Pashtun had always ruled the country. Karzai needed Pashtun votes. But Taliban violence threatened to keep the Pashtuns from coming out to vote. In the 1990s, the Taliban (most of whom were also Pashtun) had butchered many non-Pashtuns in the north and west, but now the north was relatively peaceful. Turnout in the non-Pashtun areas was expected to be high, which could make the future parliament ethnically unbalanced and hurt Karzai's vote. So U.S. Marines and British soldiers undertook a large-scale offensive in Helmand to drive out the Taliban so the Pashtuns there could vote safely. The fighting was heavy. In early July, eight British soldiers were killed in twenty-four hours. Forty-seven Americans were killed in August, the deadliest month in the war for the U.S. military. These soldiers' deaths were portrayed in their home media as deaths for the sake of a free and fair Afghan election.

On August 20, election day, the turnout was just 38 percent—far less than what it had been in 2004. Few people in the south actually turned out to vote. Local officials and Karzai tribal loyalists stuffed ballot boxes where nobody voted and even created hundreds of fake polling stations that recorded thousands of votes. In one district, polling stations were opened for an hour, then closed, and then all 23,900 ballots were forged for Karzai. Actual voter turnout in the Pashtun south was estimated at between 1 and 5 percent—but high-intensity ballot stuffing for Karzai at some polling stations recorded more than 100 percent turnout! The Taliban inflicted some damage—they killed twenty-six Western and Afghan soldiers in seventy-three attacks—but they could not disrupt the election.

But the rigging defied even the worst expectations. In the previous months, Karzai had aligned himself with warlords, drug traffickers, and provincial officials who were terrified of losing their lucrative jobs. In 2004, the UN had had control over the election, but this time Karzai had demanded that the UN hand over control to the Afghan-run Independent Election Commission (IEC), which was beholden to Karzai, as he appointed its members. The international community's biggest mistake was to agree to this demand. Some UN and U.S. diplomats warned of massive rigging but were not listened to. Within a day of the election, Karzai's aides were claiming outright victory, while Abdullah Abdullah, who believed he had won the right to a run-off election, pointed out the fraud and painted a bleak picture if the West did not recognize it. "The foundations of this country have been damaged by this fraud, throwing it open to all kinds of consequences, including instability," he said on August 29. "It is true that the Taliban are the first threat but an illegitimate government would be the second."[12]

On September 8, the Electoral Complaints Commission, which included UN members, declared that it had found "clear and convincing evidence of fraud." It threw out more than one million suspicious votes and ordered a recount of 10 percent of the returns that had led Karzai to claim he had won the election. But Karzai refused to participate in a runoff second vote against Abdullah, even if the result showed that one was needed. It took four days of persuasion by half a dozen top U.S. officials, including Holbrooke and Senator John Kerry, chairman of the Senate Foreign Relations Committee, before Karzai would agree to a runoff.

The recount was completed on October 20—two months after the election. Karzai received 49.7 percent of the vote and now faced a runoff against Abdullah, who had won 30.5 percent. On November 1, citing the "inappropriate actions of the government and the election commission," Abdullah announced that he would not participate in the second round. Karzai had won his second term as president, but the political price that he, his government, the international community, the UN, and the United States would pay was heavy. Karzai never offered an apology, never showed any remorse for the rigging, and never offered reconciliation to those Afghans who had been defrauded of their votes.

All this would have an enormous negative effect on the transition from U.S. and NATO forces to Afghan forces. The political crisis continues to this day, with no resolution in sight. The election would undermine the very surge that had been designed to protect it. Countries hostile to the U.S. presence, such as Iran and Pakistan, saw the election as Obama's failure, as did the Taliban and their supporters. By declining to hold Karzai accountable for the elections, the United States had strengthened him immeasurably. He now believed he could get away with anything. The U.S. assumption that he was a weak leader was wrong: he had become a strong president in a weak or barely existent national system.

Once again the Taliban took advantage of the political crisis, launching a series of attacks in Kabul. A suicide attack on the U.S. embassy on August 15, 2009, killed eight people and wounded more than one hundred. The worst attack came on October 28: eleven people in a UN guesthouse in Kabul, including five UN officials, were killed in a prolonged gun battle.

Unfortunately, the international community conducted no postmortem on the election, so when the parliamentary elections came around a year later, nothing had been learned or rectified, and no plan was made to deal with Karzai's determination to overrule the elections' institutional mechanisms.

Karzai again insisted on holding the parliamentary elections on time, on September 18, 2010. He wanted the elections to produce a more pliant parliament that would have a Pashtun majority, accept his plans to talk to the Taliban, and endorse his cabinet. Parliament had the right to reject the president's choices for cabinet ministers. Rigging took place on a large scale—by individual candidates, many of whom the government indirectly helped. To its lasting credit, this time around Karzai's handpicked IEC, which oversaw the poll, acted fairly. It invalidated 1.33 million votes for fraud, or nearly a quarter of the 5.74 million votes cast, and in mid-November it disqualified twenty-four candidates who had been unofficially declared winners, including a cousin of the president.

The IEC had asserted itself but left behind an intractable problem. Due to the renewed Taliban threats, turnout among the Pashtuns was very low, as a result of which the Pashtuns lost 20 percent of their seats to ethnic minorities, especially the Tajiks and Hazaras in provinces where ethnic groups were mixed. In the last parliament, Pashtuns had held 129 seats out of 249, but now they were down to just 94 seats— well short of a majority. All 11 seats in the important province of Ghazni, which has a mixed Pashtun-Hazara population, were won by Hazaras, a result that infuriated the Pashtuns and Karzai. Ghazni's results were delayed, which resulted in a long, bitter dispute be- tween the IEC and Karzai's officials, and public protests took place. Younus Qanooni, the speaker of the outgoing parliament and a prom- inent leader of the Tajik faction, described the elections "as a process of selection because some of Karzai's advisers did not get the results they wanted. But now that the government has held the elections," he added, "it cannot undermine it own elections by trying to nullify them."[13] Staffan de Mistura, the UN special representative, tried hard to find a compromise but failed, and relations between Karzai and the international community again deteriorated.[14]

When I met with Karzai in Kabul in December 2010, he clearly felt trapped and was seriously considering declaring the elections null and void, which would have created an even bigger crisis. He delayed the opening of the parliament, fearing a non-Pashtun majority that would reject any peace deal with the Taliban, amend the constitution to change from a presidential system to a parliamentary system, and reduce Karzai's own powers. The standoff continued until January 20, 2011, when the UN, the United States, and the European Union jointly expressed deep concern at Karzai's failure to open parliament and threatened that if the delay continued, they could not justify their expenditures on Afghanistan. Karzai finally backed down and opened parliament—four months after the elections had taken place.

Ultimately a kind of solution was found. The IEC dismissed nine members of parliament on account of fraud and replaced them with another nine who were acceptable to Karzai, but more than half of parliament refused to accept the new members. Parliament remained frozen and ineffective for more than a year after the elections. The legislative machinery ground to a halt, even though the parliament was and is needed to endorse a full cabinet for Karzai; to help bail out the Kabul Bank, which had given its shareholders large unsecured loans and lost hundreds of millions of dollars, as a result of which the country now faced the disruption of aid flows from the IMF; and to endorse the any post-2014 strategic agreement with the United States. The entire legislative machinery remains at a halt in the fall of 2011.

The lack of fair elections, the inequitable distribution of seats among ethnic groups, the war, and the continued economic deprivation have only intensified Afghanistan's long-running and unresolved ethnic problems. The divisions between the Pashtuns and the non-Pashtun nationalities that make up the complex weave of the Afghan national carpet remain deeply entrenched. The corruption and incompetence of the Karzai administration are still seen to benefit the Pashtuns. U.S. counterinsurgency and development spending had focused heavily on the Pashtun provinces where the Taliban insurgency was strongest, to the neglect of those dominated by ethnic minorities in the north and west. Non-Pashtuns remain furious that an estimated 70 percent of all development funds are being spent in just two provinces in the south—Helmand and Kandahar.

Meanwhile the talks between the Karzai government and the Taliban have galvanized non-Pashtuns to mount a fierce resistance led by the Tajiks, who oppose the secret talks with the Taliban and are unwilling to share power with them—the Taliban butchered them less than a decade ago and helped Al Qaeda murder their leader, Ahmad Shah Massoud. A strong grassroots movement has emerged among the non-Pashtuns that is critical of both Karzai and the Taliban. Left largely to their own devices, the Tajik, Uzbek, Hazara, and Turkoman minorities have achieved some successes (which stirs anger and resentment among the Pashtuns).

For the first time, Tajiks and Hazaras dominate the higher officer class in the army and police because not enough Pashtuns—the traditional officer class—are being recruited. U.S. recruitment policy includes a strict ratio established in 2003 among all ethnic groups. Thus Tajiks could not be over 25 percent in the army, but in 2010 they constituted some 41 percent of soldiers and officers in the army, while Tajik officers commanded 70 percent of the units.

Pashtun recruitment stood at only 30 percent, compared to the 38 percent it should be, and 50 percent of the Pashtuns recruited were from the peaceful western provinces of Nimroz and Farah, which are not considered to be the Pashtun bastions.[15] Or seen in another dimension, the southern and eastern Pashtun-dominant provinces of Kandahar, Helmand, Zabul, Uruzghan, Paktika, and Ghazni, where the Taliban are strongest, make up 17 percent of Afghanistan's population, but since 2009 only 1.5 percent of the army's soldiers have been recruited from there. Kandahar and Helmand have contributed only 1,200 soldiers since 2009, or less than 1 percent of 173,000 enlistees in that period. Uruzghan has yielded a total of 14 recruits in the same period.[16] Clearly the rapid U.S. buildup of the security forces has been a major boon to the minorities, but the new Afghan Army cannot defeat the Taliban without more Pashtuns in its units, and Pashtuns are unlikely to be recruited as long as they are intimidated by the Taliban.

The non-Pashtuns who dominate the north and west have also linked up with their neighboring states to open up road and trade networks, import electricity and gas, develop mineral extraction, and create other profitable businesses. Those benefiting are Iran and the Central Asian states of Tajikistan, Uzbekistan, and Turkmenistan. Herat, in the northwest, has forged links with Iran that have turned it into the country's most prosperous province. The same goes for Mazar-e-Sharif's links with Uzbekistan. Afghanistan's drug trade—50 percent of which travels through Iran and Central Asia—has also enriched local warlords and politicians. All this has improved lives for ordinary people in the northwest, provided independent sources of wealth for local elites that are not dependent on Kabul, and widened the ethnic rift. The Pashtuns in the south and east, by contrast, are stuck with their powerful neighbor Pakistan, which supports the Taliban with money and arms but has done little to encourage trade or development, provide aid, or improve Afghan Pashtun lives. Pakistan, mired in its own poverty, deficient in energy and water, has little to offer the Pashtuns.

Some Tajik and Uzbek warlords in the north have become so rich and powerful that they now barely listen to Karzai. Governors there have created their own fiefdoms and maintain their own militias that NATO forces based there do not touch. The most powerful man in the country after Karzai is probably the little-known Atta Muhammad Noor, a Tajik general who once fought the Taliban and who is now the governor of Balkh province, bordering Uzbekistan. Karzai would like to remove him but cannot do so, fearing a backlash. Similarly, the Uzbek general Abdul Rashid Dostum, despite being out of favor with Kabul and the United States, made a comeback in the 2009 elections with the support of the Uzbeks.

Obama ordered the first U.S. surge troops into Afghanistan to protect the election and to widen the appeal of the government. The failure of the Afghan electoral process has not only nullified that agenda, it has endangered the very process of transition and the exit of Western forces, weakened the government's authority, and diminished Karzai's standing, while it has contributed to ethnic and political polarization inside Afghanistan that could eventually erupt into another civil war. Ultimately, Obama's authority, and the U.S. reputation of being able to find its way through the Afghan thicket, have both taken a beating.

FIVE

Afghanistan: Political and Military Fault Lines

IF ANYTHING undermined President Obama's entire Afghan deployment, it was the failure to develop a comprehensive political strategy that the U.S. military could not delay or even hold hostage. In 2010, Obama decided to deploy 33,000 additional U.S. troops as part of a surge and militarily attempt to roll back the Taliban insurgency. Doing so, while at the same time setting a deadline for their return home by 2014, was a strategy fraught with risks and potential failure. Despite the euphoria in military circles about the new counterinsurgency strategy that the extra troops could now pursue, important issues were left unaddressed.

The Obama formula for Afghanistan failed to do several things: encourage Pakistan to change its policy of harboring the Taliban, build up an indigenous Afghan economy, start talks with the Taliban parallel to the military surge, and persuade Karzai to improve governance and end corruption. Not a single senior U.S. official on the Obama team had a trusting relationship with Karzai. Lacking a reliable political partner in either Kabul or in Islamabad, Obama was more dependent on the U.S. military for his policy's outcome. Obama's greatest success—using funds made available by Congress—was to rapidly build the Afghan security forces to 350,000 men, but whether these undertrained and illiterate Afghan forces could hold the country together once the Americans left was always debatable. Wars cannot be won through military means alone, especially when the occupying forces are trying to exit the country in the midst of an insurgency.

Before Obama was elected president, his admirers viewed him as a practical visionary who had seen the world, knew how it worked, and promised to move U.S. policy away from the ideological blinders of the Bush administration. Common sense and reality, not grand rhetoric, would prevail. Obama's most influential foreign policy advisers were also expected to provide realistic assessments of conditions on the ground: Thomas Donilon, the national security adviser (who replaced Gen. James Jones), his deputy Denis McDonough, and Lt. Gen. Douglas Lute, the soft-spoken senior White House adviser on Afghanistan who had also served Bush. They all believed that the United States needed to extricate itself from both Iraq and Afghanistan.

So what happened? Obama was utterly trapped by the Bush legacy of failures in Afghanistan between 2001 and 2008 and by the power and authority of the U.S. military establishment after September 11: it became arbiter, driver, and decider of U.S. foreign policy. Obama's cold sense of reality could not free itself from the Pentagon's way of thinking or doing. Another factor was more parochial. Those around him feared that the first black (and Democratic, to boot) president might be taken for a wimp when it came to dealing with the world, so Obama had better act tough and be just as militaristic as any Republican president.

In his election campaign, Obama had promised to do more for Afghanistan, both to end the war and to help develop the nation.

Once in office, he immediately increased funds for economic and so-cial development and sent civilian experts to build up the economy. Bush had done very little (as I painfully appraised in *Descent into Chaos*). According to a study by the Senate Foreign Relations Com-mittee, the Bush administration spent a total of $10.7 billion between 2002 and 2008 on economic development in Afghanistan. Obama spent $7 billion in 2009 and $10 billion in 2010 alone, but only $3.2 billion in 2011, as the recession continued in the United States. Rich-ard Holbrooke tried hard but in the midst of a countrywide insur-gency, he could not develop an indigenous economy, let alone one that could stand up to the shock of a Western troop withdrawal. The World Bank, in a 2011 report, said that 97 percent of Afghanistan's economy was related to international military spending and that once troops pulled out, it would experience a massive depression.[1]

Despite Obama's overarching commitments to Afghanistan, the U.S. military read his program to mean just one thing: more troops, which had been unobtainable while the Iraq war was at its height. Such was the expectancy of a rapid increase in U.S. troops that bases were being built even before troop numbers had been agreed upon. Secretary of State Hillary Clinton helped the military by always siding with the generals. She agreed with the Pentagon on every major deci-sion on Afghanistan, rather than listen to her own adviser and men-tor, Richard Holbrooke. Holbrooke opposed the troop buildup and pushed for resolving the Pakistan conundrum, negotiating with the Taliban, and helping Afghanistan and Pakistan with their econo-mies.[2] Unlike the military, he did not see defeating the Taliban as an option. The White House snubbed Holbrooke, even though his views were somewhat similar to those of Obama's advisers. But they hated him, and Holbrooke could never get a one-on-one meeting with the president. Some advisers even tried to get him sacked. In this debilitating state of affairs, Obama seemed to exercise no authority over his own staff. On December 11, 2010, Holbrooke collapsed in Clinton's office with a split aorta and died two days later. His friends commented afterward that the infighting had literally killed him.

In fact, relations among many leading members of the Obama team dealing with Afghanistan were dysfunctional. In Kabul, the U.S. commander, Gen. Stanley McChrystal, and the head of Central Command, Gen. David Petraeus, were barely on speaking terms with the U.S. ambassador, Karl Eikenberry. Eikenberry and Anne Patterson, the U.S. ambassador to Pakistan, were not speaking with Holbrooke. In the Pentagon, the uniformed military differed with civilian bureaucrats on policy issues. All these differences and Obama's refusal to face up to them were well known to Afghan and Pakistani leaders and to the NATO officials who exploited them. The lack of presidential control and the open infighting, in particular Obama's snub of Holbrooke, demoralized America's allies, who were having a hard enough time keeping their publics on board for the war effort.

U.S. allies around the world asked what degree of personal commitment the president actually had toward Afghanistan. For a decade, the country had been one of America's biggest foreign policy challenges. For all his misplaced ideological moorings, Bush had understood this when it came to protecting and projecting his wars. He cultivated a common touch, constantly meeting Afghans—students, women, teachers, journalists, filmmakers, or members of parliament—hosting them at the White House and asking them about their problems. His wife, Laura, played a major role in helping reopen the destroyed Afghan school system in 2002, raising education levels, and later raising funds for an American university in Kabul. She traveled frequently to Kabul on her own. The couple seemed interested in and involved with Afghanistan.

By contrast, I never heard of Obama connecting with any group of Afghans, or hosting any significant groups of Afghan civil society in the White House, or telling stories of Afghans he had met, or in any way personalizing what the war meant to him. Michelle Obama traveled the world and promoted her favorite interests involving women and children and health, but sadly none were related to Afghanistan's women and children, and Afghans noticed that, too. In his speeches, Obama always described the war in the coldest geopolitical terms or in troop numbers, never personalizing his comments, refusing to become emotional or show any passion whatsoever. He visited Kabul as rarely as possible. He failed to describe Afghan realities to the American public or to connect with the Afghan people. He may have been frustrated and disillusioned with Karzai, but such feelings should not have extended to 30 million Afghans and the American troops fighting for them. After meeting him, I had enormous personal expectations of the man, and frankly, when it came to his handling of Afghanistan, I was deeply disappointed.

Undoubtedly Karzai presented an enormous problem for Obama. Once the darling of the West and a moderate, reasonable leader who seemed to have a good chance of taking Afghanistan out of thirty years of war, Karzai had lost his way. He had been in power and isolated in the presidency for too long. Over the course of the decade, the few U.S. and international officials whom Karzai had trusted moved on, leaving the Afghan president alone with his conspiracy theories. During the 2009 presidential election, he was convinced that the Americans wanted to get rid of him, even as he stubbornly refused to correct his own failures: corruption in the top ranks of his government and family and his own lack of vision. He frequently told top U.S. officials that of the three "main enemies" he faced—the United States, the international community, and the Taliban—he would side first with the Taliban.[3] It was hardly a statement to win over Western soldiers who were living and dying battling the Taliban.

Throughout Afghan history, the hallmark of each ruler's psyche has been an overriding concern for his own political and physical survival. No recent Afghan ruler has died peacefully in his bed. U.S. diplomats of an earlier generation understood the implications: that building trust required more than just money and guns. In a prescient 1972 report, filed months before the last Afghan king, Mohammed Zahir Shah, was deposed in a coup, U.S. ambassador Robert Neumann wrote: "For the King and leadership group, survival is the first objective with all other goals considered secondary. The result is an excessively cautious governing style which invariably seeks to balance off external and internal forces perceived as threatening the regime's power."[4]

The same could be said of Karzai today. Handling a wary president preoccupied with keeping his own head requires a personal touch—something that Obama never extended. The Americans had themselves to blame for the lack of a trusting relationship with Karzai. After 2001, Western leaders had pledged never to abandon Afghanistan, but their commitments of money and manpower never matched their rhetoric. Sufficient funds to rebuild the country's infrastructure and economy never arrived, and the United States refused to deploy troops outside Kabul after the 2001 invasion, instead rearming—over Karzai's objections—the warlords who ruled the provinces like medieval barons.

The shift of U.S. resources and attention from Afghanistan to Iraq led to bitterness. During this period, I met Karzai every few months, and with each meeting his complaint grew louder: Washington was failing to help provide electricity, build roads, and rehabilitate 3 million returning refugees. U.S. resources had long been squandered in contracts for the military and civilian infrastructure; the full facts emerged only during the Obama administration. The Commission on Wartime Contracting in Iraq and Afghanistan, set up by Congress in 2008, reported that waste and fraud had affected $30 billion worth of contracts in the two countries, all of which had undermined U.S. diplomacy, fostered corruption, and tarnished the American image abroad. The United States has deployed more than 260,000 contractors, or the same number as U.S. troops, to both countries.[5] Karzai had repeatedly pointed out to Bush Pakistan's clandestine support of the Taliban. Bush declined to do anything about it, yet Karzai remained intensely loyal to Bush, who, despite his failings, made an effort to maintain close personal ties with the Afghan leader. He would videoconference with Karzai often.

Obama arrived in office giving no sign of wanting to have a personal relationship with Karzai. He canceled the videoconferences and issued a laundry list of issues that Karzai had to address: nepotism and corruption in the Afghan government, lack of good governance, and the proliferating drug trade. These were right things to ask for, but Obama asked for them in the wrong way. None of Obama's senior advisers had any experience with Afghanistan, and Karzai felt deeply insecure, as he knew nobody in Washington and nobody was making an effort to get to know him. He feared that Obama was out to replace him and so began to fear for his own political survival. Karzai was full of conspiracy theories about the Americans, which he would air to me regularly. According to one of them, the reason the United States would not deal decisively with Pakistan was that it was in league with Pakistan to weaken Afghanistan.

From Karzai's perspective, Washington treated him with a mixture of insult and confusion. During Obama's December 2010 visit to the U.S. troops at Bagram Airfield, bad weather prevented him from flying by helicopter to nearby Kabul. Rather than wait for the weather to clear—a matter of hours, perhaps—Obama left without seeing Karzai. It was a snub for the Afghans. Karzai considered the Americans hopelessly fickle, with multiple military and civilian envoys carrying contradictory messages, working at cross-purposes, and waging Washington turf battles in his drawing room. Unfortunately, the U.S. president who would try to do the most for Afghanistan militarily and economically would be the most reviled in Kabul.

Karzai got along with none of Obama's officials except for Gen. Stanley McChrystal, who showed deference to him in decision making and treated Karzai's criticism of U.S. military tactics with respect and thoughtfulness. When McChrystal was forced to resign in July 2010 over his comments in a magazine article, Karzai begged the White House not to sack him. They refused to listen. Karzai thought this was another conspiracy by Obama to sack the only friend he had made. The WikiLeaks revelations and Bob Woodward's unflattering portrait of Karzai in *Obama's Wars* based on official U.S. perceptions—the book said the CIA believed Karzai to be "manic-depressive"—were the last straw. He believed every word he read.

Karzai was his own worst enemy. He had refused to address any of the demanding issues that engulfed his administration. He failed to accept that corruption was a core problem for the country and his people. He showed little interest in improving governance and capacity in his ministries. He rarely visited the army or the bureaucracy in training. He could not say no to his brothers, who fleeced the banks and were involved in multiple property acquisitions. "He mixes the enemy in place of a friend, a friend in place of the enemy, and confuses the nation," said former presidential candidate Abdullah Abdullah.[6] Ultimately Karzai failed himself and his country.

In Washington, the real debate was not over Karzai but over whether to conduct a counterinsurgency campaign (which would require tens of thousands of troops) or a counterterrorism campaign (which would involve fewer troops but rely on drones, missiles, and surveillance to take out extremists). In 2009 and again in 2010, the military won out on obtaining more troops to do counterinsurgency. Based on the maxim "clear, hold, build, and transfer to the Afghans," counterinsurgency was meant to be people-centric—winning over Afghan peasants, protecting them from the Taliban, and rebuilding their lives. Obama's message to McChrystal was "don't clear and hold what you can't transfer, don't overextend us."[7] The Afghans were barely consulted in these internal negotiations, and the Pakistanis even less so. Both governments grew increasingly bitter as the Americans came to them with done deals.

While carrying out counterinsurgency, the U.S. military was also secretly conducting counterterrorism, which Vice President Biden had advocated. U.S. Special Operations Forces carried out night raids, killing or capturing hundreds of Taliban commanders and fighters; but civilians were also inadvertently dying. The CIA's drone strikes in Afghanistan and in Pakistan's tribal areas were also part of this secret counterterrorism war, and they caused even more civilian casualties, which ultimately increased anti-Americanism in both countries. General McChrystal, who became chief of U.S. and NATO forces in Afghanistan in June 2009, had for five years led the Joint Special

Operations Command, which conducted the night raids. Night raids were intensified, while Petraeus, as head of CENTCOM, pushed the White House for more troops. In his first report, in August 2009, McChrystal boldly wrote of the possibility that the United States would lose the war by 2010 and of the high risk of strategic defeat in the region. He was the first U.S. general to publicly admit that "a Taliban 'shadow government' . . . actively seeks to control the population and displace the national government and traditional power structures."[8]

McChrystal's shocking report made it easier for the Pentagon to ask Obama for more troops. But the White House was bewildered because it thought it had already provided the necessary number of troops—it had dispatched 17,000 just four months earlier. The generals were now loudly talking of the aim of "defeating" the Taliban rather than "disrupting and degrading" them. This was far from Obama's original mission statement. The military seemed once again to be boxing Obama into a corner and taking control of the narrative.

Starting in September 2009, over several weeks, Obama conducted a long assessment of his options. The military wanted Obama to consider only three: dispatching 10,000 trainers, sending 40,000 troops, or sending 85,000 troops. Once again there was little discussion of Afghanistan's strategic political issues, such as its growing political and ethnic divisions, its economy, relations with Karzai, or the readiness of the Taliban for talks. Pakistan occupied a lot of discussion but yielded few political answers. Instead Leon Panetta, the director of the CIA, presented a list of clandestine counterterrorism operations that the CIA wanted to conduct in Pakistan, such as stepping up drone attacks, raising the number of CIA agents and covert contractors, and even setting up a parallel intelligence organization that would be hidden from the ISI. The CIA's recommendations were accepted, but they soon led to a complete breakdown of relations with Pakistan. Once again missing from the White House debates were in-depth consultations with Pakistani and Afghan leaders.

Both the Pakistani and the Afghan governments resented the fact that a major U.S. escalation of troops was being undertaken without consulting them or soliciting their views. Instead, for the Americans, what consultations meant was sending senior officials to Kabul and Islamabad for just two days to listen to the other side. On November 11, Obama sent a letter to President Asif Ali Zardari proposing "a long term strategic partnership" that would deepen the relationship but also warning that support for the Taliban would no longer be tolerated. Zardari's reply, which ignored Obama's points, spoke of the threat to Pakistan presented by India. The two countries were talking past each other. American voices were also ignored: Richard Holbrooke and his team, as well as Karl Eikenberry, the U.S. ambassador to Kabul, who had written a long cable expressing his "reservations about a counterinsurgency strategy that relies on a large infusion of US forces." The Pentagon shoved both men into the background.[9]

On November 25, 2009, in a major speech at West Point, Obama announced his decision to enact the surge. He said he would send 30,000 more troops but would start to bring them back in July 2011, when a transition to Afghan forces would begin. The July date, added at the last minute by White House aides, without conferring with the State Department or the Pentagon, led to consternation in the region. The plan was poorly explained by Obama; all the regional countries (Pakistan, Afghanistan, Iran, and India) and the Taliban understood it to mean that the United States was on the way out and that the endgame had begun. They began to flex their muscles for future influence in Afghanistan. Obama emerged from the speech as vacillating and contrarian. He was flexing American muscle, then stopping short by putting a time limit to the surge. He insisted that any pullout be conditions-based but then gave an actual pullout date. He was going on the offensive but then announcing when that offensive would end.

He made no mention of the regional approach he had outlined in his March 2009 speech, using U.S. diplomacy to involve Afghanistan's neighbors in a noninterference pact to stabilize the region. He made no mention of reforming U.S. aid and development to Afghanistan.[10] He offered no message to Afghan civil society or the Afghan people.

At the United Nations, Obama's surge resulted in greater hostility from members. In January 2010, Kai Eide, the UN special representative for Afghanistan, presented a devastating report to the UN Security Council in which he said that the U.S. emphasis on security over social and developmental issues would doom any efforts to stabilize the country. "We will fail," he warned the UN. "What we need is a strategy that is politically and not militarily driven." Civilian deaths had risen by 14 percent in 2009, he said, compared to the previous year. "If these negative trends are not reversed and reversed soon, there is the danger that the combination of them will become unmanageable." The central government was being weakened, he said, as 80 percent of all aid was financed directly by Western governments rather than by Kabul.[11] Eide made it clear that the entire U.S. surge had been put in place in the absence of an overarching political and economic strategy.

Eide, whose term in Kabul lasted from 2008 to 2010, was a deeply honest and forthright individual who told the Americans and Karzai the blunt truth. He made it clear that the Americans had never consulted with the UN or with NATO about "critical strategy-related questions," while the Afghan authorities "had mostly been spectators" as the United States formed policy for their country. He was one of the first high-level officials convinced of the need for reconciliation with the Taliban, at a time when that idea was deeply unpopular. And, as with Holbrooke, the Obama administration chose to ignore his messages.[12]

Al Qaeda struck a major blow on December 31, 2009, when it used a Jordanian double agent to inflict the worst-ever casualties on the CIA: the man blew himself up at a U.S. base in the southeastern province of Khost, killing seven CIA officers and a Jordanian military officer. Then, on January 18, 2010, twelve suicide bombers brazenly tried to occupy shopping plazas and banks in Kabul. It took several hours of heavy fighting before they were all killed. These attacks did not alter the first target of the U.S. surge, which was Marjah, a small farming region in Helmand province. In mid-February 2010, the Marines began an offensive to clear Marjah. It was not in a populous region (it held a total of just eighty thousand people); nor was it of vital strategic importance. Most Afghans had never heard of it.

Helmand had a population of only 1.4 million people, or just one-thirtieth of Afghanistan's total, but it was a base for the heroin industry, from which the Taliban profited, as well as a major route for supplies and recruits from Pakistan. The Taliban had ruled Helmand unopposed since 1993. After their defeat in 2001, they remained in control of Helmand due to the lack of Western forces being deployed in the province. Finally in 2006, 8,000 British troops were deployed in Helmand and heavy fighting broke out with the Taliban, which continues to this day. The U.S. Marine Corps decided to move its forces to Helmand from Iraq, and as I explained earlier, the Marines had an independent command and decision-making structure within the U.S. military. Marjah was more about the Marines showing what they could do than it was part of a strategically defined offensive. Marjah had some strategic value, but because of the paucity of population, it could not be seen as part of counterinsurgency, which should have focused on the most densely populated areas. Marjah was targeted because the U.S. Marines had already decided to pacify Helmand in 2008, before they were under ISAF command, and not because of an overall strategy set by McChrystal. The Marines carried out a spectacular assault, using dozens of helicopters, and then immediately got bogged down as dug-in Taliban, suicide bombers, and mines took their toll. Three months later the 15,000 troops were still unable to secure the region. McChrystal's claim that he had a government in a box—trained Afghan officials who would jump in behind the troops and begin to govern and provide services—never materialized. No Afghan wanted to serve in Marjah, because it was so insecure. By May, only 200 Taliban were left in Marjah, but they were enough to intimidate the remaining population. Twenty-six thousand people had already fled the town. Counterinsurgency against the Taliban was not going to be easy.

A total of $19 million in aid money was earmarked for development in Marjah, but only $1.5 million was actually spent. The Americans issued vouchers to farmers that would get them free seed and fertilizer, but the farmers rejected them because they feared Taliban reprisals. The UN and other Western NGOs said they would not deploy in Marjah because the U.S. Army was running the reconstruction and the aid agencies' neutrality would be jeopardized. As a result of this debate, the military became its own development organization—a mistake that would get worse over time because it could provide neither sustainability nor longevity for projects. In a special program run by the Pentagon, U.S. commanders in the field were given cash to carry out quick-impact projects in their areas of command so they could influence the local people. For the "Commanders Emergency Response Program," a budget of $40 million was initially set aside. By 2008 this had grown to $ 750 million and by 2010 it was $1 billion, which is more than the entire revenue of the Karzai government. Nobody was consulted on how these vast free-flowing funds were to be spent. The money was "spent by military personnel without professional experience or knowledge" and without consultations with the relevant Afghans or civilian aid experts, said the UN's Kai Eide.[13]

On a visit to Marjah at the end of May, an impatient Marine officer asked McChrystal for more time to oust the Taliban. "This is a bleeding ulcer right now," McChrystal responded. "How many days do you think we have before we run out of support by the international community?"[14] His words resounded in the media and in Washington. The United States still did not have enough forces to saturate the area and evict all the Taliban; nor was there the time to win over the population, as the public in the United States and Europe was impatient for results.

In the flat, irrigated lands on both sides of the Helmand River, the Taliban's best weapons were IEDs. Despite a $17 billion U.S. military program to counter them, IEDs' use and lethality had dramatically grown. The ammonium nitrate fertilizer used in the bombs, the trigger mechanisms, and other parts came almost wholly from Pakistan, but despite frequent U.S. appeals, the Pakistanis made no attempt to shut down the manufacturers—even though the Pakistani Taliban's bombs used the same materials and parts. There were a total of 8,159 IED attacks in 2009, compared to just 3,867 in 2008 and 2,677 in

2007.[15] In 2010, the Taliban planted a staggering 14,661 IEDs, double the previous year, which killed some 268 U.S. troops and injured another 3,360. IEDs were now the Taliban's most lethal yet safest weapon.

The Taliban knew that the Marines would target Kandahar next and attempted to destabilize the city with daily bomb blasts. They assassinated senior government officials, murdering eleven in Kandahar in February and March 2010, including the deputy mayor Azizullah Yarmal, who was shot in the city's main mosque while saying his prayers. UN figures showed that in the spring of 2010, there were on average seven assassinations of public officials every week across the country, but between June and September 2010, the number jumped to twenty-one a week. Kandahar slid into anarchy, with only five out of its seventeen districts under government control. Kandahar had a corrupt local government run by the president's brother Ahmed Wali Karzai, who was alleged to be involved in protecting drug traffickers, while being on the CIA's payroll and being the government's chief interlocutor with the Taliban. But while he lived, he was a tough and ruthless administrator who held the city together. When he was killed in July 2011, there was a sudden vacuum.

Under siege in the south, the Taliban showed they could divert the West's attention by attacking in other parts of the country. They attacked the main U.S. base, Bagram, on May 19, leaving twelve American soldiers wounded. A day earlier they attacked a NATO convoy in Kabul, killing nineteen people.[16] And in Kunduz, in the far northeast, they attacked a compound housing an American contractor, killing six people, including three foreigners, in a five-hour battle. The Taliban were like a balloon—push them from one side, and they would pop out on the other. They had learned the military art of lifting pressure from one region by attacking in another. It was their answer to counterinsurgency.

As the Taliban had predicted, Coalition forces intended to tackle Kandahar next, devising a strategy that they hoped would alienate people the least yet still squeeze the insurgents out of the city. By September, 28,000 NATO forces, 10,000 Afghan troops, and 5,000 police were deployed in and around Kandahar—by far the largest military mission so far. Afghan troops were stationed inside the city of 2 million people, while the U.S. Marines set up checkposts on the outskirts. As both civilian and military casualties rose and air strikes inadvertently killed more civilians than militants, President Karzai became increasingly angry at the Coalition forces. His vitriol against NATO became critical and coarse. He urged Obama to review his strategy, saying the war could not be won by fighting in the villages of Afghanistan—it had to be taken over the border, to eliminate Taliban sanctuaries in Pakistan. Petraeus launched a media counterblitz, revealing that in a three-month period between May 8 and August 8, 2010, American special forces had killed 365 Taliban commanders and captured some 1,395 Taliban soldiers in night raids. His message to Karzai was that President Obama had not sent him to Afghanistan to seek a "graceful exit" for U.S. forces.[17] U.S. costs were also high. In the first nine months of 2010, the Taliban had killed 323 American soldiers, surpassing the 317 total killed in 2009.[18]

Marjah had taken half a year to secure, rather than a few weeks. The Taliban may have been cleared, but how long could the Marines maintain this density of troops in a small area when they were needed elsewhere? In retrospect, it was probably a mistake for U.S. forces to go for the hardest killing fields first—Kandahar and Helmand. At the time, I proposed an alternative military strategy: give first priority to securing Kabul and its surrounding districts and provinces, where some one-fifth of the population lived, then secure the major roads linking Afghan cities and the roads to the borders that were also major trade routes. Western and Afghan NGOs and aid agencies were unable to send their staff out of Kabul—even twenty miles to a neighboring province—because of security risks and Taliban ambushes. It was unsafe to travel the critical Kabul-Kandahar highway, where corrupt police, criminal gangs, and Taliban groups ran the checkpoints. NATO supply convoys moved under heavy guard with payoffs to the Taliban. Clearing the region around Kabul could have initiated a massive improvement in economic development. Several hundred of Obama's civilian experts who were stranded in Kabul could have been out and about in these provinces.[19]

The Taliban held enclaves in provinces around Kabul, such as Logar, Wardak, and Kapisa, from which they could terrorize the largely pro-government population. NATO offered no corresponding security. Moreover, the still-weak Afghan Army could have been better used to secure these areas, because many of its recruits come from these same provinces. Finally, the first military surge should have been launched not in the south but in the adjoining eastern provinces, where the Taliban were strong, their supply routes from Pakistan were significant, and there were large populations to be won over. All these opportunities were lost due to the overwhelming focus on Helmand.

By 2011, the crisis in Kabul and the seven provinces that surround the city had become far worse. Large areas (including towns) were under Taliban control, and development work had come to a standstill. Taliban who were sheltering in these provinces could easily launch sporadic attacks in Kabul, such as the suicide attack on the Intercontinental Hotel in June 2011 (which killed twenty-one people) and the brazen attack on the U.S. embassy on September 13 (which killed twenty-seven people). Stability in the Afghan heartland had steadily eroded, even though it was pivotal to a successful withdrawal of Western troops.

The Taliban were not the only problem. An added destabilizing element, according to an influential report, was "the nexus between criminal enterprises, insurgent networks and corrupt political elites, [which] is undermining Kabul's security and that of the central-eastern corridor."[20] Outside Kabul, these networks became in effect a Taliban shadow government and a hallmark of its progress. Shadow governors operated in more than half (thirty-five) of the sixty-two districts in the seven provinces. They ran a parallel government, collected taxes, administered justice, settled disputes, and appointed local leaders, sometimes just a few miles from the outskirts of Kabul. The United States had no plan or troops to combat this steady take-over by the Taliban.

Afghans argued that NATO's surge in the south had increased the levels of violence, destabilized the entire country, and given the Taliban a propaganda boost. There was truth in this, especially as the metrics of measuring the success of the surge were so controversial. Who could claim to know for certain if the areas retaken by NATO had been cleared for all time or just temporarily? Petraeus claimed that the Taliban had been driven out of their strongholds and could not return, but other commanders tactfully used the phrase "fragile and reversible" to describe the south's delicate military balance. Aid workers said the surge had been a failure because it had made a wasteland of once-viable villages and agricultural communities. Reports emerged that the Americans had destroyed entire villages, after evacuating the population, because the villages' homes and streets were so heavily laced with IEDs. Mullah Wakil Ahmed Muttawakil, the former Taliban foreign minister, told me in Kabul, "The Americans tried before with surges and failed and they will fail again. This war is not just a one-way war. If we are losing troops, so are they. If the Taliban are exhausted, so are they. If they increase their numbers, so will we. But they will wear themselves out. New Taliban recruits are more radical and more enthusiastic to fight."[21]

For the United States, the key to an eventual withdrawal lay in the successful buildup of the Afghan security forces (ASF), the army and the police. After years of going too slowly and providing inadequate funding (as I covered in *Descent into Chaos*), the Coalition was finally bringing the ASF up to speed, in terms of numbers, equipment, training, and mentoring. In 2010, the United States spent $11 billion on the ASF—the largest single-ticket item in the defense budget. The Afghan Army reached its first target of 134,000 men in late 2010 and would expand further. The police would eventually number 126,000, although they are less well trained. By October 2012, the ASF would total 352,000. In 2011, the Americans spent $11.6 billion on the ASF, equipping the army with armor and vehicles, and the following year it would spend $12.8 billion, after which there would be a rapid drawdown. (By 2012, the Americans would have spent a total of $39 billion building up the ASF.)[22] The Afghans claimed that it would cost $6 billion a year to maintain all these forces after 2014—a bill that the Americans would have to pay, as the entire Afghan state income in 2014 would not be more than $3 billion.[23]

But worrying downsides naturally affected the ability of the ASF to take on the Taliban. In early 2011, the annual attrition rate from the Afghan Army was still a staggering 24 percent: that is, one in seven newly enlisted soldiers was deserting. Eighty-six percent of the soldiers were illiterate, and drug taking was an endemic problem. The police were even worse. In June, 5,000 deserted, or 3 percent of the army, and there were no punishments for desertion. The real problem was the lack of leadership and the absence of a properly trained officer corps. In the 1980s, when the Communist Afghan Army fought the mujahedeen, there were similar large-scale desertions by rank-and-file soldiers, but the army held together because it had a core of dedicated Communist Pashtun officers who were well trained by the Soviets. That Pashtun officer class had now disappeared.[24]

Although 80 percent of army units were now partnered with NATO units, no single Afghan Army unit was ready to take full responsibility. The United States started a mass literacy campaign within the army so that soldiers could at least read basic instructions. The Americans were doing all this in the midst of an insurgency and a U.S. surge. By contrast, when the U.S. surge started in Iraq in 2007, the Iraq security forces already numbered one million men. In a highly controversial part of the U.S. buildup of security forces, Petraeus insisted on creating *arbaki*, or local self-defense forces in the villages. The Kabul government opposed the plan because it would allow warlords and militias to return to the countryside. Petraeus, basing his arguments on the Sons of Iraq program he had run in Iraq, where 100,000 militiamen had been raised, finally won support for his plan from Obama and Karzai. He planned to raise 30,000 men. But the Pashtun rural population was deeply suspicious of the militias. The program essentially put too many ill-disciplined armed men in the field.

Moreover, when the Afghan adminstrative presence in the provinces was so small, there were limits to what the ASF could achieve. The training of an Afghan civil service over the past ten years was an even worse tale of Western neglect, lack of Afghan interest, and shortage of funds and expertise. There is now a civil service academy turning out bureaucrats, but it will be years before they make a difference. The justice system was equally depleted, so the Taliban were easily able to exercise their own form of justice in the countryside. One hundred and seventeen districts were without a single judge. Ten years on, no government ministry was fully competent to run its budget or organize its personnel or spending program. All the ministries lacked capacity, trained officials, and the ability to handle money. The dependence on foreigners was enormous. In 2011, three hundred foreign advisers were still working at the interior ministry, costing the U.S. government $36 million a year.[25]

Thus the key question for the Americans before 2014 is not how many Taliban they kill but whether an Afghan state—army, police, bureaucracy, justice—neglected so badly under Bush, can be enabled to take charge of the country. Moreover, can state functionaries win the trust of a people who have put up with insecurity, corruption, and poor governance for so long? Corruption seems impossible to root out—it is endemic and everywhere. The drug trade, U.S. development contracts, oil and goods transport contracts, Western humanitarian aid—everything generates kickbacks, bribes, and payoffs, often to the Taliban themselves. In 2010, American-trained Afghan prosecutors working in secured anticorruption courts were ready to try two dozen senior Afghan officials for corruption. But the arrest of a presidential aide, who was then freed on the orders of the president himself, scuttled the entire effort. Clearly Karzai has no interest in curbing corruption.[26]

In the summer of 2011, the U.S. domestic economic crisis looms as a far larger problem for Obama than the war in Afghanistan. The American president faces a ballooning deficit, a soaring national debt, a 9 percent jobless rate, a loss of exports and production, and a housing crisis, so Americans are naturally asking why $120 billion is to be spent in Afghanistan that year—money raised not from extra taxes but entirely from borrowing, and money that could be better spent at home. Not a single Republican presidential candidate for the 2012 presidential election has endorsed maintaining U.S. troops in Afghanistan. The even more serious economic crisis in Europe stymies many NATO countries' spending on Afghanistan. The crises in Afghanistan and Pakistan are evidently going to be sacrificed on the altar of the U.S. debt. In that case, the faster the United States talks to the Taliban and works out a peaceful settlement that will allow the troops to depart in good order, the better it will be, both for the United States and for the region.

SIX

Afghanistan: Talking to the Taliban

ON NOVEMBER 28, 2010, a cold Bavarian day, in a well-to-do residential village close to Munich, German diplomat Michael Steiner was celebrating his sixty-first birthday. But this was no party. Steiner and two American officials were meeting face-to-face, for the first time in ten years, with a senior Taliban envoy—the result of intensive German diplomacy and a personal triumph for Steiner. President Obama himself had cleared the first U.S. contact with the Taliban a few weeks earlier. History might well judge that day as a turning point in the ten-year-long war in Afghanistan, no less momentous than the day the United States began talks with the Vietnamese half a century earlier, or when Britain began secret talks with the Irish Republican Army in 1972.

A flamboyant, intellectually aggressive troubleshooter for the German foreign ministry, Steiner had earned his negotiating spurs in the Balkan conflict and in May 2010 had been appointed as Berlin's special envoy for AfPak—the German counterpart to Richard Holbrooke, whom Steiner knew well from the Balkans. After many months of shuttling between capitals and meetings with the Taliban, Steiner and his knowledgeable assistant, Arend Wulff, had brought two U.S.

officials—Frank Ruggiero (from the State Department and a deputy to Holbrooke) and Jeff Hayes (from the National Security Council staff)—together with the Taliban's Syed Tayyab Agha, in his late thirties, a secretary and long-term aide to Mullah Muhammad Omar. Also present was a prince from Qatar's ruling family, whom the Taliban had asked to be present.[1]

The four-way meeting took place in a safe house belonging to the Bundesnachrichtendienst (BND), the German intelligence service, in the village where Steiner was born. The BND had cordoned off the area, but there were still spies in the village from various countries that had caught a whiff of the meeting. "If this meeting leaks out, it's dead," Steiner reportedly told the participants. Agha, who spoke English, had flown from Pakistan to Qatar on a Pakistani passport, and from there he had been whisked to Germany in a BND plane. He had worked in Mullah Omar's office in Kandahar in the late 1990s, followed by stints in the Taliban's foreign ministry and its embassy in Pakistan. Since 2001, he had been in exile in Iran and Pakistan, and he had been part of a Taliban delegation that had opened informal talks with the Karzai government in Saudi Arabia in 2008.[2]

The need for secrecy was intense because any disclosure could endanger Agha's life—Al Qaeda or some other spoiler might try to kill him. Even a close ally like Britain's MI6 was not told about the meeting. Nor was Pakistan's ISI informed of it: the Americans did not trust it to keep a secret, and Taliban leaders had become highly critical of it as well, saying that the ISI constantly threatened them and their families in Pakistan, even though it supported the Taliban war effort against the Americans. The Pakistanis would not take kindly to being bypassed. In 2009, when the Taliban had tried to talk to Karzai's brother in Kandahar without telling the Pakistanis, the ISI had arrested the Taliban interlocutor—the second-in-command, Mullah Abdul Ghani Baradar—and accused him of being a spy for the Americans. (Baradar was arrested in Karachi on February 8, 2010, and disappeared into an ISI safe house jail.)

The small group spent a total of eleven hours together—six of them in concentrated talks. They made no preconditions, assurances, or commitments, and both sides avoided actual negotiations. This was a getting-to-know-you session. At the end, Agha brought up the issue of the prisoners that the Taliban wanted freed, whom the United States was holding in Bagram, Afghanistan, and Guantánamo, Cuba. The Taliban were obsessed with getting their commanders out of jail. Steiner took the visitors on a local sightseeing trip. They were intrigued to see a typical German castle and the village church. When the meeting broke up and Agha left, the adrenaline-pumped participants horsed around. Steiner joked that the meeting should be titled "The Birthday Party"—a spoof on Harold Pinter's famous play. They were euphoric that the ice with the Taliban had finally been broken.

"Talking to the Taliban" had become the most controversial issue for all sides in the war. Hamid Karzai had promoted the idea as early as 2004, because he understood that a military victory in the conventional sense was not possible, as long as the United States continued to underfund the war effort and economic development and allowed Taliban safe havens in Pakistan to go unquestioned. Later Pakistan wanted talks because it hoped to broker the final deal that would bring the Taliban into a power-sharing agreement and keep India out of a reconstituted Afghanistan. European states with troops in Afghanistan supported the idea as a way to exit Afghanistan faster. But for years, the United States had adamantly opposed talks and continued to equate the Taliban with Al Qaeda, making no distinction between them.

By 2009–10, many Afghans and Western diplomats realized that the U.S. military surge was not working, and that the Taliban were growing stronger and spreading into every corner of the country. With the 2008 economic recession, the Europeans could not or would not maintain their troops for long. For the Americans, the cost of the war in Afghanistan—$109 billion in 2010 and $120 billion in 2011—was also becoming unsustainable, especially as it was being funded entirely with borrowed money. For some time, the Obama administration was divided between civilian advisers, who wanted talks with the Taliban and a quick military exit, and the military, which demanded another year or two of surge. Gen. David Petraeus in particular would consider talks only after the Taliban had been decimated. Admiral Mike Mullen, the chairman of the Joint Chiefs of Staff, was more open to the idea of talks but took no steps to encourage Obama to pursue that course. I argued repeatedly—both with Petraeus and with Mullen—that by the time the military got what it wanted with its degrading program, the top Taliban leaders who could lead a negotiation would be dead.

Richard Holbrooke was convinced of the need to talk, but he lacked support from anyone in the cabinet. As Bob Woodward's *Obama's Wars* makes plain, Obama's civilian advisers kept getting outmaneuvered by the generals, who demanded ever more troops for Afghanistan rather than talks with the Taliban. Only after the 2010 Lisbon NATO summit set a time limit for Western troops to be out did the idea of talks became more urgent. Naturally, many Western officials doubted that the Taliban were sincere about talks. The most common belief—and the most pessimistic—was that the Taliban had only to wait for American forces to leave, and then they could seize power in Kabul, so why should they want to talk?

But the Taliban leaders had matured considerably since the 1990s.

They remained firm that all foreign troops had to leave Afghanistan and that an Islamic system had to be restored to their country, but on both counts they were more flexible than before. Even though they had received extensive training, funding, and other support from Al Qaeda, both before and after 2001, they had now distanced themselves from it. Unlike other groups, the Afghan Taliban leadership had never sworn an oath of loyalty to Al Qaeda or to Osama bin Laden; nor had they adopted Al Qaeda's global jihad agenda or helped train foreigners to become suicide bombers, as the Pakistani Taliban and their Afghan allies, the network led by Jalaluddin Haqqani, had done. Most senior Taliban I spoke to over the years blamed Bin Laden and the Arabs for their defeat by the Americans in 2001. The Taliban stressed that they considered themselves Afghan nationalists not global jihadists. At the death of Bin Laden, the Taliban statements remained circumspect, refusing to eulogize him or call for revenge attacks.

The Taliban had mellowed on the issues of girls' education, the media, and health services for women, compared with the policies they pursued in the 1990s. In March 2010, Mullah Omar issued a decree banning attacks on all schools, including girls' schools, which did not stop them completely but much reduced them. The Taliban no longer opposed girls' schools, as long as they were separate from boys' schools, and Taliban shadow governors across the country reassured NGOs that they could build schools. Even though 400 government schools remained closed in the southern war zones, 100 new schools opened in Helmand and Kandahar in 2010–11. In 2011, 8.3 million children started the new school year in Afghanistan, 40 percent of them girls—up from 7.6 million in the previous year.[3]

The Taliban had partially adhered to a UN Peace Day on September 23, 2008, when Taliban attacks dropped by 70 percent. They had allowed the UN to conduct a medical campaign to immunize children against polio in many war-torn areas, and midlevel Taliban commanders had held meetings with UN officials in Kabul and other cities where they talked of the need for local confidence-building measures such as cease-fires. The UN special representative Kai Eide encouraged all these efforts, in particular efforts to get some Taliban leaders off the UN Resolution 1267 list, which was a list of terrorist suspects maintained by the UN Security Council since 1999.

The Taliban have also tried to reassure Afghanistan's neighboring countries that they will not host groups that are hostile to them. In an Eid message on November 15, 2010, Mullah Omar said his group has a comprehensive policy "for the efficiency of the future government of Afghanistan; about true security, Islamic justice, education, economic progress, national unity and a foreign policy . . . [to] convince the world that the future Afghanistan will not harm them."[4] In his Eid message a year later, in August 2011, after secret talks had begun with the Americans, Mullah Omar admitted for the first time that talks were going on. He said that in the interest of a peaceful Afghanistan, "every legitimate option can be considered in order to reach this goal," and he accepted that "all" ethnic groups "will have participation" in governing Afghanistan—a clear message to non-Pashtuns.[5]

The Taliban are exhausted by the long war. They have suffered terrible casualties, and they want to return home from the refugee camps in Pakistan. Moreover, they want to break free from Pakistan and the control exercised by the ISI, which they now intensely dislike. (I will deal with this complex relationship in chapter 8.) The older generation of Taliban realize that since they could not run the country in the 1990s, they will not be able to do so in the future. Rather than trying to grab power and then face international isolation and forfeit funds and aid, they now see the benefits of a coalition government with Karzai that would retain Western aid, legitimacy, and support.

The second round of talks with the Taliban took place in Doha, the capital of Qatar, on February 15, 2011. It was delayed due to the tragic death of Richard Holbrooke on December 13, 2010. The American officials, still highly mistrustful, asked Agha to prove that he had access to Mullah Omar and other leaders by getting the Taliban to deliver on a confidence-building measure that they proposed. The Americans asked Agha to see that the Taliban officially put out a certain public statement in language that had been agreed upon. A few weeks later the participants received the long-awaited confirmation: a Taliban statement containing the agreed language. Agha had delivered, confirming that he spoke on behalf of the Taliban leadership.

Three days after the Doha meeting, Secretary of State Hillary Clinton, in the most significant U.S. public statement to date, told New York's Asia Society that "we are launching a diplomatic surge to move this conflict toward a political outcome that shatters the alliance between the Taliban and Al Qaeda, ends the insurgency and helps to produce not only a more stable Afghanistan but a more stable region." It was the first tantalizing public hint that the United States was talking to the Taliban. She went on to eulogize Holbrooke, saying, "We had always envisioned Richard Holbrooke leading this effort. He was an architect of our integrated military-civilian-diplomatic strategy."[6]

A third round with the same participants took place in the same Bavarian village on May 7, 2011. Osama bin Laden had been killed in Pakistan, and Agha expressed no regret at his death. The Americans agreed to talk about the possibility of opening a Taliban office in Doha, so that more frequent talks could take place. The Taliban had been lobbying for an office outside Pakistan for more than a year. Turkey had been mooted, but the Taliban preferred Qatar. But the four parties still had to agree on the legal modalities that the office would have, while Pakistan had to be persuaded to allow the Taliban to travel freely to Qatar. This was particularly difficult because the Pakistanis, who were informed late about the dialogue, resented being neither the host nor an invited guest.

As a confidence-building measure, the Americans agreed to remove a large number of Taliban from the UN sanctions list that designated them as global terrorists. The list—called UN Security Council Resolution 1267—was first drawn up in 1999 and had 433 names on it, including 140 Taliban. The sanctions included a travel ban and an assets freeze. The entire UN Security Council had to give its agreement for any changes, which took considerable time. Some 45 Taliban names were removed in December 2010, and another 50 were requested to be removed in 2011. On June 17, 2011, in an important step, the UN Security Council decided to treat Al Qaeda and the Taliban separately and to create two separate lists. It was now much easer to scrub Taliban names from the list.

President Karzai, for his part, freed several Taliban prisoners from detention in Kabul. The Taliban then asked the Americans to free several of their leaders held at Guantánamo, including three top military commanders who had been held since 2002—Noorullah Noori, Mullah Fazel, and former interior minister Mullah Khairullah

Khairkhwa. But they could not be released because a new U.S. law prevented terrorism prisoners being removed from Guantánamo. The Taliban also demanded an end to night raids by American special forces that had killed hundreds of low-level commanders, fighters, and civilians, but the U.S. military refused to make any military concessions as yet.

In Kabul in late 2010, Mullah Abdul Salam Zaeef, the former Taliban ambassador to Pakistan, spelled out the short-term Taliban objectives to me: "The fundamental problem is between the United States and the Taliban. The Afghan government is the secondary problem. The talks we want must involve the international community and end with international guarantees. The Taliban want to discuss the system of government that will prevail after peace comes. They are not interested in sharing of power or to be in the government. It is best for our own safety to open an office in a third country so we can have a single address to meet with anyone we choose."[7]

Clearly the Taliban were serious about negotiating at least a reduction in the violence, if not an end to the fighting. The German-led peace process had begun with Steiner's predecessor, the diplomat Bernd Mützelburg, who was the German AfPak envoy until May 2010. An Afghan-born German citizen who knew Syed Tayyab Agha had contacted Mützelburg and told him that if the Germans were interested in talking to the Taliban, he could arrange it. Mützelburg and Tayyab Agha had their first secret meeting in Dubai in September 2009. Mützelburg's first task was to confirm Agha's identity and that he had access to the Taliban leadership. He had a number of meetings with Agha, building trust and an understanding of what the Taliban wanted. In February 2010, after being sure about Agha's identity, Mützelburg conferred with Holbrooke. After that, the results of each meeting were reported to the Americans and to Karzai. Steiner held two more meetings with Agha in the gulf before the Americans were ready to come to the table. Steiner was convinced of the Taliban's sincerity, in part because Agha never asked for money, and beyond a few travel expenses, the Germans did not pay him a penny.

Steiner had asked the United States to guarantee that Agha would not be harassed while traveling from Pakistan to the gulf. He got this guarantee, demonstrating early White House support for the talks. Although only a few U.S. officials knew about the talks, the power play in Washington among senior officials who supported or rejected them remained a major problem. The Germans could move no faster than the Americans were able to, and the Americans moved very slowly. The Germans frequently asked the Americans to speed up the process, especially as Chancellor Angela Merkel was following it closely. When she invited me to dinner in Berlin, she peppered me with questions about the prospects for peace in Afghanistan.

The Taliban's first demand was the release of their prisoners held by the Americans. When the United States was unable to deliver prisoners held in Guantánamo, Steiner went to Karzai: if they could not deliver on the first confidence-building measure that the Taliban asked for, the talks might collapse. Karzai said he would free some Taliban prisoners as a unilateral gesture, a step that generated enormous goodwill from the Taliban. The International Committee of the Red Cross was brought in to facilitate the prisoners' release.

When the time came to talk to the Americans, the Taliban set down two conditions on a single sheet of paper. The first was that the talks remain top secret: no leaks or revelations would take place, or the dialogue would be broken off. The second condition was that no Taliban members who took part in the talks would be arrested or harassed. Ultimately all the participants knew that the talks would be later transformed into an Afghan-led process. The Taliban, from their side, also asked that a representative from the Qatari royal family be present at all meetings. The Taliban considered Qatar to be neutral because it had never interfered in Afghanistan's affairs. Both the American and the German leaders had excellent relations with the emir of Qatar, as the world was to see later when Qatar joined NATO to help Libyans free themselves from the Muammar Gaddafi regime. The United States agreed to these conditions, and the stage was set for the first meeting outside Munich.

In May 2011, after the third round of talks, a series of leaks about the talks appeared in the U.S. and German press. This posed an immediate problem for Agha, as he was named as the Taliban interlocutor.[8] The leaks came from some of Karzai's ministers who were opposed to the talks and from American officials in both the State Department and the Pentagon who were opposed to the talks. The leaks disturbed the talks, and the fourth round was not held until August. There was an agreement that a Taliban office could open soon in Doha, but its legal position had yet to be worked out.

The leaks prompted the Germans and the Americans to level with the Pakistanis and the ISI for the first time, in May and June 2011. U.S. officials met with General Kayani in Rawalpindi, telling him about the contacts with the Taliban and asking him to protect Agha. Kayani promised to do so, but he knew about the talks already. He and ISI chief Ahmed Shuja Pasha were angry that their Western allies had gone behind their backs to make contact with the Taliban. This was the role that the ISI had always wanted to play—offer the Americans talks with the Taliban, thereby demonstrating Pakistan's importance in any future settlement. The Pakistanis were doubly angry with the Taliban, who had shown that they were not fully under their control. The ISI became convinced that the United States wanted to undermine it by cutting the one hand it had to play—bringing the Taliban to the table. Paradoxically, the Pakistan Army's relations with the Americans and the Taliban worsened at the same time. But more of this later.

Talking to the Taliban was far from a new idea. Lakhdar Brahimi and Francesc Vendrell, the UN mediators who had negotiated the Bonn Agreement (establishing a provisional government in Afghanistan after the U.S. invasion) a decade earlier, in 2001, had soon afterward admitted that their biggest mistake had been omitting the Taliban from the table at Bonn. Including them might well have achieved a peace that avoided the revival of the Taliban insurgency in 2003, but at the time the Americans were not interested.

The first peace offer came in 2002, just after the Taliban's defeat, from a group of senior Taliban, including Agha and the movement's number two, Mullah Abdul Ghani Baradar. The group wrote a letter to Karzai accepting his nomination as president and expressing a willingness to surrender if they received immunity from arrest. Both Karzai and Baradar came from the same Popalzai tribe of the Durrani Pashtuns in Kandahar. The United States and the Northern Alliance, which dominated his cabinet, told Karzai to ignore the offer.[9] Subsequent attempts by other Taliban groups to talk to Kabul were also squashed, either by infighting within the Taliban or by the ISI, which wanted to exercise control over any talks that the United States might decide to hold with Taliban dissidents.

Karzai continued to hanker after an accord with the Taliban, as he quickly understood that a military victory against the Taliban was not possible—as long as their safe havens remained in Pakistan. The United States was unwilling to put pressure on Pakistan but continued to discourage Karzai from pursuing any dialogue with the Taliban. He also did not have the full support of his cabinet colleagues. Nevertheless he persisted, and in 2005 he set up a Peace and Reconciliation Commission, headed by the aged former prime minister and mujahedeen leader Sibghatullah Mojaddedi. Its aim was to lure moderate or disgruntled Taliban out of the movement and help them resettle as peaceful citizens by offering them jobs; but the committee had neither funds, nor a plan, nor sufficiently talented staff to make the project successful.

Holding more direct contacts with the Taliban became the domain of two of the president's brothers, Qayum Karzai, a member of parliament and a businessman, and Ahmed Wali Karzai, the powerful head of the provincial council in Kandahar and a key interlocutor with the U.S. military and the CIA. Both brothers had been quietly talking to local Taliban field commanders and, through them, to Mullah Baradar. With Mullah Omar rarely making an appearance, the all-powerful deputy emir of the Islamic Emirate of Afghanistan—as Baradar was now titled—was virtually commander in chief, head of treasury, and political leader of the Taliban movement. He had been a founding member of the Taliban in 1994 and had fought under Omar's command against the Soviets in the late 1980s, so Omar and Baradar trusted each other implicitly.

Baradar's main rival for the deputy slot, the bloodthirsty Mullah Dadullah Akhund, who had restarted the insurgency in 2003 from Pakistan, had been killed in a U.S. raid in May 2007, leaving Baradar as the unquestioned leader. But serious talks could not take place inside Afghanistan, which was a constant battlefield and where the Americans gave no guarantees of safety. Nor could they occur in Pakistan, where the Taliban leaders were afraid of being harassed or arrested by the ISI; they did not want to engage in a dialogue where they appeared to be under the ISI's control.

In 2008, Karzai reached out to Gulbuddin Hekmatyar, the notorious head of Hezb-i-Islami and a Taliban ally, who was based in Pakistan. Hezb's influence in Afghanistan was in no way comparable to that of the Taliban or the network of Jalaluddin Haqqani among the eastern Pashtuns. Hezb had some influence among Pashtun intellectual circles, although many Hezb figures had abandoned the party and joined the Kabul regime. In the 2005 elections, thirty-five Hezb figures were elected to the Afghan parliament—the largest single group in parliament—and some two hundred officials in the Afghan bureaucracy were also former Hezb. All these people would benefit if Hekmatyar came to an understanding with Karzai. The ISI considered Hekmatyar more pliable and dependent on Pakistani support than the Taliban. Karzai exchanged letters with Hekmatyar in 2008 and released his son-in-law Ghairat Bahir from a Kabul jail in May. Bahir then met with Karzai, UN officials in Kabul, and other diplomats, but the Americans stayed well away from these contacts.

Karzai fully understood that without the Taliban, peace with Hekmatyar was next to useless. In 2008, he wrote to Saudi king Abdullah bin Abdul Aziz, asking him to use his influence with the Taliban and provide a venue for talks. The task was given to Prince Muqrin bin Abdul Aziz, the head of Saudi intelligence, while an important initiative was also taken by Abdullah Anas, an Algerian Islamist who had once worked with Bin Laden, had fought in the Afghan war against the Soviets, was married to the daughter of Abdullah Azam, the mentor of Bin Laden, and was eventually given political asylum in Britain. Anas used his former Saudi, Al Qaeda, and Afghan contacts to approach the Taliban. The Saudis at first insisted that the Taliban denounce Al

Qaeda before they came to the table, but this demand was seen as an end condition to talks rather than a precondition. At the request of the Taliban, the Saudis had also kept Pakistan out of the process, much to the chagrin of the ISI. Saudi intelligence—a close ally of the ISI—had itself become mistrustful of the ISI for continuing to tolerate on Pakistani soil militants and Al Qaeda, whom the Saudis were battling.

A series of meetings took place in Jeddah during the fasting month of Ramadan and the festival of Eid in September and October 2008. Those present included Afghan officials from Kabul, Afghan legislators including Qayum Karzai, and former Taliban—retired figures rather than those active in the Taliban's leadership council. Nevertheless the Saudis had secret contacts with senior active Taliban, including Baradar. Ultimately this initiative fizzled out because the Saudis did not know how to take it forward, they mistrusted the Afghans, and having just defeated Al Qaeda in Saudi Arabia, their heart was not in this difficult task. Meetings between Karzai's brothers and some Taliban leaders, including Agha, continued in Dubai, which were supported by the United Arab Emirates, but they did not move the process forward.

By the spring of 2009, U.S. and NATO military commanders had finally accepted the need for a better-funded "reintegration" policy that would take willing Taliban off the battlefield by offering them money, jobs, and resettlement.[10] In the process, the false idea emerged that there were so-called moderate Taliban as opposed to extremist Taliban, a distinction that disregarded the Taliban's basis of loyalty to its leaders and their fervent belief in the cause of expelling a foreign army of occupation. Taliban commanders would not surrender because it would require them to accept an Afghan government that they considered a stooge of the United States and, second, to break their oath of fealty to Mullah Omar, which they declined to do. Even those Taliban who were in prison or retired refused to break with or denounce Mullah Omar.

But the U.S. military's assessment was that 70 percent of the Taliban could be reintegrated because they were young, jobless men fighting for money or other practical—i.e., nonideological—reasons. According to this U.S. analysis, only about a thousand fighters, or 5 percent, were hard-line religious ideologues who would not settle for peace. But in the next three years, despite concerted attempts and lavish funds, only 2,700 Taliban availed themselves of the amnesty program. The American mistake at the time was to endorse reintegration but not reconciliation or talking to the Taliban. For the U.S. military, the template was still Iraq, where Sunni insurgents had been peeled away successfully from Al Qaeda, itself a Sunni organization that had committed terrible excesses. They believed that the Taliban could be peeled away from their leaders in the same way, but the conditions and the forms of tribal society in Afghanistan were very different from those in Iraq.

At another International Conference on Afghanistan—this time in London on January 28, 2010—the international community announced a new Peace and Reintegration Trust Fund of $140 million for reintegrating Taliban. A flurry of international activity around reintegration led nowhere. Reintegration could work only if it was part of reconciliation. Mullah Baradar issued a withering riposte to President Obama for trying to peel away Taliban rather than talk to them. "We remind Obama to avoid wasting your time on ways which are not pragmatic but focus on ways, which provide a down-to-earth and realistic solution to this issue [of talks]," Baradar said in November 2009. "Pull all your forces out of our honorable country and put an end to the game of colonization."[11]

In Washington, the idea of talking to the Taliban became more acceptable, largely due to the efforts of Richard Holbrooke, his deputy Frank Ruggiero, his adviser on Afghanistan Barnett Rubin, and Douglas Lute at the National Security Council, who all battled to win over other parts of the U.S. government. Holbrooke's successor, Marc Grossman, also quickly became deeply involved in the talks process. In Europe, there was stronger public pressure on governments to talk to the Taliban and seek a political settlement to end the war. "Success will not be achieved by military means alone," British foreign secretary David Miliband told an American audience. He asked the Americans for "a workable reconciliation strategy" and urged the Afghan government "to pursue a political settlement with as much vigor and energy as we are pursuing the military and civilian effort." Such speeches showed that Europe was way ahead of the Americans in wanting a quick resolution to the war.[12]

The British had repeatedly tried to get the Taliban to talk but had blundered badly in November 2010, when MI6, the British secret service, brought a supposed Taliban leader, Mullah Akthar Mohammed Mansour, to Kabul for talks, only to discover he was an impostor who charged the British $65,000 for every one of the three trips he made to Kabul.[13] It is still not known whether the ISI or the Taliban perpetrated the fraud, but its discovery led to severe humiliation and embarrassment for Britain and NATO. Norway had established its own secret dialogue with a representative of the Taliban but did not ask the Americans to join. The UN's special representative for Afghanistan, Staffan de Mistura, had expected the Americans to empower him in a mediating role, but Washington decided to do without the UN, even though Mistura's predecessor, Kai Eide, had earlier met with Taliban representatives.

In June 2010, Karzai held a National Consultative Peace Jirga, which aimed to bring all ethnic groups together to establish a national consensus for peace talks with the Taliban. But there were significant absences among the non-Pashtuns: the Tajiks, Uzbeks, and Hazaras did not believe in talking to the Taliban. In September, Karzai constituted a seventy-member High Peace Council, headed by the Tajik religious leader and former president Burhanuddin Rabbani, which was tasked to negotiate with the Taliban. Once again the group was supposed to be representative of all ethnic groups and women, but many of its members were former warlords whom the Taliban and the public despised. Karzai never fulfilled his promise to expand the national dialogue to include members of civil society, women, and minorities. "Instead of expanding the national conversation about reconciliation, Karzai has narrowed the avenues of public participation," wrote one expert.[14]

Once the Lisbon summit set a withdrawal date for 2014, all the neighboring countries set in motion what everyone had feared: a battle for influence in Afghanistan. Separately Pakistan and Iran wanted to ensure that when U.S. forces pulled out, they would shape the region's future. But the most dangerous source of instability was the escalation of the proxy war between India and Pakistan over future influence in Afghanistan. I will deal with the regional challenge in chapter 9. For the ISI, what was most important was to try to keep control of the peace process and any talks with the Taliban.

On February 8, 2010, the ISI infuriated Karzai by arresting Mullah Baradar in Karachi, along with a dozen senior Taliban figures who were loyal to him. It was a joint ISI-CIA operation, but senior Pakistani military officials told me later that the real reason for his arrest was not to please the Americans, but rather the ISI's conviction that Baradar had held secret talks with the Americans and had received a $5 million bribe from the CIA without informing the ISI. In fact, Baradar had only been talking to Karzai's brothers and would never have double-crossed Mullah Omar by talking to the Americans.[15] "With these measures, the Pakistani military de facto claimed a veto on all negotiations with the Taliban and therefore on Afghanistan's political future," wrote Thomas Ruttig.[16] The UN representative Kai Eide later called his arrest "a devastating blow," saying "there was no doubt in my mind that the ISI . . . had taken action to prevent the continuation of such discussions."[17]

Taliban leaders in Pakistan went underground, talks between Kabul and the Taliban stopped, and relations between Pakistan and Afghanistan worsened. In March, when Karzai visited Islamabad, he told me he had bluntly told the Pakistanis that they were "sabotaging and undermining my efforts to talk to the Taliban."[18] The Pakistani military angrily told him that if he wanted Pakistani cooperation, he should reduce Indian influence in Afghanistan by shutting down the Indian consulates in Kandahar and Jalalabad, which bordered Pakistan.[19] Pakistan was making it clear that it wanted to direct any talks with the Taliban and that it wanted something in return for doing so. Within days, the Indians in Kabul were under attack. On February 26, a suicide attack on two Kabul guesthouses killed sixteen people, including seven Indian doctors and nurses and two army majors. Afghan and Indian officials accused Jalaluddin Haqqani's network and the Punjabi group Lashkar-e-Taiba, which was now cooperating with Haqqani and Al Qaeda, of carrying out the attack. Later U.S. officials said that the attackers had been in direct contact with ISI officers in

Pakistan. Despite ISI denials, the governments of neighboring countries read the attack as a clear signal that the Pakistani military would
protect its interests.

Pakistan's obvious attempts to control any peace process among
the United States, Kabul, and the Taliban were in fact reducing its
influence and leading all the regional and Western powers to mistrust
its intentions. The attempt to isolate India from Afghanistan, where
it had spent over $1.5 billion in development aid, was shortsighted,
as the United States, Europe, and Japan—the major aid donors to
Afghanistan—rated India as a strategic ally and a major aid donor.
Nevertheless, as I will describe in chapter 9, India's interests in Afghanistan were hardly benign but were intended to keep Pakistan
under pressure. But for a long time, India, Iran, and Russia were averse
to any U.S.- or Karzai-led talks with the Taliban because they saw
such a process as only giving Pakistan greater leverage in the region.

Pakistan still holds many of the Taliban cards. Although Taliban
leaders want to go home, after long years of exile, many of them have
put down roots with their families in the border towns of Pakistan.
They have bought property, set up businesses and shops, and run bus
services—all of which makes them vulnerable to the ISI, which has
not hesitated to arrest entire Taliban families and clans in order to put
pressure on certain commanders. In Pakistan, the ISI allows the Taliban to have the supply and support network that they need to sustain
their war effort, as well as a constant pool of Afghan and Pakistani
recruits. Many of the suicide bombers used in Afghanistan are Pakistani, while the majority are trained in Pakistan. Moreover, the ISI
allows a stream of Pashtun and Punjabi militants to fight for the Afghan Taliban. The Pakistan Army, in its operations in the tribal areas,
has never attacked those Pakistani groups or militants who are pre-

pared to fight the Americans in Afghanistan but who decline to fight the Pakistan Army—something that constantly irks the United States and NATO.

Pakistan also has another reliable card: the network run by Jalaluddin Haqqani, which is based in Miranshah in North Waziristan. Haqqani, over sixty years old and now bedridden, comes from the Khost district of eastern Afghanistan and was an elder of his tribe, the Zadran. His family migrated to Pakistan in 1971, and he took part in the 1975 Islamic uprising against Afghan president Mohammed Daoud Khan. He fiercely resisted the Soviets and set up a Zadran-led battlefront, stretching across several eastern provinces, that the CIA and ISI armed and supplied with funds. In the civil war in the 1990s, at the behest of the ISI, he sided with the Taliban and became a minister in their government in 1996, but throughout he retained his independence and his close links to the ISI and to Al Qaeda. After 9/11, he refused to join the anti-Taliban alliance, although both the CIA and the ISI approached him to do so. Later he helped Al Qaeda militants escape from Afghanistan, gave them refuge in Miranshah, and set up a separate front to fight U.S. forces although remaining nominally loyal to Mullah Omar.

The Haqqanis became multimillionaires from their legitimate businesses in Pakistan and Afghanistan but also profited from kidnapping, extortion, and protection rackets for construction and transport firms that received U.S. aid money. Pakistan tried hard to promote Haqqani and his sons Sirajuddin and Badruddin as the Taliban leaders to hold talks with, but initially the Americans demurred because of his hand in many suicide attacks against U.S. targets and in particular his involvement in a suicide bombing that killed seven CIA officers at a U.S. base near Khost in December 2009.[20] The ISI did

succeed in persuading Karzai to hold talks with Haqqani representatives in 2010, which resulted in a pledge by them not to attack Kabul,
although that cease-fire lasted only nine months.

It was a significant effort by Karzai and the ISI that did not involve
the Americans, but the short-lived cease-fire did not produce any substantial talks between Karzai and the Haqqani clan. The ISI appeared
reluctant to push Haqqani into talks with Karzai; rather, it waited for
the Americans to come on board. Instead, in every meeting that Admiral Mullen had with General Kayani he urged the Pakistanis to
break with the Haqqanis and go after them—which was highly unlikely given the commitment the Pakistanis and the Haqqanis had
to each other. Jalaluddin Haqqani is also the only Taliban leader
to publicly allude to the threat that Pakistan faces from India—
something that has obviously endeared him to the Pakistanis. Just
after September 11, 2001, Haqqani said, "On Pakistan's Eastern border
is India—Pakistan's perennial enemy. With the Taliban government
in Afghanistan, Pakistan has an unbeatable two-thousand-three-
hundred-kilometer strategic depth. . . . Does Pakistan really want a
new government, which will include pro-India people in it, thereby
wiping out this strategic depth?"[21]

The U.S. military, and especially Admiral Mullen, tried hard to
persuade General Kayani to break links with Haqqani. But in 2011, the
Haqqanis are working closely with Punjabi militant groups, including
Lashkar-e-Taiba, that have been allowed to set up camps in North
Waziristan. In 2009, when it became apparent that the Quetta Shura,
or mainstream Taliban, were trying to start secret talks with the
Americans and Karzai, bypassing Pakistan, the ISI came to depend
more on the Haqqani network for its loyalty to Pakistan, its successful
military operations, and its potential as a partner for talks with Kar-

zai. The Quetta Shura is the name given to the council of Taliban leaders and elders, many of whom after 2001 settled in and around Quetta, the capital of Baluchistan province. From here they would enter and leave Afghanistan. The Haqqani network claims to be part of the Quetta Shura and operating under the Taliban leader Mullah Muhammud Omar, but the Americans assume that the Haqqani network is autonomous in deciding its targets for attacks on U.S. forces.

The U.S. military and the CIA have been decidedly less enthusiastic than the diplomatic side about talks with the Taliban. The military would prefer to stay on the offensive for as long as possible, or at least until 2014, which could entail another two years of intense conflict. Meanwhile Karzai sees his political survival as depending on ending the war as soon as possible through talks. In December 2010, I pointed out to General Petraeus that the more Taliban the Americans kill, the more he will radicalize the movement, bringing in younger and more militant commanders who owe nothing to the older leadership and who will be easier for Al Qaeda to manipulate. But he remained firm in his belief that the Taliban could be broken, fragmented, and split off one by one.[22]

In the summer of 2011, the U.S. military saturation of the south prevented any major Taliban guerrilla attacks (except for another successful jailbreak in Kandahar in April, when 476 Taliban escaped after tunneling under the jail wall and a major highway). Instead the Taliban carried out high-profile assassinations of Afghan officials, a policy intended to terrify and paralyze the Afghan government. On May 28, 2011, a suicide bomber killed Gen. Daoud Daoud, the charismatic and popular police chief in northern Afghanistan.[23] Maj. Gen. Markus Kneip, the head of German forces in the north, was wounded in the attack, and two German soldiers were killed. In August 2011, the ISI persuaded the CIA to meet with a representative of the Haqqani network in Dubai, but clearly nothing evolved, as a month later the U.S. embassy in Kabul was attacked by the Haqqanis.

But the most devastating murder was that of the Tajik religious leader and former president Burhanuddin Rabbani, at his home in Kabul on September 20. Rabbani had headed the High Peace Council that was negotiating with the Taliban on behalf of Karzai. It was not clear which Taliban group carried out the killing, but it resulted in a suspension of talks, a massive loss of prestige for Karzai and his dialogue initiative, a rise in Tajik and other minority anger and activism against the Afghan Pashtuns and Pakistan, and thus a widening of the ethnic divide. There will always be spoilers who will try to derail the talks, but the death of Rabbani holds the direst implications.

Peace will have to be built layer upon layer, district by district, and group by group, in the Afghan way rather than through grand conferences.[24] Despite the violence, the faster all sides, including the U.S. military, can develop confidence-building measures and act on them, the faster the peace process will develop. Providing an office for the Taliban negotiators would be a major step. But ultimately, with Western forces leaving Afghanistan and the weak Kabul government clearly unable to carry out its responsibilities, only an end to the violence and a political deal with the Taliban can ensure the survival of the Afghan state. The future of Afghanistan and the region depends on whether that will be possible or renewed civil war will follow the Western withdrawal.

SEVEN

A Sliver of Hope: Counterinsurgency in Swat

MAKING MY way to President Asif Ali Zardari's presidential palace in the heart of Islamabad for dinner in June 2009 was like running an obstacle course. Pakistan's once-sleepy capital, full of restaurant-going bureaucrats and diplomats, was now littered with concrete barriers, blast walls, checkpoints, armed police, and soldiers; as a result of recent suicide bombings, the city resembled Baghdad or Kabul. At the first checkpoint, two miles from the palace, they had my name and my car's license number. I had seven more checkpoints to negotiate along the way.

Apart from traveling to the airport by helicopter to go abroad, the president stays inside the palace these days; he fears threats to his life by the Pakistani Taliban, by Al Qaeda, and even by the intelligence services. Every day he remembers his wife's murder at the hands of perpetrators whom nobody has yet fully identified. Zardari's isolation and insecurity only add to his growing unpopularity, his indecisiveness, his fear of making decisions without the military's consent, and his hopeless disconnect from the public mood. Zardari has also become a know-it-all, refusing to listen to advice, asking nobody's opinion, and talking nonstop even to visiting dignitaries. Corruption scandals, like those that dogged him in the 1990s and put him in jail for over a decade, are once again rife in the Islamabad rumor mill, although the corruption stories now extend to his chosen prime minister, Yousaf Raza Gilani, and his wife and children. Zardari has totally sidelined the senior figures in the Pakistan Peoples Party who were close to his wife and replaced them with his old friends and business cronies—many of them tainted by corruption.

Zardari has become an excellent behind-the-scenes wheeler-dealer, enlarging his coalition government by bringing in new political parties in order to undermine his old rival Nawaz Sharif, whose younger brother Shabaz controls Punjab. Important national decisions are delayed or never made as the country slips into chaos. Pakistan's entire top leadership—Zardari, Gilani, and General Kayani—are in a state of denial about the reality of what Pakistan is becoming. They have begun to take violence and chaos for granted. "We are not a failed state yet, but we may become one in ten years if we don't receive international support to combat the Taliban threat," Zardari told me indignantly, pointing out that the United States had given Musharraf $11 billion between 2002 and 2008, but he had received only a pittance. "We have no money to arm the police or fund development, give jobs or revive the economy. What are we supposed to do?"[1] Zardari believes that the United States owes it to Pakistan to bail it out with billions of dollars.

But the government does not accept the need for improving governance, undertaking economic reform, increasing direct taxes, or raising greater revenue at home, which are the main demands of the international community. One Western ambassador told Zardari bluntly that there is no free lunch: "Why should our taxpayers pay for you, when neither you nor your elite pay taxes?" Zardari always has an excuse for not reforming—invariably related to his own political survival and the need for stability. Nobody has a strategic plan for combating Islamic extremism or disarming the extremists. There is no debate between the president and the generals over the continued presence of the Afghan Taliban in Pakistan. Zardari's view is that since the army and the ISI nurtured the extremists, it is they who should deal with them and take responsibility for them before the Americans. Consequently there is no internal debate, no civilian voice trying to persuade the army to change course on its foreign policy; and no political government is dedicating itself to improving people's lives. After eight years of military rule, Pakistanis crave good governance, competence, and honesty from a democratic government that will help change the army's way of thinking. To date, it has not happened.

The figures speak volumes about the precarious nature of the state. In 2009, Pakistani civilian deaths at the hands of insurgents rose to 3,021—for the first time topping the number of civilians (2,412) killed in Afghanistan and 33 percent more than those killed the previous year in Pakistan. Another 7,300 people were wounded. A staggering 87 suicide attacks took place in 2009, the largest number to date, as well as 67 sectarian attacks that killed mainly Shia Muslims.[2] Pakistan's Human Rights Commission reported that in Karachi alone during the year, 747 people were gunned down, including 7 journalists. In Baluchistan province, where a five-year insurgency is under way, 118 civilians and 158 security personnel were killed.[3] Pakistan is already on the edge of a precipice: killings, mayhem, and the breakdown of state control spread across the country, while the government seems to ignore it all.

Everywhere one looked in the spring of 2009, a sense of unreality prevailed, with the government denying there was any risk. Even as the Pakistani Taliban were storming southward from their mountain bases in FATA, Prime Minister Gilani told parliament that they posed no threat and there was nothing to worry about. Interior Minister Rehman Malik deliberately lied when he claimed that the Afghan government, India, and Russia were backing the Pakistani Taliban. The economy was spiraling out of control with drastic power cuts, industry shutdowns, and rising unemployment. In Khyber-Pakhtunkhwa province, state institutions had been shut down or paralyzed for more than a year, one million people had fled their homes, and the provincial government in Peshawar had gone into hiding because of assassination threats. In the first three months of 2009, there were two hundred kidnappings for ransom in Peshawar. Yet Pakistanis were still told that all was well.

Meanwhile, the various tribal militias that made up the Pakistani Taliban were coalescing into a new organization. On December 12, 2007, in North Waziristan, some forty tribal leaders who commanded separate militias had met to form the Tehrik-e-Taliban Pakistan, or Movement of the Pakistani Taliban. They chose a young militant, Baitullah Mehsud, as their leader. Their stated objective was to unite their militias and establish a centralized organization, fight NATO forces in Afghanistan, and wage a defensive jihad against the Pakistan Army. They claimed to have 40,000 men under their command. Their early successes and hold on territory attracted young extremists from the Punjab and Sind, all determined to topple the government.

The goal of the Pakistani Taliban in the summer of 2009 was to capture the scenic Swat Valley and its adjoining districts, just ninety miles north of Islamabad. Over the past three years, the Taliban movement in Swat had grown enormously, its ranks swelled by Afghans, Central Asians, Al Qaeda, and tribesmen from FATA. The army had twice tried and failed to oust them from Swat. In 2008, just 3,000 Taliban drove 12,000 troops out of Swat, blew up a hundred girls' schools and other public buildings, and caused the mass exodus of one-third of Swat's 2 million people. In 2009, in a sign of abject defeat, the KP provincial government signed a controversial deal allowing the Taliban to impose sharia law in Swat's courts, in return for the Pakistan Army's withdrawal from Swat.

As expected, the Taliban imposed their brutal interpretation of sharia, a code of conduct that has taken on the weight of law: it allows for executions, floggings, and destruction of people's homes and girls' schools. Pakistanis were shocked when videos of Taliban brutalities appeared on YouTube. Yet Zardari had parliament approve the implementation of sharia on April 14 without even a debate. Within days, thousands of new Taliban arrived in Swat, taking control of the local administration, police stations, and schools—which was not part of the deal. On April 19, Sufi Muhammad, a longtime radical preacher from Swat who had led his followers to fight the Americans in Afghanistan in 2001 and had subsequently been jailed and freed, declared that democracy, the legal system, and civil society should be disbanded, since they were all "systems of infidels." His son-in-law, Maulana Qazi Fazlullah, had become the undisputed leader of the Swat Taliban. A former ski-lift operator and self-appointed mullah, Fazlullah had spread his message over FM radio stations for the past three years without the army trying to stop him.

American officials were in a state of panic, while Pakistanis berated the government for its lack of action. Secretary of State Hillary Clinton bluntly said in Baghdad on April 25: "One of our concerns . . . is that if the worst, the unthinkable were to happen, and this advancing Taliban . . . were to essentially topple the government for failure to beat them back, then they would have the keys to the nuclear arsenal of Pakistan. . . . We can't even contemplate that."[4] Defense Secretary Robert Gates and Admiral Mullen issued similar dire statements. A furious General Kayani responded that the army was fully capable of defending the country.

Al Qaeda and the Pakistani Taliban were eager to expand out of FATA into KP's settled areas, where more facilities and better communications are available. The Swat Valley is a beautiful tourist destination but also a strategic transit route: to the east, it opens into Indian Kashmir, and to the west, into Afghanistan. It is conveniently out of range of U.S. drone strikes. Capturing Swat would give the Taliban and Al Qaeda control over northern Pakistan and roads that run to all the major cities, including Islamabad, as well as a new route to the battlefields of Kashmir and Afghanistan. A confident Fazlullah even invited Osama bin Laden to come and live in Swat under his protection.

On April 21, the Taliban moved into Swat's adjoining districts of Buner, Shangla, and Dir, from where they threatened several major towns in the province. The politicians finally began to address the issue, and parliament passed a resolution declaring full support for an army offensive against the militants. General Kayani said he had been waiting for just such a political endorsement before he moved in the army. On April 28, President Obama called a meeting of his cabinet to discuss the crisis in Swat. He said he was "gravely concerned" and that "the civilian government right now is very fragile."[5] It was the strongest statement Obama had yet made about the security of Pakistan.

On May 7, after forcing the evacuation of most of the population, the Pakistan Army launched a major air and ground offensive in Swat,

dropping bombs and firing artillery around Mingora, where an estimated 4,000 Taliban fighters had dug in. Some 30,000 troops, or
three times the number of those used in two earlier offensives, moved
into Swat, in the largest operation ever undertaken against the Pakistani Taliban. For the first time, troops were drawn from the Indian
border, after India pledged not to heighten tensions with Pakistan.
The army had sufficient numbers and air power, while troop morale
and motivation were high on account of the atrocities the Taliban had
committed against soldiers. The operation had public support and
international help as the UN and other aid agencies dealt with the
huge humanitarian crisis.

By June, the army had pushed the Taliban militants out of the Swat
Valley, in fierce fighting that left more than 300 soldiers and 2,000
militants killed and hundreds more injured. The leaders of the Swat
Taliban managed to escape to FATA and Afghanistan. But some 1.5
million refugees from Swat who had fled the valley earlier finally
started going back home. It had been the worst internal displacement
in the country's history.

The Americans were pleased, and Admiral Mullen felt he was finally making headway with Kayani and the army. Kayani had agreed
to rotate all army units through a six-week course on counterinsurgency, taught by Pakistani officers, while two hundred U.S. and British
officers were allowed to conduct a train-the-trainers program for the
Frontier Corps (FC). American special forces built up a new 700-man
FC commando force. The 60,000-man FC received the latest counterterrorism equipment as part of a U.S. military aid program, their sal-
aries were raised, and medical care on the battlefield was provided.

The war in Swat was the first, and so far the only, time the Pakistan
Army successfully completed a counterinsurgency campaign accord-

ing to the book: the militants were killed, captured, or driven out, the area was secured, the displaced population returned, their homes were rebuilt, and the civic administration was revived. The army had finally learned the principles of "clear, hold, build, and transfer"—the mantra of General Petraeus's counterinsurgency strategy in Iraq and Afghanistan—and could carry them out when it had the will to do so. In the words of British ambassador Sherard Cowper-Coles, "Successful stabilization requires strategic stamina, massive resources, lots of time and plenty of ambition."[6] The militants made several attempts to return, but the army still had 25,000 troops stationed in the valley two years later, in the summer of 2011.

The important difference between the campaigns in Swat and FATA was that in Swat the army had no need to differentiate between so-called friendly Taliban and those who were enemies of the state. There was no double game in Swat, no Haqqanis network or local commander such as Hafiz Gul Bahadur to protect. In FATA, every military offensive had allowed the enemy Taliban to retreat and come under the protection of Afghan or Pakistani Taliban whom the army supported; thus the enemy Taliban had been able to escape from one tribal agency, only to reemerge in another to continue the fight. The Americans hoped that the battle for Swat signaled a shift in the army's attitude, but Kayani still refused to launch an offensive into North Waziristan, where the Haqqani network and their Pakistani Taliban allies were strongest.

The Obama administration accelerated a strategic dialogue with the military and the civilian government. Richard Holbrooke set up intensive discussions between all departments of the U.S. government and their Pakistani counterparts. Secretary Clinton conducted a total of three ministerial-level meetings with Pakistani officials during

2010—something that had never happened before. The two countries identified thirteen sectors, such as energy and education, where the Americans promised help. Military aid was separated from economic aid. On May 6 and 7, the United States held a trilateral summit in Washington that brought together Presidents Karzai, Zardari, and Obama and General Kayani, where they discussed greater cooperation and laid the groundwork for what would later become a dialogue between Pakistan and Afghanistan on reconciling with the Afghan Taliban. On July 18 at another ministerial presided over by Hillary Clinton, Pakistan and Afghanistan signed a Transit Trade Agreement, which would open up bilateral trade across all borders between Afghanistan, Pakistan, and India.

But U.S.-Pakistan relations were still not set to improve over the long term, and the problem once again was dissatisfaction felt by the Pakistan military. At the end of the year, the Enhanced Partnership with Pakistan Act of 2009 was ready to be signed into law: it would give Pakistan's civilian sector $1.5 billion in aid every year for five years.[7] The bill, called the Kerry-Lugar-Berman aid bill after its major sponsors in Congress, would be a huge boost to the civilian government in Islamabad. In the past, the Americans had frittered aid away in small projects, but Holbrooke was convinced that starting a few megaprojects would show that the United States was involved in Pakistan's economic development.

For the first time, the United States, rather than just throwing money at the military, displayed a commitment to a Pakistani civilian government and the democratic process. But the bill carried the conditions that the U.S. president had to affirm every year that Pakistan remained a democracy and continued to help in the war against extremism; it thereby ruled out another military coup or Pakistani favoritism toward some Taliban. At the last minute, Kayani and the army objected to these conditions. They manipulated the Pakistani media to condemn the bill as outrageous interference in Pakistan's domestic affairs. On October 7, Kayani and his nine corps commanders "expressed serious concern regarding clauses [of the bill] impacting on national security," and said it was unacceptable.[8]

The Pakistani government was bankrupt and surviving on an $11.3 billon loan from the IMF. But President Zardari, rather then defend the bill and stress its importance, once again succumbed to the military. His government condemned the conditions attached to the bill, as did all the political parties. The ISI launched a massive public relations exercise, briefing TV talk show hosts and journalists as well as politicians, encouraging them to whip up anti-American feeling. The U.S. Congress was livid, as was the administration and particularly Richard Holbrooke, who had staked his reputation on bringing Pakistan closer to the United States. After some haggling, a consensus between the U.S. government and Pakistan was reached, and Congress passed the bill. Nevertheless, the fact that the Pakistan Army could veto even a simple measure such as aid to civilian institutions demonstrated its power to the public and to the international community. The money, after all, would only have helped do what Pakistan's elite had failed to do: set priorities for social reform, energy, education, health, governance, and justice.[9] In the aftermath of the successful Swat operation, relations between the Pakistan Army and the United States were worsening into mistrust—a harbinger of more to come.

Tensions between the United States and Pakistan also escalated over the use of drones. On a trip to Washington, General Pasha, the head of the ISI, had criticized the CIA for not targeting Pakistani Taliban leaders. On August 7, a U.S. drone fired a missile that killed Baitullah Mehsud, the leader of the Pakistani Taliban. The missile had caught him and his wife at night on the roof of a house in North Waziristan. Ten others were killed in the house. On August 22, a forty-member *shura* (gathering) chose Hakimullah Mehsud, age twenty-six, a ruthless militant commander, as the new chief of the Pakistani Taliban. When the United States next urged the army to advance into North Waziristan, the army declined, saying it would do so at its own choosing and in its own time.

The Pakistani Taliban took brutal revenge for Mehsud's killing. In October, nine suicide attacks hit Pakistan's security forces—among them a devastating attack on army headquarters in Rawalpindi on October 10. The Taliban militants were all Punjabis, and the sole survivor was a former soldier of the army medical corps. On a single day later that month, the Taliban mounted three attacks in Lahore, in which 150 people were killed and several hundred were injured. On December 4, the Taliban struck the army again in Rawalpindi: four suicide bombers attacked an army mosque during Friday prayers. Thirty-seven people were killed, including five senior army officers. The militants in each case seemed to come in under the radar, having inside information as to where to attack and who would be there.

The attacks raised embarrassing questions about the army's competence, its intelligence apparatus, and gaps in its chain of command. But no one in the army was held accountable—no one was court-martialed or punished for basic security lapses. Chief of Staff Musharraf, for all his weaknesses, had at least been decisive, punishing or sacking anyone who failed. In contrast, Chief of Staff Kayani's indecisiveness and apparent inability to hold anyone within the army accountable were his biggest weaknesses. When Osama bin Laden was killed and the ISI chief General Pasha offered his resignation,

Kayani refused to accept it. Ultimately nobody was punished for Bin Laden's six-year-long presence in Abbottabad.

Month after month the tensions between the United States and Pakistan seemed to grow as their respective intelligence agencies waged a clandestine war. In September, two NATO helicopters crossed the border into Khurram Agency and killed three FC soldiers, causing relations again to fray. That month NATO made two more air intrusions. In retaliation, Pakistan closed the Khyber Pass to all NATO supply traffic. Hundreds of NATO container trucks and oil tankers were stranded on the Pakistani side of the border, while the ISI encouraged gangs of young men to attack and burn parked NATO trucks across the country, sending a blunt message to the Americans. On October 1 in Shikarpur in northern Sind—where there was no Taliban presence—twenty-five NATO oil tankers were burned to a cinder. Two days later dozens of tankers were burned near Islamabad, the capital. The State Department finally apologized to Pakistan, and after ten days the road was reopened.

The large number of U.S. drone attacks—twenty-two in September alone, twice the largest previous monthly total—also infuriated the military. Obama had secretly ordered this escalation, and now the CIA was carrying out drone strikes without clearance from the Pakistani military, breaking the original Musharraf-era agreement between the CIA and the ISI. Gen. David Petraeus, who commanded U.S. forces in Afghanistan, also asked for a stepped-up CIA campaign against militant hideouts in FATA. Meanwhile the American special forces were carrying out night raids in Afghanistan to kill Taliban commanders and, it soon became apparent, frequently crossing over into Pakistan. "Frustration with Pakistan is reaching the boiling point," said Bruce Riedel, the former CIA analyst. "The risk that we run here is that at some point we're going to overload the circuit in Pakistan and they're going to say, 'too much.'"[10] Petraeus was carrying out a dangerous policy of brinkmanship with Pakistan, as he was desperate to show progress in the war effort, and targeted the Haqqanis as his main opponent. Moreover, political deadlines loomed for Petraeus and Obama at the end of a year in which they had to show results: preparing an assessment of the war for Congress and announcing the start of troop withdrawals.

The Pakistani Taliban stepped up their attacks, this time on Sufi religious shrines in Lahore, Karachi, Peshawar, and other major cities. A love of saints is part of the Sufi or mystical tradition in Islam; most Pakistanis are imbued with it, but the militants, with their extremist interpretation of Islam, abhor what they consider saint worship. The government could have used the attacks on the shrines to educate the public about the Taliban threat, but the military was more interested in rallying public support for its standoff against the Americans. After the army's success in Swat, the United States redoubled its efforts to persuade it to mount offensives in South and North Waziristan. The army had demonstrated that it was competent, could carry out counterinsurgency, and could persevere once an objective was set, despite taking high losses. "This progress is much appreciated, but there is a need now to do more, and the Pakistanis have proved that they can do more," Richard Holbrooke told me in August 2009.

Army casualties restricted how far Kayani could go in ordering fresh offensives from his troops. There was a growing reluctance to fight a war that was being described in army officers' messes as "America's war." Haider Mullick, an adviser to the U.S. military, later wrote, "Anti-Americanism, always high, has reached unprecedented levels within the military's ranks, especially amongst junior officers.

This is because most young officers are unaware of the past deals their generals have made with the Americans, and some may act independently in the name of national pride against an American incursion into Pakistan to target militants."[11]

In the previous decade, the Pakistan Army had suffered considerable losses. Kayani later admitted that between 2002 and 2010, 2,273 Pakistani soldiers had been killed and 6,512 had been injured, while 73 ISI officers had been killed—far higher casualties than those suffered by the Americans or NATO in Afghanistan.[12] These very high losses, along with the penetration of some army units by militants, fed the anti-Americanism growing in the ranks. Demoralized officers and men were reluctant to continue fighting indefinitely in what they constantly described as America's war—even though the Taliban had killed more Pakistani soldiers than Americans. By contrast, the Taliban in FATA had a keen sense of protecting themselves against infiltration. They launched a bloody campaign against Pashtun tribal elders who sided with the government or raised anti-Taliban militias. They publicly executed local tribesmen whom they suspected of spying for the Americans or providing intelligence for the drone strikes. Electronic chips guided drone attacks, and anyone caught with a suspicious chip of any kind was immediately killed. Starting in 2004, the Taliban executed more than a thousand Pashtuns without trial. They also established a centralized system to train dozens, then hundreds, of suicide bombers, some as young as eleven years old, for the war fronts in Afghanistan and Pakistan. Suicide bombers could be bought for as little as $4,000, and much of the training was done in North Waziristan.

In Afghanistan, the number of IED blasts in 2010 was staggering: 14,661. The main component of the mines and IEDs that the Taliban use is ammonium nitrate fertilizer, which is manufactured in prodigious quantities in Pakistan. The Americans have tried to get the Pakistani government to shut down the factories, but it refuses to oblige, even though IEDs are killing its own soldiers in FATA. In January 2010, Afghanistan banned the use, storage, or import of the fertilizer, and Afghan security forces have captured truckloads of it coming from Pakistan.

The Pakistani Taliban have also netted a large war chest through a criminal network of kidnapping for ransom. Prominent Pakistanis who were kidnapped have fetched million-dollar ransoms. The victims are invariably moved to North Waziristan, where they live in Haqqani's camps side by side with Pakistan Army units. The army has made no more attempt to finish off these criminal networks than it has the fertilizer suppliers.[13]

In Washington, the Obama administration debated whether to take a harder line toward Islamabad or to try once more to improve relations. Finally in November 2009, Obama wrote a letter to Zardari suggesting that if Pakistan were to go into North Waziristan, the two nations could become "long-term strategic partners." The letter was hand delivered by General James L. Jones, the national security adviser, who also delivered a warning that the United States would strike anywhere in Pakistan if senior Al Qaeda leaders were discovered. Zardari deferred to the military, and his late reply to Obama was noncommittal. In retrospect, Pakistan had lost an opportunity, because it was the last time Obama would offer something more than a threat-filled relationship.

———

When Kayani's three-year term as army chief was due to expire, the Pakistani government had the option of appointing a new army chief and retiring Kayani. Instead, on July 22, 2010, Zardari and Gilani gave Kayani a three-year extension. This angered many people, including some army officers, who felt their promotions were now blocked, while others considered Kayani's tenure as chief not particularly successful. Kayani had already given three other generals who were about to retire one-year extensions, and he had given two extensions to General Pasha—something that had never been done before. An institution that had once been the byword for accountability now seemed to lack it altogether. Army officers viewed the extensions as sheer favoritism on the part of the army chief. At the time there were reports that Admiral Mullen had pushed for an extension for Kayani, but Mullen told me later that he had never tried to influence the decision. There is little doubt that his unprecedented extension in service seriously diminished his stature in the armed forces and among the politicians; Kayani felt less secure in ordering his troops into combat against the Taliban. Zardari had only made sure that by extending Kayani's time in office he had rendered any political intervention or coup by Kayani controversial and problematic. He had also ensured that Kayani now owed his extra time in uniform to Zardari's goodwill.

In retrospect, the political leadership might well have been better off if it had brought in a new chief who may have improved relations with the United States and redefined Pakistan's attitude toward terrorism. But as it is, Kayani will now remain chief until the end of 2013, by which time he will have been at the center of power for nine years. (In October 2004, he was appointed head of the ISI—a hugely powerful position—and he became army chief in October 2007.) Zardari and Gilani see his extension as an insurance policy for their own personal safety and for the survival of the regime. Zardari calculates that because he did Kayani this favor, he will support Zardari's reelection as president in 2013. But Pakistan's history has proved that such assumptions are risky bets, because even the most loyal and subservient army chiefs have turned against their political benefactors when the need has arisen.

The government and the army and their relations with the United States underwent another major test with the devastating floods in the summer of 2010. Torrential rains and snowmelt loaded up the country's north-south river system beyond its capacity. The average annual rainfall in KP province is 38 inches, but in six days in July it received 136 inches of rain. A huge wave of water that began in the Swat Valley swept down the narrow rivers and poured into the mighty Indus—on the way, overflooding banks and destroying homes, farmlands, bridges, and roads. When the wall of water reached the flat plains of Sind, it flooded thousands of miles of farmland. On August 6, Prime Minister Gilani told the nation that 12 million people were displaced without shelter and that 1,600 had died. In mid-August, the World Food Program said that 3 million people needed urgent food assistance and that one-fifth of the country, or 62,000 square miles, was under water—the equivalent of an area stretching from Spain to Holland. By the end of August, the floods had affected 20 million people or 12 percent of the population.

The public response to help the victims was massive, but the government handled it with enormous incompetence and lack of leadership. Zardari chose this moment to take a vacation, both in London and at his French château, Manoir de la Reine Blanche—pictures of which were beamed back on TV to an infuriated public. The army, with help from the UN and from Pakistani and international NGOs, conducted the most effective relief work. Despite opposition in Washington, Richard Holbrooke persuaded the U.S. military to provide thirty helicopters from Afghanistan to airlift survivors and food. The relief effort did much to rehabilitate the army in the eyes of the public, and the Americans also won enormous goodwill.

But the antics of Zardari and Gilani hampered their efforts to raise international aid, as Western donor countries demanded economic reforms. Both inside and outside Pakistan, Zardari's appeals for a massive bailout fell on deaf ears. Holbrook bluntly told the government on August 15 that the world could raise only 25 percent of what Pakistan needed; it would have to raise the rest itself, through new taxes and reforms. "The U.S. Congress needs to know that you are taxing yourself," Holbrooke said repeatedly.[14] On September 19, representatives of twenty-five countries—led by U.S. secretary of state Hillary Clinton, UN secretary-general Ban Ki-moon, and World Bank head Robert Zoellick—met at the United Nations in New York to discuss further aid to Pakistan; their message was that Pakistan had to do more for itself. A UN appeal to raise $2 billion from the international community for relief work was not even half fulfilled.[15] A year later new floods hit Sind that rendered 3 million people homeless.[16]

In 2010, the Pakistani Taliban were becoming far more dangerous than even the military reckoned on: the ISI's loss of control over the groups in FATA is telling. In South Waziristan, a Punjabi militant group kidnapped two well-known retired ISI officers, Col. Sultan Amir Tarar and Khalid Khawaja (both of whom had been involved with the Afghan resistance since the 1980s and had helped train the Taliban), and subsequently executed them for being U.S. spies. The ISI, the Afghan Taliban, and even Jalaluddin Haqqani called for clemency, but the groups ignored them, indicating the military's overall loss of control over the region. The Pakistani Taliban have made it clear that unlike the Afghan Taliban, they are ready to work with Al Qaeda to train Western militants who will carry out attacks in their home countries. The Pakistani Taliban are now not merely trying to overthrow the Pakistan government—they have become part of the global jihad.

An Afghan immigrant, Najibullah Zazi, age twenty-five, planned to bomb the New York subway system on the anniversary of 9/11 in 2009; U.S. government surveillance foiled the plot. Zazi had learned to make explosives from the Pakistani Taliban in FATA. In November 2009, an American Muslim officer, Nidal Malik Hasan, gunned down thirteen people at Fort Hood, Texas. On May 2, 2010, Faisal Shahzad, a Pakistani-born U.S. citizen, tried to explode a car bomb in Times Square in New York. Well-to-do and educated, with a father who was a senior officer in the Pakistan Air Force, Shahzad had also learned bomb-making techniques from the Pakistani Taliban in FATA. The bomb was defused before it exploded; he was caught as he was about to fly out to Pakistan. He had been motivated by U.S. drone strikes in FATA that were killing innocent civilians. Hillary Clinton warned Pakistan that if any such attack was ever successful, the United States would be forced to act militarily. She further infuriated Islamabad by presciently claiming that officials there knew where Osama bin Laden was hiding: "I'm not saying that they're at the highest levels, but I believe that somewhere in this government are people who know where Osama bin Laden and Al Qaeda is, where Mullah Omar and the leadership of the Afghan Taliban is, and we expect more co-operation to help us bring to justice, capture or kill those who attacked us on 9/11."[17]

A few days later, on May 28 in Lahore, the Taliban wrought terrible havoc on the Ahmedis, a Muslim minority community. Heavily armed gunmen and suicide bombers attacked two of their mosques during Friday prayers and slaughtered ninety-five Ahmedis. Thereafter Hakimullah Mehsud, the Pakistani Taliban leader, warned that he would strike at more U.S. and Pakistani cities. The Pakistan Taliban were morphing from a loose tribal-based structure into a much more organized and sophisticated organization with links across the country and abroad. The security forces in both Pakistan and Afghanistan were clearly caught unawares. The American focus was increasingly on Lashkar-e-Taiba. Admiral Mullen warned in July, on a trip to Islamabad, that LT had become "a very dangerous organization and a significant regional and global threat." He said it was expanding into Afghanistan, adding that "the Haqqani group is the most lethal network faced by the US . . . in Afghanistan."[18]

In October 2009, U.S. authorities arrested David Headley, a Pakistani-born American citizen who claimed to have worked as an informant and a scout for the 2008 Mumbai attacks on behalf of LT and the ISI. That created a crisis with the United States and India. The Indians accused the ISI of having organized the Mumbai massacre, which Pakistan denied. India filed fresh charges in Indian courts against the LT leader Hafiz Muhammad Saeed, its military commander Zakiur Rehman Lakhvi, and four others, including two Pakistan Army officers allegedly working for the ISI. In another case filed by relatives of two Jewish American victims of the Mumbai massacre, a New York court summoned General Pasha and Hafiz Saeed to answer charges, which both men refused to do. Pasha was angered by the court case, which he saw as a trap laid by the CIA. The ISI retaliated in May 2011 by disclosing the name of the CIA station chief in Islamabad: they got a FATA-based tribesman to file a lawsuit against the station chief, claiming that he was responsible for drones that killed his relatives. The station chief left Islamabad after receiving death threats. The ISI and the CIA were now fighting in public—an ominous development.

The last straw for Kayani and Pasha was probably the release of 92,000 U.S. government documents related to Pakistan and the Afghan war as part of the WikiLeaks disclosures. The classified diplomatic cables and reports in WikiLeaks described in detail Pakistan's support for the Afghan Taliban and Haqqani and the ISI's covert operations. Kayani was already livid at the publication of Bob Woodward's book *Obama's Wars*, which showed him and the military in a poor light, while U.S. leaders' analysis of the relationship and Kayani was brutally critical.

WikiLeaks also exposed the Pakistan Army's complicity with the United States in the use of drones over Pakistani territory and the army's ongoing cooperation with the CIA—just as it was trying to convince the public it was getting tough with the Americans. The most damaging cables referred to the political tensions between Kayani and Zardari and exposed Kayani's cynical views about all Pakistani politicians, which the American diplomats had duly reported. WikiLeaks was a public relations disaster for the army and a personal disaster for Kayani, Pasha, and Zardari. Ultimately WikiLeaks did not shock the public, because it revealed what they had presumed anyway—that the ISI was in bed with the CIA on the drones issue, and that Kayani and the army held civilian politicians in contempt, and that Zardari was deemed corrupt. Nevertheless Kayani retaliated in a furious off-the-record briefing to selected Pakistani journalists on November 28, 2010. There he listed the complaints that the "people of Pakistan"—in reality, the army—had against the United States. These included the following: the United States has a "transactional" relationship with Pakistan, which is "the most bullied ally of the Americans"; the United States wants to perpetuate a state of "controlled chaos" in Pakistan; and the "real aim of United States strategy is to de-nuclearize Pakistan." The last item had become an obsession with the military, and stories bolstering this narrative were constantly being fed to the media.

On Afghanistan, Kayani said the United States needs to "clearly identify and state the end conditions" for its war there—something that the Pakistanis themselves have failed to do. The Americans lack clarity on the end conditions because "either they aren't willing to state them or they don't know themselves." Pakistan, he said, "is deliberately being kept in the dark regarding peace efforts." He was deeply pessimistic about Afghanistan, declaring that "peace may never be complete, there may be no permanent stability, and uncontested power may never establish itself." On relations with India, he said that "the people of Pakistan measure the strength of US-Pak relations on the scale of [the] US-India partnership." Although Pakistan cannot afford to be in perpetual conflict with India, he said, it has to "strike a balance between defense and development."[19] India remains the devil, as far as the army is concerned.

This briefing, the most candid one Kayani ever gave, led to a storm of protest by U.S. and Western diplomats in Islamabad when its contents were reported. The fact that the army chief was already so hostile to the United States, and his mind-set so rigid regarding India and Afghanistan, made a collapse of relations with U.S. inevitable. Bin Laden's killing in Abbottabad would be the torch that set the relations ablaze. On December 13, two weeks after Kayani spoke, Richard Holbrooke, the one man in the State Department who could have prevented a breakdown in U.S.-Pakistan relations, died of a burst aorta.

It was sadness personified, but perhaps fitting that he was spared having to see his dream of crafting a new U.S.-Pakistan relationship sink into the weeds in the months ahead. Holbrooke had been trying to enlist Pakistan as a friend rather than an enemy, but he, too, understood perfectly that Pakistan's strategic policies had to change.

EIGHT

Pakistan: Broken Relations, Crimes, and Misdemeanors

AS OF fall 2011, relations between the United States and Pakistan are utterly breaking down, even as the levels of violence escalate in Pakistan and Afghanistan. The two countries' differing interests collide daily. While the United States asks for the elimination of all terrorist groups on Pakistani soil, the army insists on maintaining the Taliban and the Haqqani network until a suitable Afghan settlement has been reached that satisfies the Pakistani military. Neither side sees a way to bridge the widening strategic and ideological gap. Much more is needed than just Admiral Mullen landing in Islamabad, holding the hand of General Kayani, and urging him to "do more." "Each crisis has inflicted more damage, weakened the relationship and added another layer of complication to already fraught ties," wrote Pakistan's former ambassador to Washington Maleeha Lodhi. "Once described as strategic, relations seemed to have slipped from being transactional to coercive. At the heart of the crisis lay the divergence between the two countries over the appropriate strategy for Afghanistan—the United States intent on waging more war even as it declared its desire to move towards a negotiated peace and Pakistan wanting a de-escalation of kinetic activity to pave the way for peace making." Meanwhile Pakistan was still unwilling to do anything about the safe havens. Pakistani officials said that the sanctuaries were a consequence, not the cause of the insurgency, and they were right when they criticized the mishandling of the policy in Afghanistan by the United States over the years.[1]

The Pakistani military has failed to notice that its options are becoming fewer as the country subsides into chaos; and it fails to grasp that U.S. unilateralism will necessarily increase, in the shape of military actions and possibly sanctions to degrade the Taliban and the Haqqani network. Instead, Pakistan's generals bury their heads in the sand and pretend no such threat will materialize and that the brinkmanship they pursue with the Americans can continue indefinitely. Their position is that if they cannot get what they want out of an Afghan settlement, nobody will get an Afghan peace. Blinded by ideology, they resist any forward-looking strategic thinking. Pakistan's military does not want to deliver peace except on its own terms; its civilians have no hope for reform without it. "The ISI should be under no illusion it will be able to influence, much less control, anything in post-American Afghanistan," wrote Ayaz Amir.[2]

Even as they wished the Americans would leave Afghanistan, the army also wanted them to stay because of the cash cow Washington had become for the military. The army receives more than $2 billion every year in various kinds of military aid from the United States, and losing that could prove to be destabilizing in the army itself. But it was clear even in 2009 that the economic crisis in the West would determine how long Western forces would stay on.

The United States, too, lacks a strategic vision for Afghanistan and the region that it could share or discuss with Pakistan. Nobody knows what the Americans want in the long term. Will they leave in 2014?

Or will they turn Afghanistan into the new South Korea, with bases and thousands of troops stationed there permanently? The Americans appear to have made little effort to calculate the repercussions of unilateral military action: that Pakistan could become even more belligerent and that a final rupture could take place. At times, both sides seem to have an underlying death wish—both have had enough of the relationship, both are defiant, yet each needs the other; neither wants to revive the relationship under false pretenses, yet neither can muster enough vision or assume enough responsibility to discuss a new paradigm. At times, each side convinces itself that it can do without the other, which of course is wishful thinking.

For Pakistan and its elite, much more is at stake than worsening relations with the United States. A huge internal crisis—economic, social, religious and political—that has been building since Musharraf's time is erupting. A particularly troubling sign is the escalating intolerance of non-Muslim minorities—an index of the rapid deterioration in the very idea of Pakistan. When Jinnah founded the country, the white stripe down the side of Pakistan's green flag represented the minorities or non-Muslims, whom the majority Muslim population would protect and treat as equal citizens. Yet Christians who can afford to do so are now leaving the country in droves because of their persecution. The Ahmedis, a Muslim minority sect, have been relentlessly persecuted by the state and the mullahs alike.[3] The Ismailis, a Shia sect led by the Agha Khan, have seen their professional and business class targeted by extremists. These groups, mainstream Shias, and the few Hindus are all trying to leave the country.

In 2010 and 2011, Sunni extremists killed more than five hundred Shias, many of them Hazaras from Afghanistan who live peacefully in Baluchistan province.

The extremists want to redefine the state of Pakistan as an Islamic jihadist venture, and for that they must create an atmosphere of total intolerance. Ayaz Amir wrote, "In our journey towards nationhood we eschewed the rational and chose instead to play with the semantics of religion. What Pakistan has become today, a fortress not so much of Islam as of bigotry and intolerance, is a fruit of these sustained endeavours."[4] The most immediate issue is the controversial and outdated law on blasphemy, which many in the ruling Pakistan Peoples Party want to reform. The law is a catch-22 because it allows anyone to charge anyone else with blasphemy, which leads to automatic arrest by the police. Yet the charge, or proof of it, can never be named, because it is blasphemous. At any given time, more than one thousand people are in jail on charges of blasphemy, some Christian but many Muslims. The loudest voice for amending the law was that of Salman Taseer, the outspoken governor of the largest province, Punjab. On January 4, 2011, he was gunned down in Islamabad; his own bodyguard, Malik Mumtaz Qadri, a policeman from the Punjab Elite Force, shot him twenty-seven times in the back and head. Other bodyguards refused to shoot Qadri dead, as he surrendered and declared he had carried out a virtuous act.

The massive public acclaim that the killer received shocked millions of Pakistanis and was a watershed for the country. As the killer went to jail, he was applauded and garlanded, and five hundred lawyers pledged to defend him in court. No *maulvi* (prayer leader in a mosque) in Lahore would read Taseer's funeral prayers. The country's rulers were too frightened to come to Taseer's funeral. For the first time, the silent majority of Pakistanis who had never been extremist, never supported the Taliban, and never voted for the religious right seemed either to be shifting their stance or to be too frightened to react.

Rather than take a stand, the government bent over backward to appease the extremists, saying that it had no intention of reviewing the blasphemy law, which it had actually promised to do. Gilani forced Sherry Rehman, a leading PPP liberal politician, to withdraw her amendment bill in parliament. Then on March 2, gunmen shot dead Shahbaz Bhatti in Islamabad. He was the PPP minister for minorities and the only Christian in the federal cabinet. Outraged political leaders from around the world, including Pope Benedict, demanded that the government protect Christians and withdraw the blasphemy law. In the meantime, extremists targeted shrines of the Sufi saints, which the vast majority of Muslims deeply revere. In 2011, every symbol of moderate Islam in Pakistan since its founding is under attack.

Baluchistan, Pakistan's poorest and most neglected province, is home to an insurgency as radical but secular Baluch leaders demand separation from Pakistan. The Baluch tribes have rebelled against the Pakistan Army five times since 1947, but each time the insurgency has been put down brutally; that has only further alienated the Baluch, while their political and economic grievances remained unaddressed. In August 2006, the army killed Nawab Akbar Khan Bugti, a powerful tribal chief and politician, and thirty of his men, which triggered a wider insurgency. When Zardari came to power in 2008, he promised reconciliation talks with the Baluch militants, but there has been no follow-up and no talks, and the insurgency has become more violent.

The fighting has been low-key but brutal. While Baluch militants have targeted the security forces with ambushes, assassinations, and land mines, they have also killed non-Baluch settlers, including teachers, shopkeepers, and bureaucrats. Non-Baluch have fled the province. Amnesty International and Human Rights Watch have described a "kill and dump" policy, by which the security forces pick up, detain, torture, and kill Baluch nationalists, activists, and ordinary civilians and students. Their bullet-ridden bodies are dumped on the roadside at a rate of about twenty a month. In October 2010, Amnesty International issued a damning report demanding that the government investigate "the torture and killings of more than forty Baluch leaders and political activists over the past four months."[5] Human Rights Watch says that hundreds of Baluch have disappeared since 2005. Often their bodies are not even found. "This is not counterinsurgency—it is barbarism, and it needs to end now," says Brad Adams, the group's Asia director.[6]

The military has long demanded that the U.S. government place Baluch insurgent groups on the State Department's list of terrorist groups—which the United States has declined to do, noting that the Baluch have not targeted anyone outside the region. Increasingly the Pakistani military has viewed the Baluch insurgency through the myopic lens of the Indian presence in Afghanistan, rather than treating it as a political issue. Pakistan claims that the RAW—India's intelligence agency—is arming and funding the Baluch insurgents from Indian consulates in Afghanistan. As early as 2007, former president Musharraf told the Americans that a hostile India was arming the Baluch from Kabul.[7] India denies the charge. In all past Baluch insurgencies India has had a hand in providing some level of support—usually money for the insurgents in a tit-for-tat return for Pakistan's support for Kashmiri militants. There is every reason to suspect that India is also involved in this insurgency, possibly providing money to Baluch insurgent leaders who are living in Europe and the Gulf emirates. However, these facts still do not deter the Baluch from their central position that they have been poorly treated, their grievances have not been addressed, and there is no political process by which they can be heard in the corridors of power in Islamabad.

Some Baluch militants have taken refuge in Afghanistan. In 2009, the Afghan interior minister, Hanif Atmar, admitted that some five hundred Baluch and Sindhi dissidents were living in a refugee camp in Kandahar, but said they were not allowed to carry out any hostile act against Pakistan.[8] Pashtuns inhabit Baluchistan's border with Afghanistan, and it is here—and in the capital, Quetta—that the Taliban have their homes, mosques, madrassas, businesses, and training camps. Most of the Taliban leaders have families living in or around Quetta, under constant monitoring by the ISI. The Taliban have been careful to maintain excellent relations with the Baluch and have refused to get involved in the civil war in Baluchistan.

The "disappearances" of hundreds of people by the intelligence agencies and in Baluchistan, even by military units such as the Frontier Corps, are a reflection of the utter failure of the judiciary. The judiciary is a broken instrument incapable of handing down judgments to the real criminals. A U.S. State Department report says that in Pakistan, three in four defendants on terrorism charges are acquitted, either because the prosecutors lack proof or because the judges are intimidated. The failure of the courts has frustrated the military, which has increasingly taken the law into its own hands, summarily jailing or executing not just antistate terrorists but any political opponents of the army or the ruling party.[9]

The city of Karachi is another fast-burning fuse that could detonate the entire country. Karachi is an extraordinary metropolis, one of "the great economic engines of South Asia"—holding the country's major port, its stock market, and more than half its industry.[10] Its 18 million people generate 70 percent of the country's revenue and 30 percent of its GDP, but every year its ethnic melting pot—the majority Mohajir community, who are settlers from India; Pashtun and Baluch tribesmen; Punjabi businessmen; and smaller groups from all over South Asia—is mired in ethnic violence. Mafias, criminal gangs, car thieves, and Taliban and sectarian extremists all carry out their turf wars and protection rackets. The kinds of violence witnessed in Karachi are seen nowhere else in Pakistan—targeted mass killings and torture using electric drills. Victims' heads, genitals, and limbs are severed, stuffed into sacks, and dropped on the road. Every year since the 2009 election, an average of 1,200 people have been killed. An orgy of violence erupted in the summer of 2011; 300 people were killed just in July.

The political parties of the ethnic groups lead the fight. The main conflict is between the Pashtuns (represented by the Awami National Party), the Mohajirs (led by Altaf Hussain, who has headed the Muttahida Quami Movement, or MQM, from exile in London for the past twenty years), and the Baluch and Sindhis (who support the PPP). In between are extremists like the Taliban. The ethnic ghettos have become so entrenched and fortified that even Karachi ambulance services have to send out drivers of the same ethnicity as the victim or they could get killed. The Taliban, with their thousands of madrassa students, could quite easily take over parts of Karachi when they feel the time is right. The MQM is constantly talking about separating urban Karachi and Hyderabad from Sind province and creating a Singapore-like state—a move that would, however, lead to a civil war with the rural Sindhis.

Karachi port is also the main gateway for supplies for U.S. and NATO troops in Afghanistan. After 2001, almost 80 percent of all military goods destined for the Aghan war were sent to Karachi and then trucked up to the border crossings in northwestern Pakistan. Now with new routes through Central Asia, the Karachi port caters to only 50 percent of the goods, and that proportion will diminish further by the end of 2011. The economic impact will be significant, with the loss of customs revenues, transport contracts, and jobs. Karachi is a microcosm of what is wrong with the country—the growing weakness of the state, the breakdown of the social contract, ethnic conflict, and the growing war between modernity, business liberalism, and extremism. These divisions can only get worse if the country dissolves into further lawlessness.

The government pushed through one major reform in April 2010. Achieving agreement from all the political parties in parliament was a major achievement for the Pakistan Peoples Party leader Raza Rabbani, who led the initiative. Since the 1973 constitution was established, Pakistan's military rulers had created many anomalies. But in April 2010, parliament passed a bill amending it, with 102 different clauses that rectified the anomalies. The bill also allowed for political devolution and greater powers to the provinces—which had been promised in the 1973 constitution but were never acted upon. This was a very important step in defusing interethnic rivalries, but it cannot be implemented, because the provinces lack the money to set up the necessary departments of government that have devolved from the center.

But the most pressing issue that will determine Pakistan's future, and especially its relationship with the United States, is the economy. The country is extremely dependent on American goodwill for its economic survival—even beyond the nearly $3 billion in annual military and economic aid that it has received since 2001. It also needs the United States to maintain its loans from primary lenders such as the IMF, the World Bank, the Asian Development Bank, the European Union, and Japan. A confrontation with the United States could mean that Pakistan loses $4.8 billion annually in foreign assistance; moreover, according to top economist Akmal Hussain, capital would flee abroad.[11] In its current tensions with the United States, the government insists that it will take the path of self-sufficiency, but it gives no sign of adopting the large-scale economic and tax reforms, revenue-raising measures, or defense cuts that will be needed before Pakistan can stand on its own two feet. So the question of where the money will come from is unanswered. Over one-third of the population is living below the poverty line, and the majority is deprived of basic services. The economy is tanking, with GDP growth at barely 2.6 percent for 2011, high inflation, a huge fiscal deficit of over 5 percent, and up to sixteen hours daily of no electricity—all of which have helped to reduce production and increase joblessness.

Since the 1980s, Pakistan's revenues have never been sufficient even to meet current expenditures; the entire development budget has been financed through foreign loans. Debt servicing and defense now take up some 60 percent of the budget. Borrowing from abroad or from the State Bank has become the norm. Since 1988, Pakistan has sought bailouts from the IMF eleven times, yet it has failed to complete any IMF programs, except for one in 2001.[12] It signed on to its current $11.3 billion IMF loan program in November 2008, but it failed to honor its commitments to reform. Zardari said people could not take any more hardship, and he would face elections in 2013. The IMF program has ended, and most other investment has come to a grinding halt. By February 2012, Pakistan will has to start repaying the most recent IMF loan and earlier ones, too. A drawdown of reserves will create financial panic, accelerate capital flight, and force the country into default—unless it signs up for another IMF loan.[13] "Instead of seriously tackling fundamental problems of resource scarcity," says senior diplomat Maleeha Lodhi, "the government is embarked on doing more of the same—borrowing its way out of a dire situation. . . . This approach also seems to be reaching a dead-end."[14]

Yet many leaders, including Zardari, naively believe that the Americans will ultimately persuade the IMF to bail out Pakistan. The journalist Ayaz Amir has described him as "a master of masterly inactivity, his forte presiding over a state of paralysis and construing it as cleverness."[15] Considering the dire international economic climate, and the fact that even badly run countries carry out major reforms before they receive loans, help for Pakistan looks less likely than ever. A White House report to Congress in April 2011 said bluntly, "The deterioration of Pakistan's economy and slow progress on economic reforms poses the greatest threat to Pakistan's stability over the medium term."[16] In the meantime, Islamic extremists have wisely made the dire condition of the economy and inflation a very effective rallying cry, targeting the government for its widespread corruption and waste, raising the issue of rich versus poor, and emphasizing the Islamic way of sharing wealth versus dependence on loans from the West.

These multiple crises are arising as Pakistan's relations with the United States decay. The CIA's long-running disputes with the ISI came to a head in early 2011 with the case of Raymond Davis. A contractor working out of the U.S. consulate in Lahore, Davis on January 27 shot dead two Pakistanis who were trying to rob him, while a U.S. car ran over a third Pakistani. Davis was arrested, but the United States claimed that he had diplomatic immunity and should be freed.

Pakistan declined to define his status and held him in jail. Davis, in fact, was part of a covert CIA-led task force collecting intelligence on militant groups without permission of the ISI. Islamic groups came out into the streets of Lahore every day to demand that Davis be hanged.

In early 2009, Obama had ordered an intensification of the drone strikes in FATA. Now it became apparent that he had also secretly authorized the CIA to conduct large-scale recruitment of Pakistanis to establish a clandestine intelligence operation, with the help of fifty CIA officers and American contractors; neither their identities nor their tasks were shared with the ISI. In other words, the Americans had set up a specific, secret, second intelligence agency to find Osama bin Laden. In telephone calls and visits, General Pasha and Leon Panetta, the respective heads of the two agencies, tried and failed to heal the rift. The ISI scaled back all intelligence cooperation with the CIA, demanding that the CIA list its three hundred agents in Pakistan and cease independent operations there—both of which the CIA declined to do.

Davis went on trial for murder in Lahore but was freed on March 16 after negotiations among the CIA, the ISI, and the relatives of the deceased, who accepted "blood money" of $2.3 million in return for pardoning Davis. (This is legal under Pakistani sharia or Islamic law.) U.S. officials said the ISI picked up the tab, as the United States did not pay blood money.[17] Davis had been in detention for forty-seven days, during fourteen of which he was interrogated by the ISI. The CIA had halted all drone strikes while Davis was in jail, but five days after his release, an angry CIA fired a barrage of drone strikes in North Waziristan that killed forty people, including some civilians. Kayani accused the Americans of conducting a strike that was "carelessly and callously targeted with complete disregard to human life." U.S. officials insisted the tribesmen were all terrorists.[18]

The CIA-ISI relationship was now speeding downward. In April, the Pakistani military told 350 CIA officers and contractors to leave the country, as well as 120 U.S. special forces trainers with the Frontier Corps. The military demanded a halt to all drone strikes and severely restricted issuing visas to U.S. officials. The ISI aimed to strip the CIA of its clandestine operations in the country, while it whipped up further anti-Americanism in the media by leaking fears that the United States wanted to undermine Pakistan's nuclear weapons capability. The CIA was forced to remove hundreds of its personnel as their visas expired.[19]

Despite Pakistan's objections, the United States pressed ahead with drone strikes. There were nineteen drone attacks in 2008, forty-six in 2009, ninety in 2010, and just forty in the first eight months of 2011.[20] The pall of secrecy that the CIA cast over the drone strikes fueled the worst suspicions among Pakistanis and Afghans and tended to mitigate whatever U.S. soldiers were doing on the ground to win hearts and minds. Controversy erupted over the number of civilian casualties caused by these strikes, something that can never be settled as long as the CIA does not explain its criteria for choosing targets. Who exactly the CIA is aiming to kill is unknown, and what legal U.S. or international rights it has to do so are also unknown.

The fact that the military under President Musharraf, despite its denials of complicity, was deeply involved in the CIA cover-up regarding the drones makes the army unpopular and untrustworthy and infuriates the Pakistani Taliban, who target the security forces even more viciously as the truth emerges. By covering up the drone strikes, the army has created the worst of all possible worlds—an irate public and a vicious, revenge-seeking Taliban.[21] At the same time, the army demands that the Americans refrain from attacking those Pakistani Pashtuns whose militias are not attacking the Pakistan Army, such as Hafiz Gul Bahadur and Maulvi Nazir Nazir. But these commanders have helped kill Americans in Afghanistan, so the United States has every incentive to continue targeting them. The CIA thinks that sharing intelligence with the ISI before drone attacks were launched often led to the victims' escaping just in time. The growing lack of trust led Bush in 2008 and later Obama to authorize attacks without informing Pakistan first.[22]

The Pakistani public is fully aware of the ISI's unconvincing denials. A bombshell statement by Senator Dianne Feinstein, chairman of the Senate Intelligence Committee, on February 12, 2009, exposed Pakistan's duplicity. "As I understand it, these [drones] are flown out of a Pakistani base," she said.[23] A few days later the *Times* of London published satellite images that showed U.S. Predator drones on a runway at Shamsi air base in Baluchistan. Not only was the Pakistani military helping with intelligence, but U.S. drones were being flown out of Pakistan to attack targets in Pakistan. There was also CIA deceit. Pakistanis were incensed after John O. Brennan, the White House adviser on terrorism, had the audacity to claim that for a year "there hasn't been a single collateral death" due to drones. According to news reports, the CIA believes that drones have killed six hundred militants but not a single civilian—a claim that is patently unbelievable to any Afghan or Pakistani.[24]

The Pakistani military's growing belligerence toward the United States is matched by a collapse of U.S. confidence in Pakistan. In an April 2011 report to Congress, the White House said that Pakistan had made no effort to support Obama's troop surge and that the army had failed to defeat the Pakistani Taliban. The army had tried three times to eliminate militants from the Mohmand tribal agency in FATA, which was, said the report, "a clear indicator of the inability of the Pakistani military and government to render cleared areas resistant to insurgency return." It concluded that "there remains no clear path toward defeating the insurgency in Pakistan, despite the unprecedented and sustained deployment of over 147,000 troops."[25] Pakistan rejected the report, saying that U.S. failures in Afghanistan were to blame in FATA's fighting its own tribesmen, the Pakistani Taliban.[26] But the truth is that the Pakistan Army was unwilling to deploy adequate numbers of troops and airpower in FATA and did not want to go up against groups whom it considered friendly, including the Haqqanis. With these double standards, Pakistan would likely never replicate its successful operation in Swat.

The plight of FATA, after four years of war, was described by Abubakar Siddique, the region's most renowned journalist: "More than one million FATA residents remain displaced by conflict. Tens of thousands of Pakistani soldiers continue to battle scores of militants. Thousands have died in the course of a seven-year insurgency in the region, with traditional tribal leaders either assassinated or chased from their home areas. FATA's status as Pakistan's backwater persists, with health, education, and other human development indicators among the lowest in Asia. And its strategic location and role as an extremist sanctuary promise to keep it embroiled in insurgency."[27]

The promise of political reform in FATA had been held out to its people since 2001, but nothing had been achieved by successive governments. FATA desperately needed to become a part of the Pakistani state by a grant of provincial status or by joining KP province. Its British-based laws needed to be brought into line with Pakistani law and the services given to the people of Pakistan, such as education and health care, needed to be made available to the FATA tribesmen. Finally, in August 2011, President Zardari amended some of the draconian British-era laws in FATA. Collective punishment for individual crimes committed by tribesmen was withdrawn, bail could be issued after arrests were made, and for the first time Pakistani political parties that had been denied access to FATA under British laws were allowed to operate there.

Overall, the contradictions of Pakistan's policies are still difficult to understand. Pakistan has suffered far higher casualties than U.S.-led Coalition forces. According to government figures, between 2001 and August 2011, a total of 36,705 Pakistanis were killed in the war on terror, including 3,840 security personnel and 11,185 civilians. The remainder, or 21,680, were counted as insurgents, although such a figure is deemed too high. The soldiers wounded totaled 8,617. By contrast, the U.S.-led Coalition suffered a total of 2,583 soldiers killed until July 2011, which included 1,626 Americans killed.[28] Moreover, at least 200 officers had been killed—1 officer for every 16 soldiers killed—an unquestionably high rate of loss. This was partly due to the traditions of bravery in the Pakistan Army, where officers were taught to lead from the front, but it was also due to the lack of training in counterinsurgency. Yet this enormous loss of life is not reflected in military gains on the ground. As long as its selective approach to extremist groups continues, the Pakistan Army's high command is throwing its soldiers into a meat grinder with no strategy or end in sight.

What are these soldiers dying for—to eliminate some groups but not others? Or to satisfy American demands and thereby keep U.S. funds rolling into Pakistan? Or to combat only the most lethal threats to the Pakistani state while ignoring others? For years people have asked these questions, but they have never received any clear answers. Meanwhile failures have multiplied, casualties have soared, and the country leans ever farther over the abyss of chaos. Every confrontation with the United States has become an excuse to further deviate from the truth and blame all Pakistani state failures on the U.S. strategy in Afghanistan and U.S. pressures on Pakistan.

Even before the killing of Bin Laden, the Raymond Davis affair had led to a severe breakdown in U.S.-Pakistan relations, and in July 2011 the United States suspended $800 million in military aid. According to Robert Blackwill, a former Republican U.S. ambassador to India, "the Pakistani military is not an ally, not a partner, not a friend of the US."[29] Lindsey Graham, the influential senator (R-SC), summed up the dilemma, saying of the Pakistani military, "You can't trust them, and you can't abandon them." The U.S. government admitted in a report that of the first year's $1.5 billion Kerry-Lugar-Berman civilian aid, only $179.5 million had been disbursed by December 2010. Corruption and incompetence were deemed so rife in the Pakistani bureaucracy that projects could not be implemented in time. But the U.S. Agency for International Development (USAID) was also slow to deliver. Of the 115 schools that USAID was supposed to build in the Swat Valley in 2009, none were completed by 2011.[30]

On April 14, General Pasha visited CIA chief Leon Panetta to see if anything could be salvaged from the rapidly deteriorating relationship. Childishly, the CIA launched a drone missile while Pasha was in Washington. As a result, Pasha left in a huff, and all conversation stalled. Two days later, in retaliation, Kayani, Pasha, and Gilani visited Kabul and tried to persuade President Karzai to dump the Americans and hold peace talks with the Taliban through Pakistan. Karzai wanted access to the Taliban leadership in Pakistan. Had Pakistan really been willing to help achieve peace in Afghanistan, it would have given both sides access to each other without interference—but the ISI refused to do that. For the past year, Kayani and Pasha had infuriated Kabul by making grandiose promises that turned out to mean less than nothing because they delivered nobody to talk to. The ISI refused to release even Mullah Baradar, the Taliban number two who had now spent more than a year in a Pakistani jail. On April 20, just days before the secret operation to kill Bin Laden would be launched, Admiral Mullen arrived in Islamabad for a last-ditch attempt to mend relations with Kayani. "[W]e cannot afford to let this relationship come apart," said Mullen. "It's just too dangerous. It's too dangerous, in each country, for each country. It's too dangerous for the region."[31] But there was no give on either side.

Several days after the U.S. attack on Abbottabad, the Pakistan Army crafted its response. First Kayani took the pulse among junior officers, who were furious with the Americans—and furious at their seniors for not retaliating. Rather than explain the complex realities to them, Kayani took the easy way out by blaming the entire episode on the Americans for breaching Pakistan's sovereignty—but he failed to answer the obvious questions: What had Bin Laden been doing in Abbottabad for six years, and why had the ISI not found him? Kayani's failure to deliver a true narrative either to his officers or to the public was compounded by his refusal to hold anyone in the army or ISI accountable for the failure. If Pakistan's sovereignty had truly been breached, then wouldn't someone have to pay for it?

Sartaj Aziz, a wise old man of Pakistani politics, advised the army that "an admission of incompetence is probably less harmful than accepting complicity," and he said some senior officers should resign.[32] In any true democracy with civilian control over the armed forces, both Kayani and Pasha, or at the very least Pasha, should have resigned, but there were no resignations, no accountability, and nobody took responsibility. The issue of Bin Laden staying in Abbottabad undetected for six years was no less important than the issue of Pakistan's sovereignty. Even more embarrassingly, it emerged that the CIA had hired Pakistanis, including a local doctor, to monitor Bin Laden's house by conducting a ruse vaccination campaign. After the raid, the ISI arrested Dr. Shakil Afridi for cooperating with U.S. intelligence, and it refused U.S. demands to free him.

On May 13, the Pakistani Taliban took revenge for the death of Bin Laden by carrying out a double suicide attack at an FC training camp in Khyber-Pakhtunkhwa province that killed 80 cadets and wounded 140. But the biggest humiliation for the military occurred on May 22, when Taliban attacked the Pakistani Navy's Mehran air base in Karachi. A six-man team of suicide attackers destroyed two U.S.-made Orion P-3C maritime surveillance aircraft worth $75 million. The battle lasted for sixteen hours; eleven sailors were killed, and two of the attackers even managed to escape. A number of foreign workers at the base, including Chinese and Americans, were rescued. It was another inside job: subsequently eight naval personnel were arrested for providing support and weapons to the attackers.

With this litany of failures, the military faced growing hostility and criticism from the Pakistani press. In May 2011, a prominent journalist, Syed Saleem Shahzad, was found tortured and murdered after having gone missing for two days. He left behind several e-mails saying that if he was killed, the ISI would be responsible. Shahzad was believed to be on the verge of making revelations that would show the extent to which Al Qaeda had penetrated the navy. An uproar ensued in the media and civil society. As the ISI denied all accusations, his death prompted a multitude of revelations from other journalists about the activities of the media cell of the ISI (whose director general was a rear admiral) in harassing and threatening journalists. Pakistan was already the most dangerous place in the world to be a journalist, according to the New York–based Committee to Protect Journalists.

Many Pakistani journalists found themselves caught in between death threats from the extremists and those from the ISI. If the state was unable to provide them with security, then they had nobody to turn to for protection. The ISI came under withering criticism, and finally a commission of inquiry headed by a judge was set up to examine the murder of Shahzad. If even some of these accusations were true, it would mean that the ISI behaved toward the press in unprecedented ways—worse even than in the darkest days of the Zia ul-Haq dictatorship in the 1980s, when journalists were flogged in public. Inflaming the controversy, Admiral Mullen said the United States had evidence that the government was responsible for Shahzad's death. Soon more journalists were reporting harassment at the hands of the ISI rear admiral, who was finally removed from his post.

The growing political crisis, the confrontation with the Americans, and the conflict between the military and the media had little effect on Pakistani politicians. President Zardari made no public statement for two months after the death of Bin Laden, and Prime Minister Gilani handed over to the army the responsibility to deal with the crisis: they conveniently assumed that since it was the army that had damaged the relationship with the United States, it was the army's job to fix it. But this would have been the moment for the civilian government to assert itself and insist that, precisely because the army had messed things up so badly, it would now take greater charge of foreign policy. Now was the moment for the government to insist on major changes in the way policy was formulated. Now was the moment for it to assert greater control over the conduct of the counterinsurgency war in Pakistan, over the peace process with the Taliban, and over relations with the Americans. Instead, Zardari and Gilani retreated into a studied, stupefied silence, fearful of taking any such risks. However, there were some attempts at reconciliation, although they proved fruitless. General Pasha organized a meeting between U.S. officials and Ibrahim Haqqani, the younger brother of Jalaluddin Haqqani, in the United Arab Emirates in the middle of August. The dialogue clearly did not lead to much and certainly not to a negotiation. The Haqqanis later claimed that the Americans' only intention was to create divisions between them and the Taliban. The Haqqanis reply came forcefully to this failed diplomatic attempt.

Instead, the crisis became worse. On September 10, the Haqqani network sent a suicide truck bomb packed full of explosives into a U.S. post in Wardak province, close to Kabul. It killed five Afghans and wounded seventy-seven American soldiers—the largest single casualty toll since the war began. Three days later (September 13) six well-trained suicide gunmen, also from the Haqqani network, occupied a partially constructed high-rise building in central Kabul and rained mortar shells, rockets, and grenades on the U.S. embassy and on the headquarters of the International Security Assistance Force. The gunmen held out for twenty hours before being eliminated. Twenty-seven Afghans were killed—no Americans—but the humiliation of having the American embassy attacked riled up the United States. On September 22, Defense Secretary Leon Panetta and Admiral Mike Mullen told the Senate Armed Services Committee that the ISI had played a supporting role in the Haqqani network's two attacks. Their comments implied, for the first time, that Pakistan was deliberately trying to kill Americans. "With ISI support," said Mullen, "Haqqani operatives planned and conducted that truck bomb attack, as well as the assault on our embassy . . . the Haqqani network acts as a veritable arm of Pakistan's ISI." Those words were to resound for months to come.

Pakistan, Mullen continued, "may believe that by using these proxies, they are hedging their bets or redressing what they feel is an imbalance in regional power, but in reality, they have already lost that bet. By exporting violence they've eroded their internal security and their position in the region. They have undermined their international credibility and threatened their economic well-being."[33] Mullen's comments were a devastating reminder to Pakistan about the long-term consequences of continuing to maintain proxy forces on its soil. Unless Pakistan went after the Haqqanis, he said, the United States would act unilaterally. It was the harshest, most direct statement ever made by a U.S. official, and it infuriated Islamabad, which lashed back against Mullen (who was due to retire that week). Kayani made it clear that he had no intention of going after the Haqqanis, and the army was placed on a high state of alert, expecting U.S. military action. F-16s were flying over nuclear facilities to protect them from possible American attacks. For a few days, the United States and Pakistan seemed to be on the verge of war, or at least skirmishes. It soon became clear that Mullen's blunt comments had not been cleared by the White House, and the State Department tried to row back the boat and keep Pakistan onside. White House spokesman Jay Carney refuted Mullen on September 28, saying it was "not language that I would use." Others spoke of Mullen "overstating" the evidence. It was yet another example showing how divided and frustrated the Obama administration was with its Afghan policy, unable to clearly define what the policy was or where it was supposed to lead. The largest split remained on reconciliation, with the military still expressing grave doubts about talks with the Taliban yielding any results.

On September 21, the crisis intensified when Burhanuddin Rabbani, a former Afghan president, was assassinated by a messenger, allegedly from the Taliban, with a bomb in his turban. Rabbani had been head of the High Peace Council, set up to hold talks with the Taliban. His death caused an outpouring of grief and bewilderment. It halted the talks process while deepening Afghanistan's ethnic divide, as Rabbani was a leading Tajik personality. At his funeral on September 24, Tajiks made fiery anti-Taliban and anti-Pashtun speeches. Ever since the death of Bin Laden, relations between the United States and Pakistan had become steadily worse. Now they were poised precariously between war and peace.

Ultimately it was left to Hillary Clinton to try to bring back some modicum of stability to the relationship. Clinton visited Pakistan in late September and brought with her several cabinet officials in order to ensure that Pakistan got a single message from all sides of the U.S. government. She was joined by the director of the CIA, David Petraeus; the new chairman of the Joint Chiefs of Staff, General Martin Dempsey; and other officials from State and Defense. Her initial message to the Pakistanis was very tough. "No one should be in any way mistaken about allowing this to continue without paying a very big price," she said in Kabul before she left for Islamabad on October 22. She said Pakistan could either help or hinder efforts to find a resolution to the war in Afghanistan. In front of his American hosts, Karzai in Kabul had weighed in with some of the bluntest criticism of Pakistan. "We believe that the Taliban to a very, very great extent are controlled by the establishments in Pakistan, stay in Pakistan, have their headquarters in Pakistan, launch attacks from Pakistan."[34]

In Islamabad, four hours of talks with the full Pakistani leadership, including Generals Kayani and Pasha, ended on a positive note with both sides claiming they had reduced their differences. The United States appeared to drop its demand that the Pakistan Army launch an attack on the Haqqanis in North Waziristan. Instead, there were more promises by the government to speed up talks among the United States, the Haqqani faction, and the mainstream Afghan Taliban. Clinton described what U.S. policy would be in the months ahead: "talk, fight, build." The United States now finally realized that Pakistan would not give up on the Haqqanis and that it wanted a seat at the table whenever negotiations did take place. However, many officials on the U.S. side did not trust the Pakistani military and wanted to promote the idea of containment. Yet at the same time, the Americans intensified drone strikes against North Waziristan, coming threateningly close to bombing Miranshah, the main city for the Haqqani network, where some 15,000 Pakistani troops were also based. Until now Miranshah had been off-limits for U.S. drone attacks because of the presence of Pakistani troops.

Many U.S. officials and experts were to take a still more aggressive line by advocating a policy of containment. Containment, expressed best by Bruce Riedel, the former Obama adviser, would recognize that the United States and Pakistan were not allies, that their strategic interests were in conflict, and that the Pakistan Army's ambitions in Afghanistan had to be contained. Riedel wrote that the army had "concluded [that] NATO is doomed to give up in Afghanistan leaving them free to act as they wish there . . . that the sooner America leaves the better it will be for Pakistan. They want Americans and Europeans to believe the war is hopeless, so they encourage the Taliban to speed the withdrawal with spectacular attacks." The United States would move toward containing Pakistan and conduct a policy of "focused hostility."[35] Such a policy might force the army to be more helpful on Afghanistan, but it would undermine Pakistan's social and political fabric, rapidly increase anti-Americanism, and give the extremists greater support.

Even as Clinton urged greater dialogue with the Pakistan military, the Pentagon released its twice-yearly report on the war in Afghanistan, which clearly stated that "safe havens in Pakistan remain the insurgency's greatest enabler" and that these safe havens have become more virulent as the United States draws down its troops.[36]

Every attack by the Taliban and the Haqqani network seemed to strengthen those in Washington who were opposed to any dialogue with either Pakistan or the Taliban. The Haqqanis did not let up. In another devastating suicide attack in Kabul on October 29, when thirteen Americans were killed (five U.S. soldiers and eight contractors) after their bus was rammed by an explosives-packed truck, U.S. public support for the war saw a further drop. A CNN poll that week revealed that only 34 percent of Americans now supported the war—an all-time low—while 63 percent were opposed. Fifty-eight percent of Americans believed that the war was now similar to the Vietnam War, where the United States saw defeat. The lack of support for the war was clearly becoming a major issue for Obama's strategy to win the 2012 presidential elections.[37]

No intelligence agency in the world should collect intelligence, decide which operations should be carried out, and then carry out those operations unsupervised. It is the government's responsibility to study the intelligence gathered, make the political and operational decisions, and then instruct the intelligence agency on how to act. But in Pakistan, the ISI carries out all tasks, giving it excessive powers. First Musharraf and then Kayani have allowed it to step into every conceivable part of the country's political functioning. Musharraf even made ex-ISI chiefs his federal ministers and gave others plum ambassadorial jobs. Kayani has not taken that path, but he relies excessively and exclusively on Pasha, who has a one-dimensional mind that causes frustration in the army and among politicians. The ISI's vast intelligence-gathering role has extended into such things as influencing the media and promoting political campaigns; monitoring diplomats, politicians, and journalists; acting as a foreign ministry for the army; and most significant, having large-scale operational responsibilities (not just intelligence gathering) related to Afghanistan and India. To win trust at home and abroad, Kayani needs to immediately reform the ISI.

Tellingly, the ISI continues to allow the retired military class and a handful of extremist intellectuals to publicly advocate near-lunatic ideas. For some years now, a former army chief, Gen. Mirza Aslam Beg, has blamed all of Pakistan's ills on "the spy network in Afghanistan, which was established in 2001 under the RAW and supported by the CIA, Mossad, MI6 and BND."[38] He locates this massive intelligence center in Sarobi, to the east of Kabul. (I have visited Sarobi and, needless to say, found nothing of the sort.) The network's aim, Beg says, is to train dissidents to undermine Pakistan and China. He and retired general Hamid Gul, the former head of the ISI, who puts out similar conspiracy theories, are frequent guests on TV talk shows. While the ISI encourages the media to give space to such madcap theories by former generals, critical and thoughtful journalists and intellectuals are constantly harassed, tortured, or just ostracized. Under such circumstances, it is not surprising that Pakistanis are worried about their future. Where will the ideas and hopes for Pakistan's future come from if the intellectual landscape is dominated by the likes of Beg, Gul, and the mullahs?

NINE

Changing the Narrative—or Preparing for the Worst

One of the things that gets in the way of conducting good national security policy is a reluctance to call things by their right names and state plainly what is really happening. If you keep describing difficult situations in misleading or inaccurate ways, plenty of people will draw the wrong conclusions about them and will continue to support policies that don't make a lot of sense.

Stephen Walt

AS I write, in the autumn of 2011, the Karzai government is in free fall, the Taliban are terrifying the population after a summer campaign of assassinations, U.S.-Pakistan relations have broken down over the role of Jalaluddin Haqqani, ethnic divisions are widening in the wake of the murder of Burhanuddin Rabbani, Pakistan refuses to give up its Taliban sanctuaries, and the failure of the Pakistani state or a military coup looms on the horizon. A critical international conference in Istanbul in November 2011, which was supposed to receive pledges of noninterference in Afghanistan's internal affairs by neigh-boring states and establish a mechanism to monitor such interfer-ence, failed to achieve its objectives. The U.S. administration remained hopelessly divided as to the way forward. The region seems to be mov-ing inexorably toward greater conflict and contradiction rather than peaceful resolution and reconciliation.

By both action and inaction, the United States has contributed sig-nificantly to the region's dangerous instability. The Obama adminis-tration has failed to detail its aims in the region beyond 2014, thereby giving rise to speculation and conspiracy theories. The U.S. desire to maintain a small but permanent military presence or even bases in Afghanistan after 2014 has annoyed all the neighboring countries. What are Washington's geostrategic interests in the region, and to what extent is it willing to deploy troops to pursue those interests? Does the United States want to stabilize Pakistan and Afghanistan, or would it rather try to contain or even challenge Iran and China? Or would it prefer to leave the region in the hands of trusted allies like India and Turkey—a surefire way to antagonize Pakistan? Moreover, while the United States has other strategic priorities now, such as the Arab Spring, a greater commitment to East Asia, and containing China, it has far fewer resources than it once did to play a global role.[1]

The United States will have to make its choices and commitments very carefully, but it alone can answer these questions. So far the Obama administration has failed to debate a single issue in a strategic manner. As always with this administration, everything is held in tight secrecy even though debates on matters like this ought to take place in the open. Even on Afghanistan, the administration is deeply divided: hard-liners within Congress, the military, and even the State Department want to continue a militarized strategy to kill more Taliban well into 2013, while others want peace talks with the Taliban to get moving quickly.[2] Part of the tension between the United States and Pakistan is related to the short-term aims of the United States, which wants Pakistan's help up to 2014 in delivering a safe U.S. troop withdrawal. The United States refuses, however, to outline what policies it will pursue after 2014, which are essential to Pakistan's stability. A positive outcome for the region will depend on a deliberate, carefully considered Western withdrawal from Afghanistan, the existence of a political settlement with the Taliban, and Pakistan's willingness to rein in Islamic extremism and prevent a potential state meltdown. The grimmest outcome would result from a botched, overly hasty Western withdrawal, the absence of a political settlement with the Taliban, a continuing civil war in Afghanistan, the Pakistani leaders' continuing resistance to internal reform, the army's refusal to seek a compromise on Afghanistan with the United States and the Afghans, and a consequent meltdown of the Pakistani state.

The core issue is what happens in Pakistan. Its geostrategic location, its nuclear weapons, its large population, its terrorist camps, and its enfeebled economy and polity make it more important—and more vulnerable—than even Afghanistan. And yet Pakistan's plan for its national security still consists almost entirely of resisting Indian hegemony, protecting and developing its nuclear program, promoting the Kashmiri cause, and ensuring the presence of a pro-Pakistan government in Kabul. None of that has changed since 2001, despite U.S. pressure and money. As long as the ISI protects key Afghan insurgent groups, a peaceful settlement in Afghanistan is out of the question, and the deepening of democracy and economic reform in Pakistan has no chance. "Mending Afghanistan is just not possible while Pakistan continues to fall apart," writes a former ambassador.[3]

Moreover, in order to enhance its national security, Pakistan must integrate FATA into the mainstream of its polity. In 2008, President Zardari promised to change FATA's status, but only in August 2011 did he take the first belated steps, allowing political parties to operate in FATA for the first time and amending the outdated British Frontier Crimes Regulations penal code. Much more needs to be done, and quickly.

If the persistent schizophrenia in Pakistan's Afghan policy continues, the country could face breakdown. What the military gives with one hand, it takes away with the other. Pakistan has genuine national security interests in Afghanistan, and it wants the international community to take them into account. But if it follows its present chosen path—conflict with the United States and trying to dictate terms and gain supremacy over the Afghans, while being inflexible and ignoring the interests of other neighbors—Pakistan will lose everything in Afghanistan. In the past, similar uncertain policies have resulted in Pakistan's losing the endgame in Afghanistan, both in 1989, when the Soviets withdrew, and in 1992, when the Communist regime collapsed. This time the end result will be more dangerous, because Pakistan's own extremists will be immeasurably strengthened, ethnic separatists could plunge the country into conflict, the economic and social malaise will intensify, and the military itself may split, endangering its strong control over nuclear weapons. The army's obsession with Afghanistan has turned Pakistan's foreign policy on its head. No longer is foreign policy a reflection of domestic policies and the pursuit of peace in the region. Instead, foreign policy toward Afghanistan is further undermining domestic stability, making internal contradictions and conflicts worse and intensifying the conflict between civilian power and the military. Moreover, the unrealistic goals the military has set for Afghanistan have once again isolated Pakistan in the region just as it was in the 1990s, when it first backed the Taliban regime in Kabul.

These are just some of the contradictions that Pakistan's policies are riddled with. Pakistan does not want to see the return of a Taliban government in Kabul and would prefer to foster a power-sharing agreement in Kabul. But it also does not want the non-Pashtun former Northern Alliance to return to power, even though that will be impossible to prevent in a sustainable peace, as non-Pashtuns constitute more than 40 percent of the population. Pakistan fears a civil war in Afghanistan and opposes any partitioning of Afghanistan because of the dire implications for itself. But its support for the Taliban worsens the ethnic divide in Afghanistan and further alienates non-Pashtuns. Pakistan accepts only a minor role for other neighbors of Afghanistan and no role for India—yet India is the region's economic powerhouse and is the most likely investor in Afghanistan's economy. Even some Taliban are now frustrated with Pakistan for holding them back from having meaningful talks with the Americans and the Kabul regime.

Pakistan would like to see the United States withdraw from Afghanistan, but it fears the resulting vacuum and the loss of U.S. military aid to its army. Even as the Pakistani military fears a destabilized Afghanistan, it equally fears an overly strong Afghanistan: a powerful Afghan Army could cement national unity and turn the country against Pakistan. It wants the Afghan Pashtuns to be in power, but not to be so strong as to revive the idea of a greater Pashtunistan, which would include parts of Pakistan. So General Kayani has vigorously opposed the U.S. buildup of a large Afghan Army, even as he complains that the Afghan Army is not strong enough to stop the Taliban. (The Afghan Army, in any case, will have no offensive punch because the United States is depriving it of tanks and fighter aircraft.)[4]

The Pakistani military supports an Afghan-led reconciliation process with the Taliban, but it wants to be at the table, which is unacceptable either to Karzai or to the Taliban. The non-Pashtuns will never accept a peace process in which the ISI plays a major role. Yet the ISI, after a year of courting Karzai and persuading him to trust Pakistan rather than the Americans for peacemaking, has not allowed Afghan leaders to meet with any Taliban living in Pakistan. Nor has it freed Mullah Baradar, the Taliban number two, whose release Karzai has asked for half a dozen times. That the United States, with the help of Germany and Qatar, went around Pakistan to open a dialogue with the Taliban has further infuriated Islamabad. Many Afghans, including Karzai, believe that Pakistan wants a peace settlement but only on its own terms.

Pakistan must act as a normal state, rather than a paranoid, insecure, ISI-driven entity whose operational norms are to use extremists and diplomatic blackmail. The ISI has become a state within a state and must be put under civilian control. A normal state would put civilians in charge; it would employ diplomacy, nuance, and flexibility; it would view its own national security as interconnected with that of its neighbors and allies; and it would, as its first and primary task, deradicalize its own society. But normality is not what we have in Pakistan. To function as a normal state, Pakistanis desperately need a new narrative from their leaders, one that does not perpetually blame the evergreen troika of "India, the United States, and Israel" for its own ills.

We Pakistanis as a nation seem hesitant to carry out self-analysis or apportion blame according to logic and rationality rather than emotion and prejudice. The elite refuses to take responsibility for its actions or its mistakes and instead paints Pakistan as the victim, maligned and wronged at the hands of foreign powers. It presents the United States and India as wanting to subvert, undermine, and destroy Pakistan but gives no logical reason as to why they should want to do so.

It is equally vital that Pakistan change its attitude toward the region. One of the military's principal aims in an Afghan settlement is to keep India out. But India has played an influential role in Kabul since 1947, one that Pakistan cannot ignore. For example, Pakistan does not allow Indian goods and aid to flow through its territory; so after 9/11, India set out to create a new route to Afghanistan, bypassing Pakistan, through Iran. India invested $150 million in building a new 180-mile road from Delaram (in Afghanistan's Nimroz province) to Zaranj, on the Iranian border, shortening the route to the Iranian port of Chabahar on the Arabian Gulf and avoiding the longer route through Herat. By the time this new road opened in January 2009, some 50 percent of Afghan exports and imports were already moving through Iranian ports—the Afghans, too, were fed up with long delays and hassles at Karachi port. Karachi was once the only port that landlocked Afghanistan used, but no more; Pakistan has lost out badly.

In the autumn of 2008, the American scholar Barnett Rubin and I published an essay called "From Great Game to Grand Bargain," in which we advised the incoming Obama administration to foster a major regional diplomatic initiative that would bring all the neighbors—Pakistan, India, China, Iran, Tajikistan, Turkmenistan, and Uzbekistan—to the table to discuss a peace process and noninterference guarantees for Afghanistan.[5] In 2009, Richard Holbrooke embarked on such a regional initiative, visiting all the neighbors and setting up a forum of special envoys from forty countries to coordinate initiatives. But India snubbed Holbrooke and the U.S. strategy, demanding that Pakistan first eliminate terrorist groups targeting India. India also suspected that the United States was trying to push for a Kashmir settlement so that it could then ask Pakistan to eliminate its extremists. India refused to link Kashmir with Afghanistan. New Delhi's resistance forced Holbrooke to take India off its regional initiative, but despite that, the Pakistan Army did not trust the Americans. Subsequently the Taliban mounted several attacks on Indian targets in Kabul.[6] India itself has acted immaturely since 9/11, refusing to accept compromise or to see the benefits of working with the Americans and Pakistan on Afghanistan.

Pakistan is convinced that India's strategic interests in Afghanistan center on wooing separatist groups among the Baluch and Pashtun tribes to undermine Pakistan. That may well be true, because at least five hundred Baluch dissidents are resident in Kandahar. But Pakistan has elevated the Indian threat coming from Afghanistan to the equivalent of the Indian threat coming from the east. In a manner of speaking, Kabul has become the military's new Kashmir. But Pakistan will always be Afghanistan's most important neighbor, and the threat felt by the military is out of all proportion to India's actual influence in Afghanistan. Pakistan must not be permitted to make decisions that are detached from global and regional realities, or to determine which countries can be included or kept out of a peace process. If Pakistan is not more flexible and realistic, it will find the international community unwilling to accept even a minimum role for it, while the Taliban will want to distance themselves from appearing as Pakistan's stooges. In 2011, even India finally accepted the need for talks with the Taliban, something that it had opposed for many years.[7]

A peaceful solution to the Afghan war must include the participation of India.

Many Pakistanis believe that if its relations with the United States finally break down, the lost economic aid can be replaced by China. China is geographically close to Pakistan; it has in the past funded some major infrastructure projects, such as dams, ports, and roads; it has helped substantially with Pakistan's nuclear weapons and nuclear energy programs; and it has provided the military with several billion dollars' worth of heavy weapons at cut-rate prices—tanks, ships, submarines, and fighter aircraft. Not surprisingly, Pakistan calls China its "all-weather friend." After Bin Laden was killed in May and the whole world was castigating Pakistan for not being aware of his presence, China's prime minister, Wen Jiabao, issued a stunning morale booster, saying China and Pakistan "will remain forever good neighbors, good friends, good partners and good brothers."[8]

But the China-Pakistan relationship is essentially military to military, rather than people to people. (Outside the military, Pakistanis don't visit China and don't speak Chinese.) The $9 billion trade between the two countries is heavily weighted in China's favor. China wants a strategic relationship with Pakistan to balance a rising India, and Pakistan has shown a willingness to provide it. But China is not prepared to treat India as an enemy, as Pakistan wants it to; rather, China wants the two countries to live in peace, not in a state of proxy war. Once upon a time, China strongly supported Pakistan's position on Kashmir, but since the mid-1990s it no longer does. China has a massive $60 billion trade and business relationship with India, which it envisages will rise sixfold in the next ten years. China will not forsake that by throwing its support wholly and unconditionally to Pakistan.

Moreover, China cannot oblige Pakistan the way the United States does. It does not give cash or loans for budgetary support—it gave only one loan of $500 million in 2001. It does not give development aid—in fact, Beijing has no government development agency to distribute such aid. During the 2005 earthquake and the 2010 floods, China's financial help was negligible, and many Pakistanis criticized its lack of presence. The Americans provided hundreds of millions of dollars and dozens of helicopters, but the Chinese provided neither. Moreover, China lacks the clout the United States has with the international lending institutions that are so vital to Pakistan, and with the Europeans and Japan, who are Pakistan's main aid providers. China is now just as deeply concerned about Pakistan's failures and the growth of extremism there as the United States. Its diplomats discreetly point out that Pakistan cannot even protect Chinese citizens, several of whom have been killed. China is also deeply concerned about the inability of the government to carry out economic reforms.

China now faces the threat of Islamic militancy at home. Chinese Muslims, or Uighurs, from Xingjian have long journeyed to Pakistan for trade and to perform the Hajj in Saudi Arabia, along a route that was part of the ancient Silk Road. But in the 1980s, Uighurs went to study in Pakistani madrassas and then went on to fight the Soviets in Afghanistan. Now some are fighting with the Taliban. Uighur nationalism is becoming much stronger in Xingjian, but the greater Chinese fear is that Uighur Islamic extremism will grow; it is still a minor threat, but China finds it easy to blame Islamic groups for any unrest.

China considers the most potent threat to be the East Turkistan Islamic Movement (ETIM), which the UN declared a terrorist organization in 2002. In October 2003, the Pakistan Army killed ETIM leader Hasan Mahsum, and in January 2010, his successor, Abdul Haq al-Turkistani, was killed by a U.S. drone attack, both in FATA.[9] The Islamic Movement of Uzbekistan is now a pan–Central Asian group: its members are living in FATA, and it has also recruited numerous Uighurs. Another group, the Turkistan Islamic Party, posted a video in September 2011 claiming responsibility for some attacks in Xingjian. In 2009, Al Qaeda in Pakistan called for attacks on Chinese interests, after riots in Urumqui left two hundred Han Chinese and Uighurs dead. China fears that all these shadowy Uighur Islamic groups have found refuge in FATA. But whenever the ISI has been warned of Uighur militants operating out of Pakistan, it has obliged Chinese intelligence. The ISI captured and extradited to China fourteen Uighurs in 1997, seven in 2002, nine in 2009, and five in 2011, including a woman and two children, despite fears that not all were militants and despite objections from the UN that Pakistan was sending them back to certain execution.[10]

Pakistan has been hugely embarrassed by its first-ever public denunciation by the Chinese authorities. On July 18, 2011, Uighurs and police clashed at a police station in Hotan, which led to twenty people being shot dead. The official *China Daily* of August 2, 2011, wrote that "the leaders of the group learned terrorist techniques at ETIM camps in Pakistan before they penetrated into Xingjian." This prompted ISI chief General Pasha to rush to Beijing, where he reassured the Chinese that Pakistan would counter the ETIM.[11] During 2011, in what appears to be a concerted campaign, China has forcibly demanded the return of Uighurs settled in Malaysia, Thailand, Cambodia, Nepal, and Kazakhstan.

China's role in Afghanistan is important for the future because its thirst for raw materials makes it a major investor for minerals. The China Metallurgical Corporation has bought a controlling stake in the Aynak copper field in Logar province for $3 billion—one of the largest copper fields in the world. China's largest oil company has won the rights to exploit the first oil field to be tendered in northwestern Afghanistan. But China has done little to help rebuild Afghanistan's economy, giving just $130 million in aid in the last decade, although its construction companies have won Western contracts to build roads in Afghanistan. China allows hundreds of Afghan products to enter China without tariffs and has trained some five hundred Afghan officials.

China is extremely nervous about a possible future civil war in Afghanistan and a meltdown of Pakistan. Beyond repressing the Uighurs—a policy reminiscent of Stalin's tactics against Muslims in Soviet Central Asia in the 1930s—China has no constructive policies to deal with the revival of Islam and nationalism among its minorities. Thus it needs a stable Afghanistan and Pakistan to prevent infiltration by extremists. But Chinese repression fuels Muslim anger in Afghanistan and Pakistan, and the mullahs frequently denounce it. China cannot just blame outsiders like Pakistan for its internal difficulties—it must look at its own policies more closely and realize it is not just a victim but also part of the problem.

Iran shares a common border, language, and culture with much of Afghanistan, and no Afghan regime can hope to survive without yielding Iran some influence. In the spring of 2010, Iranian president Mahmoud Ahmadinejad visited Kabul and made it clear that after the American withdrawal, Iran would play a major role in the country. Iran is also of two minds about Afghanistan: it does not want it to be dominated once again by a pro-Pakistan Taliban who will persecute Afghan Shias, but it also does not want it to succeed as a Western-style democracy and an American satellite, which could then fuel the

Iranian opposition.[12] This double game has led Iran to back, at differing times, Karzai, the Shia Hazaras, some Tajik leaders, and even Taliban groups that operate along the Iranian border. In September 2011, Tehran hosted an Islamic conference that included two members of the Taliban and Burhanuddin Rabbani.

Pakistan's relations with Iran have been tense due to competition over Afghanistan. Since the 1980s, Pakistan's support for extremist anti-Shia Afghan groups such as the Taliban has marred relations. Pakistan also had to fight its own sectarian extremists, Sunni groups such as Lashkar-e-Jhangvi and Sipah-e-Sahaba, who attacked Shias. After 9/11, at the CIA's request, Musharraf allowed an Iranian Baluch dissident group called Jundollah to have bases in Baluchistan and to carry out guerrilla attacks against Iranian government targets. General Kayani later dismantled Jundollah's sanctuary, but Iran remained angry until February 2010, when it captured the Jundollah leader Abdolmalek Rigi and hanged him.[13]

In Iranian eyes, Pakistan had not only sided with the Great Satan—the United States—but had allowed its territory to be used against Iran. In retaliation, Iran cultivated some Taliban groups. The Islamic Revolutionary Guard Corps and the Quds Force provided money, weapons, and training to counter U.S. influence in the region but also to break the ISI monopoly over the Taliban. At the height of the Bush administration, when Iran was constantly threatened with a U.S. attack, Iran armed all anti-American groups in the region—Shia or Sunni—with the implicit threat that it could unleash them against the United States. After 2002, Iran gave refuge to several members of Al Qaeda and Bin Laden's family, restricting their activities but refusing to hand them over to the Americans.

Iran has an extensive development program in western Afghanistan, providing roads, electricity, and gas, and it is in the process of making it the most developed region in the country. Iran has pampered the Hazaras—the Afghan Shias—funding their leaders and institutions, particularly education. Karzai has skillfully maintained a relationship with Iran, even though Iran is the declared enemy of his U.S. protector. Karzai's visits to Tehran are usually disguised as summits of Persian-speaking countries (Iran, Tajikistan, and Afghanistan) or to celebrate Nowruz, the Persian New Year, so as not to annoy the Americans.

Obama has handled Iran with far more sensitivity than his predecessor, despite the problems he faces with Iran's nuclear weapons program. Obama realizes that threatening Iran would be counterproductive, as so much in the region is at stake: Iran is needed to secure the withdrawal of U.S. troops from Iraq and Afghanistan, stabilize Pakistan and the Arab world, and not block the Israeli-Palestinian peace process. Obama also understands Iran's paranoia of encirclement, as it is surrounded by countries that either host U.S. troops or provide bases for them. But in 2011 problems between the United States and Iran have become worse. Iran backed the hated regimes of Libya and Syria in the Arab Spring, while it refuses to agree to U.S. forces remaining in Afghanistan after 2014. In the Middle East, Iran became even more of a pariah state after it continued to support Syrian President Bashar al-Assad in putting down a growing uprising against his regime. The Arab street once in favor of Iran turned vehemently against it and Iran's continued support of the Shia group Hezbollah in Lebanon made it deeply unpopular across the largely Sunni Arab world. In October an apparent Iranian-backed plot to assassinate the Saudi ambassador to Washington was uncovered, which increased concerns among Arab states about Iran's irrational behavior. Iranian policy has become weaker and more diffuse due to the intense power struggle under way between President Mahmoud Ahmadinejad and Supreme Leader Ayatollah Ali Khamenei.

Recently Russia and the Central Asian republics have expressed themselves for the first time as wanting to discuss the future of Afghanistan. This regional debate has become more heated ever since Washington and Kabul declared that they were negotiating a long-term strategic security pact and that U.S. troops would stay on in Afghanistan beyond 2014—which none of the regional countries desire. The weak and fragile states of Tajikistan, Kyrgyzstan, and Uzbekistan fear that the Afghan and Pakistani Taliban are supporting Central Asian militants who once took refuge in FATA and are now trying to reinfiltrate Central Asia. Much of the Taliban actions against U.S. forces in northern Afghanistan are carried out by these Central Asian militants. Even far-removed Kazakhstan, with its massive oil wealth, Western investment, and relatively prosperous society, has not been immune from several suicide bomb blasts that were set off in Kazakh cities in 2010 and 2011, allegedly by Islamic militants. The short-term fear of the Americans is that these radicals will try to disrupt the northern NATO traffic that brings supplies across Russia and Central Asia to Afghanistan. On November 19, 2011, the first terrorist attack on this route took place when a bomb exploded the railway line between Termez in southern Uzbekistan and Kurgan-Tyube in Tajikistan. More such attacks are bound to follow. The Arab Spring has generated a genuine political revival in the Middle East, but what shape it will take—authoritarian, democratic, or Islamic—remains unknown. In Egypt the Muslim Brotherhood (now renamed the Freedom and Justice Party) and in Tunisia the Islamist Renaissance Party (Nahda) have emerged as the most organized political parties, largely because they stayed organized when they were banned. In the first free and fair elections in the Arab world, which took place in Tunisia on October 23, 2011, Nahda won 41 percent of the vote, resulting in 90 seats of the 217-seat constituent assembly that would draw up a new democratic constitution. Despite winning the elections and taking power on its own, Nahda showed immense maturity by offering to create a government of national unity. Other Islamist parties are likely to emerge out of the struggles in Syria, Yemen, Bahrain, and Libya. Also highly visible are the Wahhabis and Salafis, funded by the Saudis. For the time being, these Islamists and Islamic extremists are on the side of popular people's revolts, but how long such goodwill lasts is an open question. Later Egypt's Muslim Brotherhood was to win a majority in the controversial Egyptian elections, while in Morocco an Islamist party also won the elections, and the king appointed its leader as prime minister.

There are wider dangers. Those Arab countries that have successfully overthrown their regimes—Tunisia, Egypt, and Libya—have no tradition of democracy or power sharing, and they are divided by deep sectarian and tribal rivalries.[14] While tribalism seldom oversteps its borders, Shia-Sunni sectarianism haunts the entire Muslim world and remains toxic in Pakistan. Shias are demonstrating for their rights in Lebanon and Bahrain and are being shot down by the regimes, while Sunnis are demonstrating for more rights in Iraq and Syria and are being shot down there. While many Shias and Sunnis live in harmony across the Muslim world, its main cheerleaders—Iran in defense of the Shias, and Saudi Arabia for the Sunnis—are at daggers drawn.

One remarkable fact about the Arab Spring is the minimal violence where those revolutions have occurred, as compared to the wars in Afghanistan and Pakistan. In Tunisia, with a population of 10 million, the regime of President Zine el-Abidine Ben Ali and his rapacious wife was overthrown after 219 deaths. In Egypt (population 80 million), the regime of President Hosni Mubarak was overthrown with 850 deaths. In Libya (population 6 million), the eight-month-long war, replete with NATO bombing, took a far heavier toll—probably several thousands killed. In Syria (population 20 million) and Yemen (population 24 million), thousands have been killed. The other remarkable factor is the lack of either pro- or anti-Americanism. Obama and Washington have barely figured in the calculations of the protesters. Even Obama's slow response in support of the uprisings did not lead to derisive comments. Nobody seemed to care. An uprising in Pakistan and Afghanistan would, in contrast, be bursting at the seams with anti-American rhetoric, and there would be no guarantee that at the end of the day democracy would triumph.

The Arab Spring has the potential to create major new problems for Pakistan. Young Pakistanis could well emulate the cry for democracy, freedom, and jobs voiced by millions of young Arabs, as they have seen an equally uncaring elite plunder their own country. Half of Egypt's 80 million people are under the age of twenty-four, while two-thirds of its population have never held a job—about the same statistics as in Pakistan. But for the moment, any kind of mass movement that arose in Pakistan would immediately be taken over by the extremists, their madrassa cohorts, and well-armed and well-funded militiamen. Their demands would be for an Islamic revolution or at least a stricter interpretation of Islam that would divide Pakistan further and plunge it into conflict. A civil society or middle class strong enough to counter them is still missing.

Another problem is that the Pakistan Army is already being asked to help protect the Arab Gulf emirates, much as when the Saudis hired Pakistan Army units in the 1980s. The Shia-Sunni unrest in Bahrain prompted the hiring of 3,000 Pakistani ex-servicemen to join the local police force. If Pakistan does rent out its regular forces to any Arab state, the Iranian backlash will be fierce. Pakistan could well be dragged into an Iran-Arab rivalry in the region, a sectarian war in the Middle East that would inflame sectarian tendencies in Pakistan.

For an example of what success could look like in a volatile region, Pakistan's leaders need look no farther than Turkey, its oldest friend in the Muslim world and now a model for how a Muslim country can regenerate itself. In the summer of 2011, the Arab world seemed to be going through a "Turkish moment," as leaders studied how Turkey had turned from a military dictatorship into a thriving democracy that was run by moderate, modern Muslims and that had a booming economy that registered a 9 percent GDP growth rate in 2010 despite a global recession. Turkey's prime minister, Recep Tayyip Erdogan, age fifty-seven, is a new hero for the Arab and Muslim world, taking on Muslim dictatorships like Syria, defending the Palestinians, tilting against Israel, yet firmly wedded to the West and the United States through NATO and other alliances; it is even up for membership in the twenty-seven-nation European Union. In June 2011, Erdogan and his Justice and Development Party (AKP) were reelected for the second time since first winning in 2002.[15] His party calls for a foreign policy that wants "zero problems with the neighbors."[16]

In September 2011, Foreign Minister Ahmet Davutoglu, describing the new order in the Middle East, said Turkey was now one of the most relevant players in a region in the midst of transformation. Turkey "is right at the center of everything," he said. "This will not be an axis against any other country ... this will be an axis of democracy."[17] Such is Turkey's regard in the Arab world that it is generating enormous envy from Iran, which it is replacing in the hearts of the Palestinian, Lebanese, and even Shia minorities. Arab leaders recently freed from dictatorship are rushing to Turkey to seek its advice. Secretary of State Hillary Clinton sings Turkey's praises. "Turkey's history serves as a reminder that democratic development also depends on responsible leadership," she said in Istanbul in July 2011.[18]

In 1947, Turkey befriended Pakistan, and the militaries that ruled their respective countries for decades became extremely close. Pakistan could depend on Turkey for spare parts for its American-built tanks whenever a U.S. embargo banned sales to Pakistan, and for Turkish air bases where it could park its aircraft during wars with India. But the story of Turkey's transformation is even more relevant to Pakistan: it has shed the grip of its military, turned away from its historic enmity with Greece, and become the truest democracy in the Muslim world. Civilian power is now supreme in Turkey, and the military respects it. Moreover, it is a heavily Islamized civilian power—a world away from the founder of modern secular Turkey, Mustafa Kemal Ataturk, whom the military and secular Turks still idealize. These are all lessons that the Pakistani military has failed to learn. Former president Musharraf was particularly fond of Turkey, having grown up there, but he never learned Turkey's essential lesson, which is how to transform from military to civilian rule.

In Afghanistan, Turkey has tried to promote regional peace, first by bringing together Pakistan and Afghanistan in a series of summit meetings, then by holding wider meetings to discuss a regional agreement on noninterference in Afghanistan. Pakistan encouraged Turkey to play such a role in 2009, but when Turkey invited India to attend regional meetings, Pakistan's military objected and refused to attend. The result has been Turkey's growing frustration with

Pakistan. As the Afghan endgame approaches, Russia and the Central Asian republics have also made themselves visible in wanting to be part of the discussion. This regional debate became even more heated after Washington and Kabul declared that they were negotiating a long-term strategic security pact and that some U.S. troops would stay on beyond 2014.

In Pakistan, the reactionary forces of Islamic extremism of course reject any change in strategy, any new foreign policy of good neighborliness or plans for enforcing modernity and reform at home; but sadly the military often does not support such changes either. Unlike Turkey, the Pakistani military spurns any change in strategic thinking as a devious attempt by the United States, India, and others to subjugate Pakistan, as change undermines its own vast economic interests, its large share of the budget, and its overwhelming influence over foreign policy. And as long as the civilian political elite also remains wrapped in its feudal mind-set, an unchanging Pakistan faces an ideological dead end. One new element on the Pakistani political scene has been the rise in popularity of Imran Khan, the world-famous cricketer and social worker. His popularity, marked by highly successful rallies that he held in late 2011, are a reflection of the growing public and especially middle-class frustration with the existing political parties and their failure to offer any constructive reform. Imran Khan's politics are a mishmash of economic reform and a dependence on advisers from both the extreme secular right and the religious right wing. His politics are at best confusing and contradictory; he is authoritarian in his approach to building a political party and has few candidates who could win elections. Moreover, his detractors claim that he is a tool of the military, something that he denies strongly. Whether he will win the next election, in 2013, is unknown, but there is no doubt that he is a phenomenon that cannot be ignored, and his emergence now after two decades of failed politics is a reflection of public frustration with the feudal political class and the crisis that Pakistan faces.

Unless both the military and the political parties put change and reform on the agenda, Pakistan will face a loss of political control, growing anarchy and violence in the provinces and among ethnic groups, enormous economic catastrophe for tens of millions of people, natural disasters made worse by lack of government, and the ever-looming threat of militant Islam, which could in time overwhelm the security apparatus. Most critical of all for a country whose army guards its nuclear weapons arsenal, potential coup makers in the ranks, linked to the extremist parties outside, may threaten the army's cohesion and unity. Pakistan poses a much more dangerous situation than even Afghanistan.

The region is beset with crises that are getting worse, but there is still time before 2014 to rectify the situation. First and foremost, the United States has to get its strategy right and share it with its allies. It must clarify what relationship it wants to have with Afghanistan, Pakistan, and the wider region after its withdrawal in 2014. It must push forward with a comprehensive dialogue with the Taliban, even though spoilers such as Al Qaeda would like to scuttle such talks. It must build a more stable relationship with Pakistan. It must bring India and Pakistan closer on the Afghanistan issue, and it must initiate a dialogue with Iran. Given the time frame, the lack of resources, and the mood back in the United States, a military option no longer exists; hence a political strategy and dialogue are absolutely necessary. By the summer of 2012, 33,000 U.S. troops will depart Afghanistan, leaving behind 65,000 troops, who will leave by the summer of 2014.

Recently President Obama has kept his distance from Afghanistan, allowing his subordinates to fight over the policy, which has led to confusion in Washington and abroad. Having overseen the deployment of more U.S. troops in 2009 and the surge, he has not lately been a hands-on president for perhaps the most important foreign policy crisis he faces, one in which the lives of 100,000 American and 40,000 NATO troops are at stake. If there is to be a peaceful withdrawal of U.S. forces and a way out of the quagmire, this distancing is clearly not acceptable.

President Karzai has to do far more than he is doing at present to convince his fellow Afghans, the Taliban, and the neighboring states that he genuinely intends to find a peaceful solution or at least a substantial reduction of violence in his country. His primary task is to heal the ethnic, political, and social divide in Afghanistan and to bring all groups on board in a genuine national discussion and consensus building on how to end the present war. Karzai's past wheeling and dealing must give way to a transparent political strategy that is visible to and shared by the entire nation. Beyond that, in the time left before the Western withdrawal, he must initiate better governance so that a functioning Afghan government, hopefully less corrupt and more competent than before, will be able to deliver goods and services to the people.

A key component of peace making with the Taliban has to be confidence-building measures, to reduce the unacceptably high levels of violence emanating from conflict. The Taliban could stop assassinating senior Afghan government officials in exchange for a halt in night raids by American special forces. These U.S. commando raids, late at night, try to kill or capture Taliban fighters and commanders but claim large numbers of civilian casualties; they have set a terrible precedent in the Pashtun south. By day, the U.S. Army tries to win hearts and minds; by night it is undermining its own actions by launching raids that terrify the population and cause resentment and anger against the United States and the Afghan government.

Between February 2009 and December 2010, night raids increased fivefold, with an average of 19 but sometimes as many as 40 raids per night.[19] Even more recently, from January to August 2011, American special forces launched 1,879 night raid missions, killing or capturing 916 Taliban, compared with 1,780 missions in all of 2010.[20] The lack of transparency and information about who exactly is being killed or captured raises immense suspicions among the public, not least that many Afghan civilians are being trapped or targeted. Military-related confidence-building measures between the Taliban and U.S. forces could initially be limited or have a time frame (they could last a month before being extended) and an area frame (they could be restricted to one province for a certain period). Once both sides have proved their good intentions to each other about controlling and reducing the violence, longer-lasting measures can be taken that actually bring violence down on a permanent basis. In November 2011 a special session of the loya jirga, or traditional Afghan assembly, called by Karzai to discuss the upcoming strategic pact with Washington, demanded that the United States stop night raids and take other measures to reduce the violence. The jirga also endorsed talks with the Taliban.

Ending the West's military deployment in Afghanistan in a constructive way also depends heavily on Pakistan's willingness and ability to deal with extremism. For too long, Pakistan has distinguished between good Taliban and bad, good extremists and bad, those who fight Pakistani forces and those who do not. These distinctions have to end. Ultimately all extremists are a threat to the state and to neighboring states. But not all have to be eliminated. Many can be deradicalized in programs of a kind that have been successful in Saudi Arabia. Pakistan's internal conundrum of military versus civilian power must be slowly resolved in favor of civilian, but civilian politicians must be much more responsible to the nation than they have been so far. For those who hoped for better civilian governance and policy making after a decade of military rule under Musharraf, the present government has been an unmitigated disaster; but then, when civilians are out of power for so long, it is difficult to expect anything better in the short term.

The tensions between the civil and military power brokers increased markedly by the end of 2011. Husain Haqqani, Pakistan's ambassador to Washington, was forced to resign in November after the release of an alleged memo that he was supposed to have had sent to Admiral Mullen in May asking for U.S. help to overthrow Generals Kayani and Pasha after the death of Osama bin Laden. Also involved in the scandal was Mansoor Ijaz, a Pakistani-born American who was renowned as a wheeler-dealer and gave the so-called memo to the ISI. The scandal, whether based on truth or not, created even greater mistrust between the government and the military. However, these tensions were temporarily covered up by another crisis with the United States.

On November 26, twenty-four Pakistani soldiers were killed by accident in bombing raids by NATO planes. The Pakistani military, already deeply frustrated with the Americans, took swift action, shutting down two NATO supply routes to Afghanistan that ran through Pakistan; telling the Americans to vacate Shamsi air base in Baluchistan, which some drones were flying from; cutting off all military and intelligence cooperation with the United States; and abandoning two liaison centers on the Afghan border that were manned jointly by American, Pakistani, and Afghan officers.

At the same time there was an outpouring of anti-U.S. public feeling on the streets, which was partly fueled by the military. Public anger was stoked by the fact that Obama refused to make a public apology to Pakistan, offering instead only "condolences" in private to President Zardari. The military clearly wanted to use this opportunity to make a decisive break with the Obama administration, and there was talk of creating a new relationship on Pakistan's terms and demands. The memo and the bombing incident left the civilian government even more fragile and vulnerable. As opposition leaders Nawaz Sharif and Imran Khan demanded early elections by 2012, there appeared to be a growing consensus among the military, the judiciary, and the opposition political parties that the government had lost its credibility and its usefulness.

Prime Minister Gilani railed against a conspiracy against democracy, but he was unable to stem the growing criticism. If Pakistan enters another phase of quasi-military rule brought about either through a military coup or a constitutional coup by the Supreme Court declaring President Zardari unfit to rule, Pakistan may well tip over the brink. No illegitimate government brought in through the courts or the army will have the authority or the legality to carry out the reforms that are so badly needed by a desperate public. Instead, such a government will become a pawn in the hands of the military and the ISI as they continue to seek the best advantage for themselves from the U.S. withdrawal from Afghanistan. The generals remain obsessed with Afghanistan, and a change of government in Islamabad that gives them a free hand to indulge in that obsession will not bring peace to that troubled country; it will only increase tensions among Afghanistan's neighbors and ultimately backfire on Pakistan.

The bitter public disappointment with Asif Ali Zardari and Yousaf Raza Gilani must not become a public rejection of democracy; extremist ideology must not replace democratic aspirations. Elections must be held in 2013 or before without interference from extremists or the military, and a new government must take office and be allowed to govern, one hopes with better results. Pakistan needs several elections and several elected governments before democracy will become the acceptable mode of governance. Governments must also tackle the myriad problems to which years of neglect, bad government, and poor distribution of resources have led. For too long the military and the political parties have neglected their one single task, which is to make life better for their people.

NOTES

ONE | Osama and Obama, Legacy and Inheritance

1. Micha Zenko, "Bin Laden's Death: One Month Later," Council on Foreign Relations, June 1, 2011. The best report of the attack is Nicholas Schmidle, "Getting Bin Laden," *New Yorker*, August 8, 2011. The first to be killed was the courier Abu Ahmed al-Kuwaiti, who was spotted in an outside guesthouse. Then his brother Abrar and his wife Bushra were killed in the entrance to the main house. Khalid, Bin Laden's son, was killed on the staircase after firing on the Americans.
2. Catherine Philip, "Bin Laden Had Cash and Telephone Numbers," BBC, May 4, 2011.
3. "236,000 Killed," Costs of War, September 2011, Costsofwar.org.
4. Ahmed Rashid, *Taliban*, 2nd ed. (New Haven, Conn.: Yale University Press, 2010).
5. Ahmed had had a phone conversation with someone being monitored by U.S. intelligence. That person asked why Ahmed had been out of circulation for so long, and Ahmed replied, "I am back with the people I was with before." Bob Woodward, "Death of Osama Bin Laden," *Washington Post*, May 7, 2011.
6. Zahid Hussain, "Pakistan Identifies Two Key Aides," *Wall Street Journal*, June 1, 2011.
7. Dean Nelson, "Osama bin Laden Dead: The Humble 'Buyer' Whose Uncle Was World's Most Wanted Man," *Telegraph*, May 5, 2011, www.telegraph.co.uk.
8. Nasir Jamal, "Musharraf Rules Out Pakistan Link to Blasts Abroad," *Dawn*, July 25, 2005, www.dawn.com.
9. See Mohammed Waseem, "Patterns of Conflict in Pakistan: Implications for Policy," Brookings Institution Working Paper, Washington, D.C., January 2011. The army has ruled 1958–71, 1977–88, and 1999–2008.
10. Farzana Shaikh, "Client Country's Descent into Chaos," *Times of India*, September 11, 2011.
11. Mehreen Zahra-Malik, "Paradise Lost—Pakistan's Government Blew Its Chances," *Newsweek*, May 27, 2011.
12. *Financial Times*, available at: http://www.ft.com/intl/cms/s/0/576ee506-7583-11e0-8492 -00144feabdco.html#axzz1dydme6sm.
13. Statement by Inter-Services Public Relations of the Pakistan Army, Rawalpindi, May 5, 2011.
14. Zahra-Malik, "Paradise Lost."
15. "Al-Qaeda Statement on Death of Osama bin Laden," Associated Press, May 3, 2011.
16. Declan Walsh, "Pakistan Under Strain as Attack Hits Too Close to Home," *Guardian*, May 3, 2011.
17. Brian Knowlton, "U.S. Officials Back Ally as Its Reliability Is Questioned," *New York Times*, May 4, 2011.
18. The dead included seventeen Navy SEALs, five support staff for the SEALs, three Air Force Special Operations personnel, a helicopter crew of seven and seven Afghan com-

mandos, an interpreter, and a military dog. See Thom Shankar and Ray Rivera, "Airstrike Kills Afghan Insurgents Linked to Deadly Attack on Helicopter," *New York Times*, August 11, 2011.

19. Michael Kugelman, "The Most Lethal Bomb," *Dawn*, June 28, 2011, www.dawn.com.
20. Michael OHanlon, "Success Worth Paying For in Afghanistan," *Washington Post*, June 3, 2011.
21. White House, "Overview of the Afghanistan and Pakistan Annual Review," December 16, 2010.
22. Ahmed Rashid, *Descent into Chaos: The United States and the Disaster in Pakistan, Afghanistan, and Central Asia* (New York: Penguin, 2008).

TWO | Pakistan in Crisis

1. Part of this opening was delivered by Ahmed Rashid, Tanner Lectures, Brasenose College, Oxford University, February 13, 2010.
2. Daniel Dombey and James Lamont, "U.S. Reinforces Links with Pakistan," *Financial Times*, May 11, 2011.
3. Ambassador Anne Patterson, "U.S. Thinks Anti-Americanism Rife in the National Defence University," confidential cable, 2008, via Wikileaks, *Dawn*, May 25, 2011, www.dawn.com.
4. Benazir Bhutto, "When I Return to Pakistan," *Washington Post*, September 20, 2007. The quote is taken from "After Bhutto's Murder: A Way Forward for Pakistan," International Crisis Group, Asia Briefing no. 74, January 2, 2008, www.crisisgroup.org.
5. U.S. Senate, Armed Services Committee, Hearing on Worldwide National Security Threats, February 27, 2008, testimony of J. Michael McConnell, Director of National Intelligence.
6. Sheila Fruman, "Will the Long March to Democracy in Pakistan Finally Succeed?" United States Institute of Peace, July 2011, www.usip.org.
7. Fareed Zakaria, "'Pakistanis know I can be tough': Interview with President Pervez Musharraf," *Newsweek*, January 12, 2008.
8. President Barack Obama, remarks on Iraq and Afghanistan, *New York Times*, July 15, 2008.
9. Peter Spiegel, "Pakistan Tribal Area Called Likely Source of Next Attack on U.S.," *Los Angeles Times*, June 11 2008.

THREE | Pakistan: Who Betrayed Whom?

1. Sarmilla Bose, *Dead Reckoning: Memories of the 1971 Bangladesh War* (London: Hurst & Co., 2011).
2. I was the first to outline this ISI support base for the Taliban as early as 2003, when I wrote a cover story for the magazine I worked for. The army reacted instantly, issuing a spate of denials. Two weeks after the article was published, the army flew Western ambassadors to Quetta to show them that there was no Taliban presence there. See Ahmed Rashid, "Afghanistan and Pakistan Safe Haven for the Taliban," *Far Eastern Economic Review*, October 9, 2003.
3. Craig Whitlock, "U.S. Turns to Other Routes to Supply Afghan War as Relations with Pakistan Fray," *Washington Post*, July 3, 2011.
4. Peter Bergen and Katherine Tiedemann, "Washington's Phantom War: The Effects of the U.S. Drone Program in Pakistan," *Foreign Affairs*, July–August 2011.

5. Charlie Savage, "White House Split over Terror Fight," *New York Times,* September 16, 2011.
6. Greg Miller and Julie Tate, "CIA Shifts Focus to Killing Targets," *Washington Post,* September 2, 2011.
7. Farzana Shaikh, "Extraordinary Times for Pakistan," *Times of India,* May 7, 2011.
8. "Clinton Urges India to Expand Influence," Associated Press, July 20, 2011.
9. Shaun Gregory, "Terrorist Tactics in Pakistan Threaten Nuclear Weapon Safety," Combating Terrorism Center at West Point, June 1, 2011, www.ctc.usma.edu.
10. Susanne Koelbl, "Musharraf Is Not Telling Truth," *Der Spiegel,* November 8, 2008.
11. Susanne Koelbl, "'We may be naïve but we are not idiots': Interview with A. Q. Khan," *Der Spiegel,* June 28, 2011.
12. R. Jeffrey Smith, "Pakistan's Nuclear-Bomb Maker Says North Korea Paid Bribes for Know-How," *Washington Post,* July 7, 2011.
13. Walter Ladwig III, "A Cold Start for Hot Wars? The Indian Army's New Limited War Doctrine," *International Security* 32, no. 3 (Winter 2007–8).
14. Ahmed Rashid, "Pakistan's Continued Failure to Adopt a Counterinsurgency Strategy," Combating Terrorism Center at West Point, March 15, 2009, www.ctc.usma.edu.
15. Mahmood Adeel, "Pakistan's Dark Ages," *New Pakistan,* September 11, 2011, New-pakistan.com.
16. David Ignatius, "Pakistan Is Missing the U.S. Message on Terrorism," *Washington Post,* May 13 2011.

FOUR | Afghanistan: The First Surge and the Failure of Elections

1. Senator Joseph Biden, speech at the Council on Foreign Relations, New York, February 25, 2008.
2. "Mullen: Afghanistan Isn't Top Priority," statement to House Armed Services Committee, Associated Press, November 12, 2007.
3. President Barack Obama, remarks on Iraq and Afghanistan, *New York Times,* July 15, 2008.
4. Greg Jaffe, "U.S. Is Losing a Savvy Leader in Afghan War Effort," *Washington Post,* April 19, 2011.
5. Ann Scott Tyson, "Petraeus Mounts Strategy Review," *Washington Post,* October 16, 2008.
6. Bob Woodward, *Obama's Wars* (New York: Simon & Schuster, 2010).
7. Britain appointed Sherard Cowper-Coles (its former ambassador to Kabul and Jeddah); France, Pierre Lellouche; Germany, Bernd Mützelburg; and Japan, Motohide Yoshikawa (its former ambassador to Spain).
8. Woodward, *Obama's Wars.*
9. Sherard Cowper-Coles, *Cables from Kabul: The Inside Story of the West's Afghanistan Campaign* (London: Harper), 2011.
10. President Barack Obama, "Transcript of Remarks by the President on a New Strategy for Afghanistan and Pakistan," *New York Times,* March 27, 2009.
11. Martine Van Bijlert, "How to Win an Election: Perceptions and Practices," Afghan Analysts Network, February 2009, aan-afghanistan.com. Elections, wrote Van Bijlert, were "fixed by a combination of international interference, deals between political leaders and fraud."
12. The quotes from this section are drawn from Ahmed Rashid, "The Afghanistan Impasse," *New York Review of Books,* October 8, 2009. Also see "Afghanistan: Elections and the Crisis of Governance," International Crisis Group, Asia Briefing no. 96, November 25, 2009, www.crisisgroup.org.

13. Younus Qanooni, interview by author, Kabul, November 12, 2010.
14. Ahmed Rashid, "The Way Out of Afghanistan," *New York Review of Books*, January 13, 2011.
15. Ibid.
16. Ray Rivera, "A Shriveling Army in the Taliban's Shadow," *New York Times*, September 7, 2011.

FIVE | Afghanistan: Political and Military Fault Lines

1. Ken Dilanian, "U.S. Risks Wasting Billions More in Afghan Aid, Report Says," *Los Angeles Times*, June 17, 2011.
2. Once again I am indebted to the excellent article by Ryan Lizza for some of these ideas. Ryan Lizza, "The Consequentialist: How the Arab Spring Remade Obama's Foreign Policy," *New Yorker*, May 2, 2011.
3. Some of this material is drawn from Ahmed Rashid, "How Obama Lost Karzai," *Foreign Policy*, March–April 2011.
4. I am extremely grateful to Ambassador Neumann for sending me his father's quote. Ronald Neuman, Jr., followed in his father's footsteps and was U.S. ambassador in Kabul from 2005 to 2007.
5. Dan De Luce, "Pentagon Under Fire over War Contracts," AFP, August 30, 2011. "Tens of billions of taxpayer dollars have been wasted through poor planning, vague and shifting requirements, inadequate competition, substandard contract management and oversight," wrote the co-chairs of the panel, Christopher Shays and Michael Thibault.
6. "After a Decade of War, No Clear Answers," Associated Press, June 26, 2011.
7. Bob Woodward, *Obama's Wars* (New York: Simon & Schuster, 2010).
8. For these paragraphs I have used Woodward, *Obama's Wars*; Ahmed Rashid, "Afghan-Pakistani Doubts over Obama Plan," BBC News Online, December 3, 2009; and President Barack Obama, "Address on the War in Afghanistan," December 3, 2009.
9. Woodward, *Obama's Wars*.
10. See Ahmed Rashid, "Afghanistan, the Missing Strategy," *New York Review of Books*, December 2, 2010.
11. Neil MacFarquhar, "U.N. Envoy to Afghanistan Warns of Peril of Emphasizing Security over Social Issues," *New York Times*, January 7, 2010.
12. Kai Eide, *The Power Struggle over Afghanistan* (New York: Skyhorse Publishing), 2011.
13. Ibid.
14. Dion Nissenbaum, "McChrystal Calls Marjah a Bleeding Ulcer in Afghan Campaign," McClatchy Newspapers, May 26, 2010.
15. Rick Atkinson, "Left of Boom: The Struggle to Defeat Roadside Bombs," *Washington Post*, September 30, 2007.
16. Those killed included two NATO colonels and two lieutenant colonels, the highest officer death toll in a single attack.
17. Jorge Benitez, "ISAF Briefing Reveals 365 Taliban Leaders Killed in Last Three Months," Atlantic Council, August 29, 2010, www.acus.org.
18. In total, 490 foreign soldiers had been killed by September 1, compared with 521 total for 2009.
19. Ahmed Rashid, "It Is Time to Rethink the West's Afghanistan Strategy," *Financial Times*, June 24, 2010.
20. "The Insurgency in Afghanistan's Heartland," International Crisis Group, June 27, 2011, www.crisisgroup.org.
21. Mullah Wakil Ahmed Muttawakil, interview by author, November 13, 2010.

22. David Cloud, "Pentagon to Drastically Cut Spending on Afghan Forces," *Los Angeles Times*, September 12, 2011.

23. Maria Abi-Habib, "U.S. and Allies Cut Plans for Funding Afghanistan's Forces," *Wall Street Journal*, July 4, 2011.

24. Joshua Patlow, "More Afghan Soldiers Deserting Army," *Washington Post*, September 4, 2011.

25. Government minister, interview by author, Kabul, November 11, 2010.

26. Dexter Filkins, "Endgame," *New Yorker*, July 4, 2011.

SIX | Afghanistan: Talking to the Taliban

1. My sources for this section include American, German, and Afghan officials involved in the peace talks process, as well as officials in Kabul who were briefed on the talks.

2. I met Tayyab Agha briefly in 1998. Born in Kandahar (where I also met him), he was a young, educated boy who had come out of a Pakistani madrassa. He had spent time in exile in Iran and Pakistan.

3. Ray Rivera and Taimoor Shah, "Filling Classes with Learning, Not Fears," *New York Times*, June 9, 2011.

4. Amir ul Momineen Mullah Muhammed Omar, "Eid Message to the People of Afghanistan," Taliban press release, November 15, 2010.

5. Ahmed Rashid, "What the Taliban Want," *New York Review of Books*, August 29, 2011.

6. Hillary Clinton, Richard Holbrooke Memorial Addresses, Asia Society, New York, February 18, 2011.

7. Mullah Zaeef, former Taliban ambassador to Pakistan, interview by author, Kabul, November 11, 2010.

8. The leaks were in Karen DeYoung, "U.S. Speeds Up Direct Talks with Taliban," *Washington Post*, May 17, 2011; and in Susanne Koelbl and Holger Stark, "Germany Mediates Secret U.S.-Taliban Talks," *Der Spiegel* Online, May 24, 2011.

9. Thomas Ruttig, "The Battle for Afghanistan: Negotiations with the Taliban," New America Foundation, May 23, 2011, Newamerica.net.

10. Christina Lamb, "Quiet Crawl to Peace on the Afghan Shuttle," *Sunday Times* (London), March 15, 2009.

11. "Remarks of Esteemed Mullah Barader Akhund Made to Media About Obama's New Strategy," Taliban statement, November 2, 2009.

12. Peter Dizikes, "In MIT Visit, Miliband Presses for Afghan Peace Deal," MIT News Office, March 11, 2010.

13. Some key diplomats in Kabul gave me the details. See also Dexter Filkins and Carlotta Gall, "Taliban Leader in Secret Talks Was an Impostor," *New York Times*, November 22, 2010.

14. Candace Rondeaux, "Reconsidering Reconciliation in Afghanistan," *Washington Post*, September 21, 2011.

15. The ISI rounded up a dozen or more top Taliban commanders living in Pakistan, including for a time Tayyab Agha. The ISI wanted to know who else was involved in the so-called plot to talk to the Americans. It was clear from then on that the ISI would never trust the Americans. I spoke to Karzai and other Afghan officials several times over this period, and they were flabbergasted at the ISI's response.

16. Ruttig, "Battle for Afghanistan."

17. Kai Eide, *The Power Struggle Over Afghanistan* (New York: Skyhorse Publishing), 2011.

18. Ahmed Rashid, "Why the U.S. Must Talk to the Taliban," *Washington Post*, March 18, 2010.

19. Since the British period, all the neighbors of Afghanistan were allowed to maintain four consulates in the cities of Kandahar, Jalalabad, Mazar-e-Sharif, and Herat. The Pakistanis had four consulates, as did the Indians and the Iranians. The ISI had continually propagated the claim that India had more than a dozen consulates, which was false.

20. Sirajuddin, who is called Khalifa, a religious title, is respected and feared for his military ruthlessness and acumen. He is in his early thirties, and his mother is an Arab. He has always been close to Al Qaeda. Badruddin, also in his thirties, is from a Zadran mother and deals mostly with finances.

21. Aslam Khan, "Interview of Jalaluddin Haqqani," *The News*, October 20, 2001. Also see Melissa Skorka from the author's unpublished paper, "Haqqani Reintegration and Transition in Eastern Afghanistan."

22. See Ahmed Rashid, "The Way Out of Afghanistan," *New York Review of Books*, January 13, 2011.

23. Top officials assassinated included Haji Ramzan Aka, the commander of the border police in Spin Baldak in Kandahar province, on January 7; Abdul Latif Ashna, the deputy governor of Kandahar province, on January 29; Abdul Rahman Syed Khili, the police chief of Kunduz province, on March 10; Khan Mohammed Mujahid, the police chief of Kandahar province, on April 15; Gen. Daoud Daoud, the police chief for northern Afghanistan, in Thakar, on May 28; Abdul Wali Karzai, the stepbrother of President Karzai, in Kandahar, on July 12; Jan Mohammed Khan, the leading elder and Karzai ally, in Uruzghan province, on July 17; Ghulam Haider Hamidi, the mayor of Kandahar, on July 27; and Burhanuddin Rabbani, in Kabul on September 20.

24. Ahmed Rashid, "The U.S. Must Choose to Talk or Fight the Taliban," *Financial Times*, November 2, 2010.

SEVEN | A Sliver of Hope: Counterinsurgency in Swat

1. Ahmed Rashid, "Pakistan on the Brink," *New York Review of Books*, June 11, 2009.

2. Pakistan Institute for Peace Studies, Pakistan Security Report 2009, Islamabad, January 13, 2010.

3. Human Rights Commission of Pakistan, Pakistan Security Report 2009, Lahore, January 20, 2010.

4. This quote appears in Rashid, "Pakistan on the Brink." Also see Declan Walsh, "Taliban Reaches Beyond Swat Valley in Pakistan," *Guardian*, April 25, 2011.

5. Helene Cooper and Jeff Zeleny, "Obama Voices Concern About Pakistan," *New York Times*, April 30, 2009.

6. Sherard Cowper-Coles, *Cables from Kabul: The Inside Story of the West's Afghanistan Campaign* (London: Harper), 2011.

7. Ahmed Rashid, "Pakistan Civilian-Military Ties Hit New Low," BBC Online, October 16, 2009.

8. Statement issued by the army's Inter Services Public Relations, Rawalpindi, October 7, 2011.

9. Saeed Shafqat, "Saving Pakistan: Devising an Agenda for Counter Terrorism Strategy," *Quarterly Research and News: Center for Public Policy and Governance*, Forman Christian College, Lahore, April 2011.

10. Greg Miller, "CIA Backed by Drones in Afghanistan," *Washington Post*, October 3, 2009.

11. Haider Ali Hussain Mullick, "The U.S., Pakistan and the Perils of Brinkmanship," *Foreign Policy*, October 24, 2011.

12. General Kayani gave these figures in a meeting with Pakistani journalists on February 3, 2010.

13. Ahmed Rashid, "The Afghanistan Impasse," *New York Review of Books*, October 8, 2009.
14. Richard Holbrooke, telephone conversation with author, August 16, 2010.
15. The United States had given $340 million, Britain $200 million, and the European Union $315 million, while India contributed $25 million for the first time. China and the Gulf Arab states, Pakistan's closest allies, contributed paltry amounts. The total contributed was only just over $1 billion.
16. Ajay Chhibber, "Pakistan's Flood Victims Still Need Support," *Washington Post*, August 13, 2011.
17. Rob Crilley, "Pakistani Officials Know Where Bin Laden Is Hiding: Hillary Clinton," *Telegraph*, May 11, 2010.
18. "Lashkar-e-Taiba Has Become a Global Threat: Mullen," Indo-Asian News Service, July 25, 2010.
19. Cyril Almeida, "Pakistan 'the Most Bullied U.S. Ally,'" *Dawn*, November 30, 2010.

EIGHT | Pakistan: Broken Relations, Crimes, and Misdemeanors

1. Maleeha Lodhi, "Crux of the Crisis," *The News*, October 4 2011.
2. Ayaz Amir, "With Democracy Failing What Is Succeeding?" *The News*, October 7, 2011.
3. Abdus Salam, a theoretical physicist, won the Nobel Prize for physics in 1979, but because he was an Ahmedi, the state ignored him. He is unknown in Pakistan, and nobody mentions him in official histories, as Ahmedis are portrayed as enemies of Islam. In contrast, Abdul Qadir Khan, who never won any international award, stole secrets about how to make nuclear weapons, and then sold them to other countries or rogue states, is considered a national hero.
4. Amir, "With Democracy Failing What Is Succeeding."
5. "Pakistan: Investigate Murder and Torture of Baloch Activists," Amnesty International, October 26, 2010, www.amnesty.org.
6. "Pakistan: Balochistan Atrocities Continue to Rise," Amnesty International, February 23, 2011, www.amnesty.org. Also see "Pakistan: Disastrous Year for Rights. Militant Attacks, Judicial Misconduct Mark the Year," Human Rights Watch, January 24, 2011, www.hrw.org.
7. Musharraf was speaking to Deputy Secretary of State John Negroponte in September 2007. Ambassador Anne Patterson, cable to State Department, WikiLeaks, September 21, 2007.
8. U.S. Embassy Kabul, dated August 19, 2009, WikiLeaks, reported in "Kabul Admits Having 500 Baluch, Sindhi Separatists in Afghanistan," *Dawn*, June 7, 2011, www.dawn.org.
9. "Pakistani Courts Let 3 out of 4 Terror Suspects Go: US State Dept.," *Express Tribune*, September 1, 2011, Tribune.com.pk. See also "Pakistan: Balochistan Atrocities Continue to Rise," Amnesty International, February 23, 2011, www.amnesty.org; "Pakistan: Disastrous Year for Rights," Human Rights Watch, January 24, 2011, www.hrw.org.
10. Matthew Green, "The Killers of Karachi," *Financial Times*, August 17, 2011.
11. Akmal Hussain, "The Political Economy of Confrontation," *Express Tribune*, September 26, 2011, Tribune.com.pk.
12. See http://tribune.com.pk/story/230499/imf-programme-we-tried-we-failed-we-give-up/.
13. This year Pakistan is expected to earn $24 billion from exports, while remittances from overseas Pakistanis will set a record of $11 billion. But these windfalls will start declining rapidly next year, as the economic effects of loss of production, energy, and loans kick in.
14. Maleeha Lodhi, "Roots of Economic Dysfunction," *News*, August 15, 2011, Jang.com.pk.
15. Ayaz Amir, "Smashing the Conspiracy of Silence," *News*, August 31, 2011, Jang.com.pk.

16. David Sanger and Eric Schmitt, "White House Assails Pakistan's Effort on Militants," *New York Times,* April 5, 2011.

17. Carlotta Gall and Mark Mazzetti, "Hushed Deal Frees CIA Contractor in Pakistan," *New York Times,* March 16, 2011.

18. Salman Masood and Pir Zubair Shah, "CIA Drones Kill Civilians in Pakistan," *New York Times,* March 17, 2011.

19. Jane Perlez and Ismail Khan, "Pakistan Tells U.S. It Must Sharply Cut C.I.A. Activities," *New York Times,* April 11, 2011.

20. South Asia Terrorism Portal, Institute of Conflict Management, www.satp.org.

21. In a letter to the *New York Times* on August 12, 2011, Gabor Rana, international legal director of Human Rights First, said that "the problem with the drone debate is that the government doesn't explain its criteria for targets. Until it does, any dispute about the number of civilian casualties, or their proportionality to properly targeted individuals, can't be settled."

22. Brian Glyn Williams, "Death from the Skies: An Overview of the CIA's Drone Campaign in Pakistan," *Jamestown Terrorism Monitor* 7, no. 29 (September 25, 2009), www.jamestown .org.

23. "Drones Fly out of Pakistan," *Dawn,* February 14, 2009, www.dawn.com.

24. Scott Shane, "CIA Is Disputed on Civilian Toll in Drone Strikes," *New York Times,* August 12, 2011.

25. Sanger and Schmitt, "White House Assails Pakistan's Effort."

26. "Pakistan Rejects U.S. Report," *Daily Times,* April 8, 2011, www.dailytimes.com.pk.

27. Abubakar Siddique, "Pakistan's Tribal Areas Reforms Too Little, Too Late," Radio Free Europe/Radio Liberty, August 20 2011.

28. The government of Pakistan presented these figures as an advertisement on September 11, 2011, in the *Wall Street Journal.* It is not known what prompted this action.

29. Daniel Dombey and James Lamont, "U.S. Reinforces Links with Pakistan," *Financial Times,* May 11, 2011.

30. Jane Perlez, "U.S. Aid Plan for Pakistan Is Floundering," *New York Times,* May 1, 2011. The report came from the Government Accountability Office (GAO).

31. "Ties Can't Be Allowed to Unravel: Mullen," *Dawn,* April 20, 2011, www.dawn.org.

32. "Redefining Pakistan-U.S. Relations," *Dawn,* June 28, 2011, www.dawn.org.

33. Elisabeth Bumiller and Jane Perlez, "Pakistan's Spy Agency Is Tied to Attack on U.S. Embassy," *New York Times,* September 22, 2011.

34. Both quotes are from Steven Lee Myers and Jane Perlez, "A U.S.-Pakistani Battle of Will over War," *New York Times,* October 23, 2011.

35. Bruce Riedel, "A New Pakistan Policy: Containment," *New York Times,* October 14, 2011.

36. Reuters, "Pakistan Safe Havens Challenge U.S.-Afghan Effort," Washington, October 28, 2011.

37. Paul Harris, "Poll Shows Decline in US Support for War," *Guardian,* October 29, 2011.

38. Gen. (Ret.) Mirza Aslam Beg, "Proxy War and Politics in Pakistan," *Nation,* August 28, 2011, www.nation.com.pk. The CIA is the Central Intelligence Agency, the Mossad is Israel's external intelligence service, MI6 is Britain's, and the BND is Germany's.

NINE | Changing the Narrative—or Preparing for the Worst

1. I would like to thank, for some of these ideas, Anthony Cordesman, "Time to Get Real About the Future in Afghanistan," *Washington Post,* September 23, 2011.

2. Ahmed Rashid, "Once Again U.S. Afghan Policy Is Hobbled by Divisions," *Financial*

Times, September 19, 2011. When this article appeared, it caused a considerable uproar in Washington.

3. Ann Wilkens, "Another Pakistan Is Needed," Afghanistan Analysts Network, September 11, 2011, aan-afghanistan.com.

4. I am grateful to Alexander Evans for raising some of these points although in a different context. Alexander Evans, "Pakistan and the Shadow of 9/11," *RUSI Journal*, August–September 2011.

5. Barnett Rubin and Ahmed Rashid, "From Great Game to Grand Bargain: Ending Chaos in Afghanistan and Pakistan," *Foreign Affairs*, November–December 2008.

6. U.S., Indian, and Afghan intelligence traced two major attacks on the Indian embassy in Kabul to the Haqqani network and ISI involvement. In July 2008, a car bomb aimed at the embassy killed fifty-four people, while in October 2009, suicide attackers killed seventeen people and wounded sixty-three near the embassy. In February 2010, a suicide attack killed nine Indians in Kabul.

7. As late as June 2011, WikiLeaks revealed that a senior Indian official told the Americans that India saw no benefit in talks with the Taliban, adding, "It is quite clear to India that Pakistan views Afghanistan as a zero sum game and they want India out of Afghanistan." He said that India would not leave Afghanistan because it has strategic interests there. "India Claims Its Strategic Interests in Afghanistan," *Dawn*, June 8, 2011, www.dawn.com.

8. James Lamont and Farhan Bokhari, "China and Pakistan: An Alliance Is Built," *Financial Times*, June 30, 2011.

9. Mushahid Hussain, "Kashgar Must Not Mar Ties," *Dawn*, August 9, 2011, www.dawn.com.

10. "China: Account for Forcibly Returned Uighurs," Human Rights Watch, September 2, 2011, www.hrw.org.

11. Ibid.

12. Amin Tarzi, lecturer at the Marine Corps University, conversation with author, Washington, September 28, 2011.

13. Rigi was on a flight from Dubai to Kyrgyzstan when his plane was forced down over Iran. Iran subsequently claimed that he was under the control of the CIA and helped by the ISI and that he had recently traveled to Europe and Pakistan to elicit support for his cause.

14. Vali Nasr, "When the Arab Spring Turns Ugly," *International Herald Tribune*, August 27, 2011.

15. The Justice and Development Party's Turkish name is Adalet ve Kalkinma Partisi.

16. David Gardner, "Turkey's Newly Faltering Foreign Adventures," *Financial Times*, August 16, 2011.

17. Anthony Shadid, "Turkey Sees Alliance with Egypt as Axis of Democracy," *New York Times*, September 19, 2011.

18. Mahmood Adeel, "The Turkish Path," *New Pakistan*, July 21 2011, New-Pakistan.com.

19. "The Cost of Kill and Capture, Impact of the Night Raid Surge on Afghan Civilians," Open Society Foundations and the Liaison Office, Kabul, September 19, 2011, www.soros.org.

20. Tony Capaccio, "Afghanistan Raids by U.S. Commandos Almost Triple Since 2009, NATO Says," *Bloomberg*, August 12, 2011.

INDEX